CIMA

PRACTICE & REVISION KIT

Stage 1 Paper 1

Financial Accounting
Fundamentals

First edition 1995
Fourth edition February 1998

ISBN 0 7517 3880 8 (previous edition 0 7517 3913 8)

British Library Cataloguing-in-Publication Data
A catalogue record for this book
is available from the British Library

Published by

BPP Publishing Limited
Aldine House, Aldine Place
London W12 8AW

We are grateful to the Chartered Institute of Management Accountants for permission to reproduce past examination questions. The suggested solutions to past examination questions have been prepared by BPP Publishing Limited.

Contents

PREFACE

You're approaching your exams in May or November 1998. You're under time pressure to get your exam revision done: trying to fit in **study** as well as a **social life** around your **job** is difficult. But could you make better use of your time? Are you sure that what you are revising is entirely relevant to the exam you will be facing?

By using BPP revision material you can be sure that the time you spend revising and practising questions is time well spent. Our Practice & Revision Kits are clear, concise and effective and are focused exclusively on what you can expect to encounter in your exam.

- We offer **guidance on revision, question practice and exam technique** gleaned from years of successfully helping students to pass their CIMA exams.

- In the **key question checklist** we highlight the questions we think you must attempt if you want to pass the exam.

- We ensure that the **bank of questions is comprehensive** so that you can cover all areas of the syllabus if you have time.

- We firmly believe that you should only start practice and revision once you've acquired a certain level of knowledge and understanding of a syllabus area. The **Do You Know? checklists** let you see whether or not you really are ready to begin.

- We think it is important that you set yourself high but realistic targets. So the **basic content and the general structure of solutions** to questions are **achievable by a good student.**

- In **tutorial notes** to solutions we explain how to allocate your time, how to get the easy marks and how to avoid common mistakes.

- We include the **November 1997 exam as a test paper** for you to attempt under exam conditions – a dress rehearsal for the big day.

All in all, this Kit provides the most effective way of using revision time for your exams. It's about time. So choose BPP.

BPP Publishing
February 1998

For details of other BPP titles relevant to your studies for this examination and for a full list of books in the BPP CIMA range, including our innovative CIMA PASSCARDS, please turn to the end of the kit. If you send us your comments on this Practice & Revision Kit you will automatically be entered in our FREE PRIZE DRAW.

USING THIS KIT FOR REVISION AND EXAMINATION PRACTICE

Revision technique

This is a very important time as you approach the exam. You must remember three things.

> Use time sensibly
> Set realistic goals
> Believe in yourself

Use time sensibly

- How much study time do you have?
- Remember that you must EAT, SLEEP, and of course, RELAX.

Task: Work it out

- How will you split that available time between each subject?
- What are your weaker subjects? They need more time.
- What is your learning style? AM/PM? Little and often/long sessions? Evenings/weekends?

Task: Work it out

- Are you taking regular breaks? Most people absorb more if they do not attempt to study for long uninterrupted periods of time. A five minute break every hour (to make coffee, watch the news headlines) can make all the difference.

Task: Stop every hour

- Do you have quality study time?
- Unplug the phone.
- Let everybody know that you're studying and shouldn't be disturbed.

Task: Isolate yourself when studying

Set realistic goals

- Have you set a clearly defined objective for each study period?
- Is the objective achievable?
- Will you stick to your plan? Will you make up for any lost time?
- Are you rewarding yourself for your hard work?
- Are you leading a healthy lifestyle?

Task: Make sure the answer to all these questions is YES

Believe in yourself

- Are you cultivating the right attitude of mind? There is absolutely no reason why you should not pass this exam if you adopt the correct approach
- Be confident - you've passed exams before: you can pass them again
- Be calm - plenty of adrenaline but no panicking
- Be focused - commit yourself to passing the exam

Task: Tell yourself you can pass

Practising answering questions

Are you ready to answer questions?

Once you know a topic, you should attempt questions to consolidate your knowledge. However, there is no point in attempting questions before you are ready. Throughout the question bank, you will find one-page checklists of key points. If you are happy that you know the points on a checklist, then you can go ahead and start answering questions. Key questions are recommended on page (xx) and at the end of each checklist. Remember that attempting questions on topics you do not know will only dishearten you.

Task: Go back to your BPP Study Text and revise any topics of which you are unsure

Which questions should you do first?

This Kit includes special *tutorial questions* (which are indicated as such in the index to questions) to warm you up for key and difficult areas of the syllabus. Each tutorial question is followed by guidance notes, showing you how to tackle the question. We suggest that you read the question and then the guidance notes, and then try to apply the guidance to the question systematically. You should not worry about the time it takes to do these questions, but should concentrate on producing good answers. For this reason these questions do not carry mark allocations.

Task: Do *all* the tutorial questions for each subject area

How should you use this Kit while revising?

It is important to maintain a systematic approach to your studies, right up to the examination.

Task: Pull together your notes then tackle these activities

- Revise an area of the syllabus.

- Read the corresponding 'Do you know?' checklist, then try the key questions suggested at the end of the checklist. Do the tutorial questions without time pressure, but do the other questions under strict examination conditions. In both cases, do not look at the answer or at your text or notes for any help at all.

- Mark your answers to the non-tutorial questions as if you were the examiner. Only give yourself marks for what is on your script, not for what you meant to put down, or would have put down if you had had more time. If you did badly, try another question.

- When you have been through the whole syllabus, identify your weak areas and concentrate further question practice on them.

- When you feel you have completed your revision of the entire syllabus to your satisfaction, answer the test your knowledge quiz on pages 176 to 181. This covers selected areas from the entire syllabus and answering it unseen is a good test of how well you can recall your knowledge of diverse subjects quickly.

- Finally, when you think you have mastered the entire subject, attempt the test paper at the end of the Kit under strict examination conditions.

 BPP Publishing

Examination technique

Passing professional examinations is half about having the knowledge, and half about doing yourself full justice in the examination. You must have the right technique.

Final preparation

- Set at least one alarm (or get an alarm call) for a morning exam

- Have something to eat but beware of eating too much; you may feel sleepy if your system is digesting a large meal

- Allow plenty of time to get to the exam hall; have your route worked out in advance and listen to news bulletins to check for potential travel problems

- Don't forget pens, pencils, rulers, erasers

- Put new batteries into your calculator and take a spare set (or a spare calculator)

- Avoid discussion about the exam with other candidates outside the exam hall

Task: Tick off this list in the 24 hours before the exam

Technique in the exam hall

Satisfying the examiner's requirements

- **Do** *read the instructions (the 'rubric') on the front of the exam paper carefully*

  Check that the exam format hasn't changed. It is surprising how often examiners' reports remark on the number of students who attempt too few - or too many - questions, or who attempt the wrong number of questions from different parts of the paper. Make sure that you are planning to answer the right number of questions.

- **Don't** *produce irrelevant answers*

  Particularly with written answers, make sure you answer the question set, and not the question you would have preferred to have been set.

- **Do** *produce an answer in the correct format*

  The examiner will state in the requirements the format in which the question should be answered, for example as a report or memorandum.

- **Don't** *ignore the examiner's instructions*

  You will annoy the examiner if you ignore him. The examiner will state whether he or she wishes you to 'discuss', 'comment', 'evaluate' or 'recommend'. Refer to the meaning of examiners' instructions on page (xix).

Pleasing the examiner

- **Do** *present a tidy paper*

  You are a professional, and it should show in the presentation of your work. Students are penalised for poor presentation and so you should make sure that you write legibly, label diagrams clearly and lay out your work professionally. Markers of scripts each have hundreds of papers to mark; a badly written scrawl is unlikely to receive the same attention as a neat and well laid out paper.

- **Do** *use workings correctly*

  Show all your workings clearly and explain what they mean. Cross reference them to your solution. This will help the examiner to follow your method (this is of particular importance where there may be several possible answers).

Doing yourself justice

- **Do** *select questions carefully*

  Read through the paper once, then quickly jot down key points against each question in a second read through. Reject those questions against which you have jotted down very little. Select those where you could latch on to 'what the question is about' - but remember to check carefully that you have got the right end of the stick before putting pen to paper.

- **Do** *plan your attack carefully*

  Consider the *order* in which you are going to tackle questions. It is a good idea to start with your best question to boost your morale and get some easy marks 'in the bag'.

- **Do** *check the time allocation for each question*

  Each mark carries with it a time allocation of 1.8 minutes (including time for selecting and reading questions). A 25 mark question should be completed in 45 minutes. When time is up, you *must* go on to the next question or part. Going even one minute over the time allowed brings you significantly closer to failure.

- **Do** *read the question carefully and plan your answer*

  Read through the question again very carefully when you come to answer it. Plan your answer to ensure that you keep to the point. Two minutes of planning plus eight minutes of writing is virtually certain to earn you more marks than ten minutes of writing.

- **Do** *lay out your numerical computations correctly*

  Ensure that the layout is appropriate to the type of question and is in the manner preferred by the examiner.

- **Do** *gain the easy marks*

  Include the obvious if it answers the question and do not spend unnecessary time producing the perfect answer.

  Avoid getting bogged down in small parts of questions. If you find a part of a question difficult, get on with the rest of the question. If you are having problems with something, the chances are that everyone else is too.

- **Don't** *leave an exam early*

  Use any spare time checking and rechecking your script.

- **Don't** *worry if you feel you have performed badly in the exam*

  It is more than likely that the other candidates will have found the exam difficult too. Don't forget that there is a competitive element in these exams. As soon as you get up to leave the exam hall, *forget* that exam and think about the next - or, if it is the last one, celebrate!

- **Don't** *discuss an exam with other candidates*

  This is particularly the case if you still have other exams to sit. Put it out of your mind until the day of the results. Forget about exams and relax!

  Task: Learn this list of points for when you really need them - in the exam!

SYLLABUS

The syllabus contains a weighting for each syllabus area, and a ranking of the level of ability required in each topic. The Institute has published the following explanatory notes on these points.

Study weightings

A percentage weighting is shown against each topic in the syllabus; this is intended as a guide to the amount of study time each topic requires.

All topics in a syllabus must be studied, as a question may examine more than one topic, or carry a higher proportion of marks than the percentage study time suggested.

The weightings do not specify the number of marks which will be allocated to topics in the examination.

Abilities required in the examination

Each examination paper contains a number of topics. Each topic has been given a number to indicate the level of ability required of the candidate.

The numbers range from 1 to 4 and represent the following ability levels:

Appreciation (1)
To understand a knowledge area at an early stage of learning, or outside the core of management accounting, at a level which enables the accountant to communicate and work with other members of the management team.

Knowledge (2)
To have detailed knowledge of such matters as laws, standards, facts and techniques so as to advise at a level appropriate to a management accounting specialist.

Skill (3)
To apply theoretical knowledge, concepts and techniques to the solutions of problems where it is clear what technique has to be used and the information needed is clearly indicated.

Application (4)
To apply knowledge and skills where candidates have to determine from a number of techniques which is the most appropriate and select the information required from a fairly wide range of data, some of which might not be relevant; to exercise professional judgement and to communicate and work with members of the management team and other recipients of financial reports.'

Syllabus overview

This syllabus gives students with no previous accounting knowledge an introduction to the basics of financial accounting systems. It deals with the reasons for having a financial accounting and bookkeeping system; the processes involved in the operation of such a system; an elementary awareness of controls and audit; and some interpretation of accounting statements.

Aims

To test the candidate's ability to:

- explain the operation of financial accounting systems (manual and computerised) and prepare simple financial statements for incorporated and unincorporated businesses

- relate basic accounting concepts to financial accounting

- interpret simple financial statements and draw conclusions

- read the accounts of a company (without subsidiaries or associates), understand their main components and the reasons for external audit

Content and ability required

	Ability required
1(a) Conceptual framework *(study weighting 10%)*	
The users of accounts and the objectives of financial statements; the differing functions of financial accounts and management accounts; the accounting system	2
Statutory accounting principles (Companies Acts); fundamental concepts of accounting (SSAP 2); materiality; assets, liabilities, income, expenditure; capital and revenue; profit and cash	2
Different methods of asset valuation and their implications for the balance sheet and profitability	2
Historical cost accounting convention	2
Alternative methods of accounting	1
1(b) Accounting systems *(study weighting 40%)*	
Purpose of accounting records	2
Preparation of accounts for cash and bank; bank reconciliations; imprest system for petty cash	3
Accounting for sales and purchases including personal accounts and control accounts	3
Accounting treatment of Value Added Tax (VAT)	3
Components of gross pay and deductions from pay; accounting for payroll, including Pay-As-You-Earn (PAYE) and National Insurance (NI)	3
Fixed asset register	3
Financial accounting codes and their uses	2
Nominal ledger accounting, journal entries; trial balance	3
Interpretation of outputs from computerised financial accounts	2
Stewardship	2
The purpose of external and internal audit, and the meaning of true and fair	1
Financial controls; audit checks on financial controls; audit trails	1
Errors or fraud	1

		Ability required
1(c)	**Preparation of accounts** *(study weighting 40%)*	
	Simple profit and loss accounts and balance sheets from trial balance; income and expenditure accounts	3
	Accruals and prepayments; bad debts and provision for doubtful debts	3
	Methods of depreciation (straight line, declining balance and revaluation methods) and the basic rules of the relevant standard for depreciation)	3
	Accounting for stocks (excluding long-term contract work in progress); methods of stock valuation (FIFO, average cost)	3
	Manufacturing accounts; trading accounts; accounting for appropriations of profit; cash flow statements	3
	Completion of accounting records from incomplete data	3
1(d)	**Interpretation of accounts** *(study weighting 10%)*	
	Calculation and interpretation of:	
	return on capital employed; gross profit and net profit percentages; cost to sales ratios; asset turnover; debtors turnover, creditors' time to pay; current and quick ratios; financial gearing.	2
	Items in company accounting formats (company legislation)	1

GUIDANCE NOTES

The role of the chartered management accountant includes the preparation of information and its provision to other members of the management team. This paper is intended to lay the foundation upon which more detailed and specialised knowledge of accounting techniques may be built.

The examination paper will be divided into three sections, up to 80 per cent of which could be compulsory.

Section A will contain between ten and fifteen multiple-choice sub-questions, taken from across the syllabus.

Section B will contain two compulsory questions. The first of these will require the preparation of final accounts from a trial balance or from incomplete data. It may involve a sole trader, a company, or a not-for-profit organisation, and may include any combination of the 'final accounts' with necessary adjustments and supporting records. Although the question will be substantially numerical, there may be discursive elements included from any area of the syllabus. The other question may be from one or more syllabus areas.

Section C will contain two questions from which candidates will be required to select one to answer. These questions may include material from one or more syllabus areas and candidates must be prepared to view accounting as a whole.

Conceptual framework   *Syllabus reference 1(a)*

Candidates must appreciate the importance of the regulatory framework and its effect on the principles and practices used in the preparation of accounts. Questions in this area will be mainly discursive and may be part of a larger question which examines the candidate's knowledge of other syllabus areas, thereby increasing the practical emphasis of the question.

In the examination, candidates may be required to:

- describe the main user groups of accounting information and their information needs;

- demonstrate an appreciation of the effects of changing price levels on accounting statements and on capital maintenance, and a basic knowledge of the techniques which have been used by accountants in the past to try to solve this problem;

- explain the nature, classification and write off against profits of intangible fixed assets such as purchased goodwill and research and development costs.

The following items are not examinable:

- knowledge of specific Statements of Standard Accounting Practice (SSAPs) and other regulatory statements, except for a knowledge of the fundamental accounting concepts (SSAP 2) and of the basic rules of depreciation (SSAP 12);

- the calculation of adjustments for changing price levels.

Accounting Systems   *Syllabus reference 1(b)*

Candidates must be capable of maintaining accounting records and systems efficiently and accurately.

Since those areas of this syllabus which are concerned with recording transactions are ranked at ability level 3, candidates must be able to demonstrate skill in identifying and accurately recording transactions. Questions will *not* be set which require the writing up of numerous ledger accounts, but the underlying double entry principles are important and may be tested using journal entries, control accounts or through other means which restrict the number of ledger accounts required.

In the examination, candidates may be required to:

- demonstrate the ledger entries required to record the purchase, depreciation and disposal of fixed assets, and the issue of shares at par or at a premium;

- explain and demonstrate how control can be assisted by the use of control accounts and totals, reconciliations, segregation of duties and proper authorisation procedures;

- explain the purpose of external and internal audit, and the importance of audit checks and trails, and the prevention of errors or fraud.

The following items are *not* examinable:

- the technical aspect of how computers work, but candidates may benefit from having practical experience in using computer packages and, in particular, using the controls and interpreting outputs from such accounting systems;

- specific knowledge of audit procedures or auditing standards and guidelines.

Preparation of accounts   *Syllabus reference 1(c)*

Candidates must be able to demonstrate skill in the preparation of accounts for various types of organisations, including sole traders, limited companies and not-for-profit organisations.

Many of the questions set on this section will also require knowledge and skills from other areas, particularly those involving adjustments to accounts and the preparation of accounts from incomplete records.

In the examination, candidates may be required to:

- distinguish between items of expense and appropriations of profit in the accounts of limited companies;

- demonstrate an understanding of the different natures and accounting treatment of provisions and reserves;

- deal correctly with the provision for corporation tax for the year;

- prepare cash flow statements using any reasonable format which displays the information required by the question.

The following items are not examinable:

- the preparation of accounts in a format suitable for publication;
- the calculation of the provision for corporation tax;
- partnership accounts;
- the content of FRS 1 cash flow statements;
- the LIFO method of stock valuation.

Interpretation of accounts   *Syllabus reference 1(d)*

Candidates must be able to look at a set of company accounts and gain a general understanding of the picture it portrays. They must be able to calculate various ratios as stated in the syllabus, interpret them, compare them with other ratios, and suggest possible reasons for the results obtained.

In the examination candidates may be required to:

- calculate the return on capital employed using the formula:

  Net profit before tax and interest/average capital employed

  where average capital employed includes long-term finance, but does not include short-term finance such as bank overdrafts. As additional guidance, where questions do not include any long-term finance, then any mention of interest payable can be assumed to relate to short-term finance. Where questions include both short-term and long-term finance, the Examiner will clarify the content of any figure for interest payable;

- calculate asset turnover in a variety of ways, including the rate of stock turnover;

- calculate cost to sales ratios involving the major cost headings of the profit and loss account, eg cost of goods sold, materials costs, labour costs, administration costs, etc compared to sales;

- demonstrate an appreciation of the types of headings which appear in company accounts, and the general contents of each heading.

The following items are *not* examinable:

- investors' ratios, eg earnings per share, dividend cover etc.

BPP MEETS THE EXAMINERS

On behalf of students, BPP keeps in touch with the CIMA examiners and seeks to determine the precise limits of the syllabus. On this page, we summarise the key points in question and answer form. **These questions represent information given by the examiner at the CIMA Lecturers' Conference in December 1997.**

Is the vertical format for balance sheets acceptable?

This is certainly an acceptable format - most candidates use it.

Should students present workings for the answers for the MCQ questions?

Yes, in the answer booklet.

Are marks awarded for presentation and workings for preparation of financial statements questions?

They can be.

Is the ASB's Statement of Principles examinable?

No.

THE EXAMINATION PAPER

Assessment methods and format of the paper

		Number of marks
Section A:	one compulsory question composed of 15 multiple choice sub-questions (special answer sheet provided)	30
Section B:	two compulsory questions	50
Section C:	one question from two	20
		100

Time allowed: 3 hours

Analysis of past papers

The analysis below shows the topics which have been examined in the six sittings of the syllabus and the CIMA specimen paper.

November 1997

Section A

1 Multiple choice questions - 15 questions worth 2 marks each

Section B (two compulsory questions)

2 Preparation of P&L and balance sheet; calculation of ratios
3 Cash book; ledger accounts; provision for doubtful debts

Section C (one out of two questions)

4 Valuation of assets and liabilities
5 Income and expenditure account; depreciation

This paper forms the test paper at the end of the Kit so only an outline of its contents is given here.

May 1997	*Question number in this Kit*
Section A	
1 Multiple choice questions - 15 questions worth 2 marks each	81
Section B (two compulsory questions)	
2 Prepare trial balance, P&L and balance sheet; capital maintenance	47
3 Imprest; day books; sales ledger control accounts	16
Section C (one out of two questions)	
4 Capital and revenue expenditure; true and fair view, and materiality; journals	24
5 Appropriation accounts; capital side of balance sheet; working capital ratios	74

Examiner's comments

The pass rate for this exam was 60.5%, against a Stage 1 average of the other papers of 47.4%. The examiner was pleased with the overall standard, and the fact that time pressure had not been a problem. Answers to the narrative sections of questions were too brief to score highly.

Examiner's comments

The examiner was very impressed by candidates' performance. Nearly all attempted every question, with some scoring over 90%.

The multiple choice questions were not as well answered as on previous occasions. Questions 2 and 3 were well answered, but more problems were experienced in the optional questions 4 and 5.

Examiner's comments

Candidates' performance was in line with expectations. All candidates handled the accounts preparation question well, and the preparation of the sales ledger control account.

The optional questions and the parts of the questions requiring explanations let some candidates down, but gave others a chance to shine.

Introduction

Examiner's comments

In general the standard of scripts was very reasonable, with the average mark just above the 50 per cent level. The compulsory questions on the paper covered the most important areas of financial accounting and the examiner expected candidates to do well in these questions. Question 3 and the optional questions in Section C tended to distinguish the better candidates from the poorer ones.

Candidates generally scored well on the multiple choice questions (Section A). The majority of candidates who failed to achieve the overall pass mark on this paper performed badly on question 2 (preparation of final accounts). Question 3 was well answered. Question 4 (optional) involving a fixed assets register reconciliation was popular but not well answered. For question 5, however, the reverse applied.

THE MEANING OF EXAMINERS' INSTRUCTIONS

The examinations department of the CIMA has asked the Institute's examiners to be precise when drafting questions. In particular, examiners have been asked to use precise instruction words. It will probably help you to know what instruction words may be used, and what they mean. With the Institute's permission, their list of recommended requirement words, and their meaning, is shown below.

Recommended requirement words

Advise/recommend	Present information, opinions or recommendations to someone to enable that recipient to take action
Amplify	Expand or enlarge upon the meaning of (a statement or quotation)
Analyse	Determine and explain the constituent parts of
Appraise/assess/evaluate	Judge the importance or value of
Assess	See 'appraise'
Clarify	Explain more clearly the meaning of
Comment (critically)	Explain
Compare (with)	Explain similarities and differences between
Contrast	Place in opposition to bring out difference(s)
Criticise	Present the faults in a theory or policy or opinion
Demonstrate	Show by reasoning the truth of
Describe	Present the details and characteristics of
Discuss	Explain the opposing arguments
Distinguish	Specify the differences between
Evaluate	See 'appraise'
Explain/interpret	Set out in detail the meaning of
Illustrate	Use an example - chart, diagram, graph or figure as appropriate - to explain something
Interpret	See 'explain'
Justify	State adequate grounds for
List (and explain)	Itemise (and detail meaning of)
Prove	Show by testing the accuracy of
Recommend	See 'advise'
Reconcile	Make compatible apparently conflicting statements or theories
Relate	Show connections between separate matters
State	Express
Summarise	State briefly the essential points (dispensing with examples and details)
Tabulate	Set out facts or figures in a table

Requirement words which will be avoided

Examiners have been asked to avoid instructions which are imprecise or which may not specifically elicit an answer. The following words will not be used.

Consider	As candidates could do this without writing a word
Define	In the sense of stating exactly what a thing is, as CIMA wishes to avoid requiring evidence of rote learning
Examine	As this is what the examiner is doing, not the examinee
Enumerate	'List' is preferred
Identify	
Justify	When the requirement is not 'to state adequate grounds for' but 'to state the advantage of'
List	On its own, without an additional requirement such as 'list and explain'
Outline	As its meaning is imprecise. The addition of the word 'briefly' to any of the suggested action words is more satisfactory
Review	
Specify	
Trace	

KEY QUESTION CHECKLIST

You may not have left yourself enough time before the examination to attempt all of the questions in this Kit. Alternatively, you may simply want to begin your practice and revision with some really key questions. You therefore need to focus on effective question practice, answering the questions most relevant to the examination you will be facing. So we strongly advise you to attempt the following key questions before any others. They cover the most important syllabus topics, test the most fundamental techniques and/or most closely reflect the examiner's question-setting style.

Of course, you should make every effort to answer *all* of the questions contained in this Kit. But if you are able to put a tick in each of the boxes below, having attempted all of the key questions, you will be well on your way to exam success. If you really cannot do so, at least précis the answers to act as last-minute revision aids.

The headings indicate the main topics of questions, but questions often cover several different topics.

Tutorial questions, listed in italics, are followed by guidance notes. These notes show you how to approach the question, and thus ease the transition from study to examination practice.

Each question in the Kit which came from a CIMA examination has the date it was set in its heading. Note that ACC in a question heading indicates an old syllabus *Accounting* question and FAC an old syllabus *Financial Accounting* question. Such questions are included because they are directly relevant to the new syllabus, and their style and level are expected to be similar to those of new syllabus questions.

		Question	Suggested solution

BPP Publishing

Questions

DO YOU KNOW? - CONCEPTUAL FRAMEWORK

- *Check that you know the following basic points before you attempt any questions. If in doubt, you should go back to your BPP Study Text and revise first.*

- The main *users* of financial information are managers, shareholders, trade contacts, providers of finance, the Inland Revenue, employees and financial analysts and advisers. The information needs of these users differ.

- *Financial accounting* provides summaries of historical data for external purposes.

- *Management accounting* aims to provide information to management to facilitate decision making.

- The *balance sheet* is a list of all the assets owned by a business and liabilities owed by a business at a particular date.

- The *profit and loss account* is a record of income generated and expenditure incurred over a given period.

- The four fundamental accounting concepts are the *going concern* concept, the *accruals* (or matching) concept, the *consistency* concept and the *prudence* concept.

    o   *Going concern* - an enterprise will carry on in existence for the foreseeable future.

    o   *Accruals* - revenues and expenses should be taken into account in the period to which they relate.

    o   *Consistency* - like items should be accounted for in the same way, even though they arise in different periods.

    o   *Prudence* - costs should be charged, and liabilities accounted for as soon as they are recognised; income should be taken into account when its receipt is reasonably certain.

- You should also be aware of the *money measurement concept* (which prevents businesses from placing a value on things they cannot measure, like their management team), and the problem of attributing monetary values to some of the items that appear in accounts (the *cost concept*).

- *Capital maintenance* is concerned with how well off a business is at the beginning and end of a period. This is important when considering the adequacy of historical cost accounting, especially in times of inflation, and possible alternatives.

    o   Current purchasing power adjusts all values by the retail price index.
    o   Current cost accounting applies different price indices to individual items.

- Present day financial accounting has been influenced by a number of forces, including company law, accounting standards, international accounting standards and the Stock Exchange.

- In order to overcome subjectivity in applying fundamental accounting concepts, accounting standards (SSAPs and now FRSs) were developed.

- Financial statements are required by law to give a 'true and fair view' . This is not defined.

- *Key questions*

    Tutorial questions 1, 5, 6, 7
    4   *Shareholder and supplier*
    8   *Explanations and illustrations*
    9   *Suggestions*

1   TUTORIAL QUESTION: USERS OF ACCOUNTING STATEMENTS

It has been suggested that, apart from owners/investors, there are six separate user groups of published accounting statements: the loan creditor group, the employee group, the analyst-advisor group, the business contact group, the government and the public.

Required

(a)   Taking any four of these six user groups, explain the information they are likely to want from published accounting statements.

(b)   Are there any difficulties in satisfying the requirements of all four of your chosen groups, given the requirements of other users?

Guidance notes

1   To answer part (a) think about what item or part of the financial statements will be of particular interest to the user group concerned. We deal with all six groups in our suggested solution, but you should only write about four.

2   To answer part (b) look back at your answer to part (a). Are the information requirements of different groups at odds with each other?

2   ACCOUNTING STATEMENTS   *29 mins*

It has been suggested that published accounting statements should attempt to be relevant, understandable, reliable, complete, objective, timely and comparable.

Required

(a)   Explain briefly in your own words, the meaning of these terms as applied to accounting.

12 Marks

(b)   Are there any difficulties in applying all of them at the same time?   **4 Marks**

Total Marks = 16

3   PURPOSE OF ACCOUNTS   *22 mins*

The following letter has been received from a client. 'I gave my bank manager those audited accounts you prepared for me last year. But he says he needs more information before he will agree to increase my overdraft. What could he possibly want to know that he can't get from those accounts? If they are not good enough why bother to prepare them?'

Required

Outline the major points which should be included in a reply to this letter.

12 Marks

4   SHAREHOLDER AND SUPPLIER   *22 mins*

'The shareholder needs a statement of financial prospects, ie an indication of future progress. However, the supplier of goods on credit needs as statement of financial position, ie an indication of the current state of affairs.'

Required

(a)   Explain the extent to which you think this statement is true   **6 Marks**

(b)   It is general practice in most countries to prepare published accounting reports either based on historical costs, or based on historical costs but with the occasional revaluation of some fixed assets. To what extent do you think that accounting reports prepared in such ways do actually meet the needs of shareholders and suppliers of goods on credit?   **6 Marks**

Total Marks = 12

5   TUTORIAL QUESTION: ACCOUNTING CONCEPTS

Dee has given you a piece of paper with four statements about accounting concepts.

(a)   A business continues in existence for the foreseeable future.
(b)   Related revenues and expenses should be matched with each other.
(c)   Income should not be recognised until receiving it is reasonably certain.
(d)   Similar items should receive a similar accounting treatment.

Required

Name the four accounting concepts described above.

Guidance notes

1   You should have no difficulty in answering this question. If you do you should not even consider continuing with this kit until you have revised properly.

2   If this is too easy, you may wish to test yourself further by trying to think of an example of the application of each of the four concepts. You will find plenty in later questions.

6   TUTORIAL QUESTION: TERMINOLOGY

A friend has bought some shares in a quoted United Kingdom company and has received the latest accounts. There is one page he is having difficulty in understanding.

Required

Briefly, but clearly, answer his questions.

(a)   What is a balance sheet?
(b)   What is an asset?
(c)   What is a liability?
(d)   What is share capital?
(e)   What are reserves?
(f)   Why does the balance sheet balance?
(g)   To what extent does the balance sheet value my investment?

Guidance notes

1   Questions requiring you to give brief, clear explanations of accounting terminology occur very frequently in examinations, usually as part of a longer question. Be ready for them and earn quick and easy marks.

2   Your own words are better for this purpose than something cribbed from a book; there is little value in rote learning definitions without properly understanding them. Most likely you will be caught out, anyway, because you will be asked to distinguish between, say, a reserve and a provision by giving, or identifying, specific examples.

7   TUTORIAL QUESTION: SSAP 2

In relation to SSAP 2, *Disclosure of accounting policies* explain, with examples, *each* of the following terms.

(a)   Fundamental accounting concepts
(b)   Accounting bases
(c)   Accounting policies

Guidance notes

1   Understanding of fundamental accounting concepts, accounting bases and accounting policies underpins all your financial accounting studies. It is essential that you do not confuse them.

2   Read the question carefully. It requires you to relate your answer to SSAP 2, and to give examples. Do not lose easy marks by failing to do one or both of these.

3   This question is broken down helpfully into parts, thus providing a structure for your answer.

4   In the examination you would probably be asked to *apply* the understanding required here, for example, by discussing a particular accounting treatment in the light of, say, the prudence concept.

8   EXPLANATIONS AND ILLUSTRATIONS (ACC, 5/94)   *36 mins*

Explain any *four* of the following, illustrating your answer, where possible, with examples.

(a)   Capital maintenance
(b)   Goodwill
(c)   Economic value of assets
(d)   Research and developments costs
(e)   Prudence concept   **4 × 5 Marks = 20**

9   SUGGESTIONS (ACC, 11/93)   *32 mins*

You have recently been appointed as assistant accountant of PQR Limited. You have assisted in preparing a forecast set of final accounts for the company whose year end is 31 December 19X7. The forecast shows that the company is expected to make a loss during the year to 31 December 19X7. This would be the first time that the company has made a loss since it was incorporated twenty years ago.

The managing director is concerned that the company's shareholders would be unhappy to hear that the company had made a loss. He is determined to avoid making a loss if at all possible. He has made the following suggestions in order to remedy the situation.

(a)   Make no further provision for obsolete stock and consider crediting the profit and loss account with the provision made in previous years.

(b)   Do not provide for depreciation for the year to 31 December 19X7.

(c)   Capitalise all research expenditure.

(d)   Do not make any further provision for doubtful debts and credit the profit and loss account with the full amount of provisions made in previous years.

Required

Consider the managing director's suggestions and draft a report to him stating whether you agree or disagree with them. Make reference to accounting concepts as appropriate.

18 Marks

DO YOU KNOW? - ACCOUNTING SYSTEMS AND ACCOUNTS PREPARATION

- *Check that you know the following basic points before you attempt any questions. If in doubt, you should go back to your BPP Study Text and revise first.*

- The accounting equation is as follows.

  o   Capital + Liabilities = Assets

- Transactions are initially recorded in *books of prime entry* like the cash book, the sales day book, the wages records or the journal. Later they are posted to the ledger accounts. For example, total wages and salaries might be entered into wages, PAYE and National Insurance control accounts in the nominal ledger.

- The nominal ledger contains details of assets, liabilities and capital, and income and expenditure. The *sales ledger and purchases ledger* contain details of the personal accounts of customers and suppliers respectively: these details are summarised in control accounts which form part of the nominal ledger.

- For every *debit* entered in the ledger accounts there must be an equal *credit* and vice versa, If this system breaks down through error or omission it will generally show up because of the existence of a suspense account or the non agreement of control accounts and memorandum accounts.

- The *trial balance* lists all the balances in every account in the nominal ledger at the end of a period. Adjustments sometimes need to be made to the balances in the trial balance to allow for amounts due but not yet paid for (accruals), amounts paid in advance (prepayments), and amounts only provided at the year end (depreciation, bad debts).

  o   Depreciation is usually calculated using the straight-line method or the reducing balance method.

  o   Debts that are known to be bad are written off in full; the possibility that other debts may not be paid is dealt with by increasing or decreasing the size of the bad debts provision, with a corresponding entry in the P&L.

  o   Other adjustments may be needed for goods on sale or return, discounts received or allowed, dividends to be paid or taxation to be provided for.

- Stocks are valued at the lower of cost and net realisable value (SSAP 9).

- To calculate cost of goods sold, the formula is:

  o   Opening stock + Purchases – Closing stock

- The cost of a fixed asset is allocated fairly between accounting periods by means of depreciation. The provision for depreciation is both;

  o   charged against profit; and
  o   deducted from the value of the fixed asset in the balance sheet.

- Intangible fixed assets are those which have a value to the business but which do not have any physical substance. The most significant intangible assets are goodwill and deferred development expenditure.

- Computers assist in all areas of financial accounting: sales and purchases ledger, payroll, nominal ledger, stock control, fixed assets or whatever. The processing involved is relatively simple but very voluminous and needs to be done quickly and accurately·

- *Key questions*

  Tutorial questions 11, 12, 21, 28, 31, 36
  13   *XY's daybook*
  19   *XW*
  24   *OBJ plc*
  33   *BC*
  34   *PQR*
  42   *Sales ledger package*

10   TUTORIAL QUESTION: THE ACCOUNTING AND BUSINESS EQUATIONS

Dave has given you some numbers extracted from the financial statements of an enterprise. He has heard of two 'equations' in which these numbers can be used: the accounting equation; and the business equation.

(a)   Profit is £1,051
      Capital introduced is £100
      There is an increase in net assets of £733

      What are drawings?

(b)   The increase in net assets is £173
      Drawings are £77
      Capital introduced is £45

      What is the net profit for the year?

(c)   Liabilities of a business are £153 whereas assets are £174.

      How much capital is in the business?

(d)   Capital introduced is £50
      Profits brought forward at the beginning of the year amount to £100
      Liabilities are £70
      Assets are £90

      What is the retained profit for the year?

Guidance note

The accounting and business equations were given on the 'Do you know' page. This question will help to drum these basics home. Most students will think that this is an easy question, but many will lose their grasp of these fundamental points when faced with more complicated problems.

11   TUTORIAL QUESTION: THE EFFECT OF TRANSACTIONS

Karen Dickson is interested in knowing what effect the following transactions would have on her balance sheet. Since liquidity and profitability are particularly important to her, she wants to know whether each individual item would alter current assets, current liabilities and profit, and if so by how much.

(a)   Purchased £2,000 of stock for cash.
(b)   Bought £15,000 of machinery by loan repayable over 8 years.
(c)   Bought new car for £6,250 by cash.
(d)   Karen withdrew £2,750 of cash from the business for private use.
(e)   Paid rates demand for £1,400 in cash.
(f)   Borrowed £1,000 cash from the bank by way of loan repayable over 5 years.
(g)   Depreciated the machinery by £500.
(h)   Sold an old car with a book value of £650 for £775 cash.
(i)   Bought £8,000 of stock on credit.
(j)   Sold stock which had cost £4,000 for £5,000 in cash.
(k)   Paid for repairs to the premises costing £820 in cash.

Required

You are to produce a table, as shown below, giving the effect of each individual transaction by stating whether the current assets, current liabilities and profit would increase or decrease (together with the relevant amount) or stay the same.

Transaction	*Current assets*	*Current liabilities*	*Profit*
(a)	Increase £2,000 Decrease £2,000	stay the same	stay the same

Guidance notes

1   This question challenges you to think of transactions not simply in terms of 'debit such and such/credit so and so' but in terms of the effect of the transaction in the financial statements as a whole.

2   Take your time with this question, because you will be developing a habit that is of tremendous practical use, as well as one that helps you to avoid foolish slips in examinations.

12   TUTORIAL QUESTION: CREDIT, CASH AND DISCOUNT

On 1 May 19X9 Marshall's cash book showed a cash balance of £224 and an overdraft of £336. During the week ended 6 May the following transactions took place:

May 1	Sold £160 of goods to P Dixon on credit
May 1	Withdrew £50 of cash from the bank for business use
May 2	Purchased goods from A Clarke on credit for £380 less 15% trade discount
May 2	Repaid a debt of £120 owing to R Hill, taking advantage of a 10% cash discount. The payment was by cheque
May 3	Sold £45 of goods for cash
May 4	Sold £80 of goods to M Maguire on credit, offering a 12$\frac{1}{2}$% discount if payment made within 7 days
May 4	Paid a telephone bill of £210 by cheque
May 4	Purchased £400 of goods on credit from D Daley
May 5	Received a cheque from H Larkin for £180. Larkin has taken advantage of a £20 cash discount offered to him
May 5	Sold £304 of goods to M Donald on credit
May 5	Purchased £135 of goods from Honour Ltd by cheque
May 6	Received a cheque from D Randle for £482
May 6	Purchased £100 of goods on credit from G Perkins

Required

Enter the above transactions for Marshall into:

(a)   sales book;
(b)   purchases book;
(c)   cash book with separate columns for discounts, bank and cash.

The records should be balanced off or totalled, as appropriate, at the end of the week. Folio numbers are not required.

Guidance notes

1   Draw up your three column cash book allowing yourself plenty of space, and enter the balances brought forward.

2   Now work through each transaction one by one. You can ignore VAT for the purposes of this question.

3   Beware of transactions like that on May 5. The balance on Larkin's account would have shown a debit of £200. This would be entirely cleared by the payment received, but how would this be posted? Return to your Study Text if you are not sure, because later questions will test this point.

4   Questions like this are not particularly taxing, but they do require a clear head, patience and neatness, and these are rare commodities under examination conditions.

13   XY'S DAYBOOK (ACC, 5/92)   *36 mins*

Shown below is the Sales and Returns Inwards Daybook of XY, a sole trader, who employs a book-keeper to maintain her personal account records but maintains the nominal ledger herself.

Date	Customer	Goods	VAT	Total
19X2		£	£	£
Feb 7	ANG Ltd	4,600	805	5,405
10	John's Stores	2,800	490	3,290
14	ML Ltd	1,000	175	1,175
17	ML Ltd	(600)	(105)	(705)
25	ANG Ltd	1,200	210	1,410
		9,000	1,575	10,575

Required

(a) Explain a possible meaning for the entry on 17 February **2 Marks**

(b) Explain how the realisation concept would have been applied in determining the above entries. **5 Marks**

(c) Post the above transactions to the appropriate accounts in the nominal ledger and in the customer's personal accounts (do not balance the accounts off). **8 Marks**

(d) Explain why a provision for doubtful debts is usually calculated in respect of debtors; support your answer by reference to basic concepts. **5 Marks**

Total Marks = 20

14 **TRANSACTIONS (5/95)** *36 mins*

Your organisation had the following transactions during the last month.

Transaction 1: purchase of raw materials on credit from J Smith, list price £3,000, trade discount 25%, rate of VAT 17.5%.

Transaction 2: payment by cheque to a creditor, L Taylor, outstanding amount £2,400 less cash discount of 5%.

Transaction 3: contra entry between sales and purchases ledger of £300, re K Green.

Transaction 4: motor vehicle worth £2,000 received in part-payment of a debt due from a customer, S Long.

Transaction 5: staff wages earned during the month of £3,000 gross, with PAYE of £450, Employees' National Insurance contributions of £120 and Employer's National Insurance contributions of £130. All payments are to be made after the month end.

Required

(a) Use the following column headings:

Transaction number	Book of prime entry	Debit entries		Credit entries	
		Account name	Amount	Account name	Amount

and, for each transaction, state the book of prime entry in which the transaction would be entered, and the ledger entries which would subsequently be made. **14 Marks**

(b) Explain what is meant by the term 'stewardship', when applied to an organisation. **6 Marks**

Total Marks = 20

15 **XY LEDGER ACCOUNTS (11/96)** *36 mins*

At 1 October 19X5, the following balances were brought forward in the ledger accounts of XY:

Rent payable account	Dr	£1,500
Electricity account	Cr	£800
Interest receivable account	Dr	£300
Provision for doubtful debts account	Cr	£4,800

You are told the following.

(a) Rent is payable quarterly in advance on the last day of November, February, May and August, at the rate of £6,000 per annum.

(b) Electricity is paid as follows.

5 November 19X5	£1,000 (for the period to 31 October 19X5)
10 February 19X6	£1,300 (for the period to 31 January 19X6)
8 May 19X6	£1,500 (for the period to 30 April 19X6)
7 August 19X6	£1,100 (for the period to 31 July 19X6)

At 30 September 19X6, the electricity meter shows that £900 has been consumed since the last bill was received.

(a) Interest was received during the year as follows.

2 October 19X5   £250 (for the six months to 30 September 19X5)
3 April 19X6   £600 (for the six months to 31 March 19X6)

You estimate that interest of £300 is accrued at 30 September 19X8.

(b) At 30 September 19X6, the balance of debtors amounts to £125,000. The provision for doubtful debts is to be amended to 5% of debtors.

Required

(a) Write up the ledger accounts for:

    (i)   rent payable;
    (ii)   electricity;
    (iii)   interest receivable;
    (iv)   provision for doubtful debts.

and bring down the balances at 30 September 19X6.   **10 Marks**

(b) Explain *two* accounting concepts which govern the treatment of the above items in the accounts of XY.   **4 Marks**

(c) State the meaning of *each* of the four balances brought down on the accounts at 30 September 19X6, *and* show how they should be treated in the balance sheet at 30 September 19X6.   **6 Marks**
Total Marks = 20

16   BH (5/97)   *36 mins*

BH commenced in business some years ago, maintaining a single ledger for all accounts, plus a cash book. His business has now expanded to the extent that he now needs to consider improving his accounting system by dividing the ledger into sections and introducing a petty cash system.

Required

(a) Describe the operation and explain the purpose of the imprest system of maintaining and recording petty cash.   **6 Marks**

(b) Explain how the use of day books can contribute to the efficiency and control of the double-entry ledger system.   **6 Marks**

(c) From the following information, draw up a sales ledger control account for the month of February 19X7.

	£
Owing by customers at 1 February 19X7	103,670
Owing to customers at 1 February 19X7	1,400
Sales, excluding VAT	175,860
VAT on sales	10,350
Returns inwards, including VAT	9,500
VAT on returns inwards	1,300
Refunds to customers	800
Cash sales, including VAT	12,950
Cheques received from debtors	126,750
Discounts allowed to customers	1,150
Contra entries to purchase ledger	750
Bad debts written off	2,300
Dishonoured cheques from debtors	1,580

In addition, BH has been notified that he will receive a dividend of 10p in the £ from a previously written-off bad debt of £3,000. The amount has not yet been received.

At 28 February 19X7, a provision for doubtful debts is to be made of 2% of the net balance which existed at 1 February 19X7.

Amounts owing to customers at 28 February 19X7 amounted to £840.   **8 Marks**

Total Marks = 20

17   TUTORIAL QUESTION: STOCKS

Statement of Standard Accounting Practice No 9 states that stocks and work in progress, other than long-term contract work in progress, should be valued at the 'lower of cost and net realisable value'. You are required to define the meaning of:

(a)   cost; and
(b)   net realisable value.

Guidance notes

1   A very straightforward question, particularly if you have a good memory!

2   You should know these definitions very well as you will almost certainly be asked to apply them to a practical problem.

3   A 'memory test' such as this may well come up as part of a longer question. It is an easy way of picking up marks, and you would be advised to do it first to give yourself confidence.

18   SMITH   *27 mins*

On 31 December 19X6, the last day of the financial year of your employer, three pieces of paper arrive on your disk. The first is an invoice for advisory services from Smith for the period July to November 19X6, for £2,000.

The second is a reminder that an estimated amount of £700 is owing for Smith's advisory services for December 19X6. The third is a note which says: 'Please transfer £10,000 of this year's profits to some special account or other, designated as being kept back for stock replacement purposes.'

Required

(a)   Prepare journal entries to record each of the above, clearly labelling the accounts concerned so as to show the effect on the reported results.   **7 Marks**

(b)   Briefly explain the terms:

      (i)   provision;
      (ii)   creditor;
      (iii)   reserve.   **6 Marks**

(c)   The three terms explained above in (b) are each illustrated by one of the adjustments made in (a). Which is which?   **2 Marks**

Total Marks = 15

19   XW (11/95)   *36 mins*

XW Ltd is a medium-sized company which is considering improvements to its methods of recording accounting transactions; one of the improvements will be the implementation of a coding system for stock records.

Required

(a)   Explain the purpose of financial accounting records.   **6 Marks**

(b)   Briefly describe *five* characteristics of a good coding system.   **5 Marks**

(c)   Explain *three* accounting concepts which govern the valuation of stock. **9 Marks**

Total Marks = 20

20   TUTORIAL QUESTION: DEPRECIATION

Explain briefly the provisions of SSAP 12 *Accounting for depreciation* where:

(a)   an asset is disposed of; and
(b)   the method of depreciating assets is changed.

Guidance notes

1   It is on the cards that you will be asked for explanations and discussions in the second half of the paper, with calculations being tested in the multiple choice section.

2   Part (b) is more difficult to explain in words than to apply in practice!

21   TUTORIAL QUESTION: ASSET DISPOSALS

(a)   On 1 January 19X1 a business purchased a laser printer costing £1,800. The printer has an estimated life of 4 years after which it will have no residual value.

Required

Calculate the annual depreciation charges for 19X1, 19X2, 19X3 and 19X4 on the laser printer on the following bases:

(i)   the straight line basis; and
(ii)   the diminishing balance method at 60% per annum.

Note. Your workings should be to the nearest £.

(b)   Suppose that in 19X4 the laser printer were to be sold on 1 July for £200 and that the business had chosen to depreciate it at 60% per annum using the diminishing balance method applied on a month for month basis.

Required

Reconstruct the following accounts for 19X4 only:

(i)   the laser printer account;
(ii)   the provision for depreciation - laser printer account; and
(iii) the assets disposals account.

Guidance notes

1   Providing for depreciation is not difficult as long as you do exactly as you are told in the question. Most accounts preparation questions offer you a few marks for doing this.

2   Straight line depreciation gives the same charge every year. The reducing or diminishing balance method charges the greatest amount in the first year.

3   Dealing with disposals requires you to take the asset(s) out of the asset account, the related accumulated depreciation out of the provision for depreciation account and to enter both in the disposals account together with any cash proceeds of the sale. Check whether you have a profit or a loss by deducting the net book value from the cash proceeds.

22   DEPRECIATION (ACC, 5/93)   *36 mins*

(a)   Prepare a report to a departmental manager, explaining the reasons for providing depreciation, with special reference to the measurement of income, capital maintenance, and the effect of changing price levels.   **10 Marks**

(b)   ABC Limited had the following balances on its motor vehicles accounts at 30 September 19X0.

	£
Motor vehicles at cost	10,000
Provision for depreciation of motor vehicles	4,000

During the year to 30 September 19X1, the following transactions occurred.

31 January 19X1	Bought a motor van (plant number MV11) costing £9,000.
24 April 19X1	Sold a motor van (plant number MV05) for £500 which had originally cost £4,000 in January 19W8.

During the year to 30 September 19X2, the following transactions occurred.

20 February 19X2	Bought a motor van (plant number MV12) costing £12,000.
31 August 19X2	Traded in van bought on 31 January 19X1 (plant number MV11) for a new van (plant number MV13) costing £14,000. The trade-in allowance was £7,400.

ABC Limited provides for depreciation on its motor vehicles at a rate of 25% per annum using the reducing balance method. It is company policy to make a full year's charge against all assets held at the end of its financial year (30 September).

You are required to show the ledger accounts necessary to record the above transactions. The form of presentation should clearly show the values which will be transferred to the company's profit and loss account and balance sheet at the end of *each* of the financial years to 30 September 19X1 and 19X2. **10 Marks**

Total Marks = 20

23 **SBJ (5/95)** *36 mins*

SBJ's fixed asset register gives the cost and depreciation to date for every fixed asset held by the company. Prior to charging depreciation for 19X4, the total net book value of all fixed assets on the register at 31 December 19X4, was £147,500.

At the same date, the fixed asset accounts in the nominal ledger showed the following balances.

	Cost	*Depreciation to date*
	£	£
Motor vehicles	48,000	12,000
Plant and machinery	120,000	30,000
Office equipment	27,500	7,500

You are told the following.

(a) An item of plant costing £30,000 has been sold for £23,500 during 19X4. The loss on disposal was £800. No entries have been made for this disposal in the nominal ledger, but the asset has been removed from the fixed asset register.

(b) A motor car was purchased on 1 October 19X4, and correctly recorded in the nominal ledger. Its cost was as follows.

List price of vehicle	£24,000
Trade discount	20%
VAT added at 17.5%	
Insurance	£360
Vehicle licence (road fund) tax	£130
Painting of company name	£100 (No VAT)

The vehicle has not been entered in the fixed asset register.

(c) Office equipment was purchased during 19X4, entered on the fixed asset register, but not in the nominal ledger. Until the omission can be investigated fully, its cost is deemed to be the difference between the balances on the fixed asset register and the nominal ledger at 31 December 19X4 (prior to charging depreciation for the year).

(d) Depreciation for 19X4 is to be charged as follows.

(i) On motor vehicles, at 25% per annum straight line on an actual time basis

(ii) On plant and machinery, at 10% per annum straight line, with a full year's depreciation in the year of purchase

(iii) On office equipment, at 10% per annum reducing balance, with a full year's depreciation in the year of purchase

Required

(a) Calculate the correct balances at 31 December 19X4, for cost and depreciation to date on the three fixed asset accounts in the nominal ledger (prior to the charging of depreciation for 19X4). **8 Marks**

(b) Calculate the depreciation for each class of fixed asset for 19X4. **6 Marks**

(c) Explain why an organisation charges depreciation on fixed assets, and the accounting concepts and principles which govern the charging of depreciation. **6 Marks**

Total Marks = 20

24   OBJ PLC (5/97)   *36 mins*

The external auditors of OBJ plc have identified several areas of weakness in the company's accounting procedures. One area of weakness is the classification of capital and revenue transactions. They feel that incorrect classification of material items could result in the failure of the accounts to show a true and fair view.

Required

(a) Explain briefly the meaning of the terms 'capital expenditure' and 'revenue expenditure'.   **3 Marks**

(b) Explain what is meant by a 'true and fair view' of an organisation's accounts *and* how the true and fair view might be affected by the concept of materiality. **5 Marks**

(c) The auditors have also identified that the following transactions have been omitted from the accounts.

    (1) Plant purchased for £18,800 cash including £500 for delivery and £2,800 VAT.

    (2) Motor vehicle purchased at the beginning of the accounting period, for £16,355 cash, including £140 for vehicle licence tax and VAT of £2,415.

    (3) Replacement engine for a commercial vehicle, costing £1,300 cash.

    (4) Sale of a fixed asset for £12,000 cash. This asset had cost £30,000 and it had been depreciated by £20,000.

OBJ plc's accountant has calculated the following figures at the year end of 30 April 19X7:

- net profit ~   £475,350
- fixed assets   £272,330

Required

    (i)   Prepare journal entries (*without* narratives) to correct *each* of the above transactions.   **6 Marks**

    (ii) Recalculate net profit and fixed assets after adjusting for the above transactions.   **6 Marks**

(Ignore any depreciation on fixed assets purchased.)

Total Marks = 20

25   GOODWILL   *36 mins*

(a) List three methods of accounting for purchased goodwill and briefly state the arguments in favour of each of the three.   **12 Marks**

(b) What are the main characteristics of goodwill which distinguish it from other intangible assets? To what extent do you consider that these characteristics should affect the accounting treatment of goodwill?

State your reasons.   **8 Marks**

Total Marks = 20

26   GOODWILL, FIXED ASSETS AND RESEARCH (ACC, 11/92)   *36 mins*

The managing director of a company has recently returned from a conference on the techniques of business valuation.

She has now realised that the accounts prepared by the company for publication probably understate the value of the company by:

(a) the exclusion of goodwill;
(b) the valuation of fixed assets at cost; and
(c) the treatment of the costs of research.

She has asked you to draft a report stating why the accounting treatment of these items understates the value of the company.

Required

Draft an appropriate report, making reference to accounting concepts where applicable.

20 Marks

27 NG NEARING (ACC, 11/94 amended) *27 mins*

You are the accountant of an engineering company.

The company has its own research and development department which comprises a research director and six technical staff. The company spends £1 million on research and development each year, which is approximately 5% of its turnover.

The research director has asked you to prepare a report explaining the accounting treatment of the costs incurred by the research and development department.

You are required to prepare this report, which should explain the principles applicable to accounting for research and development, referring to accounting concepts where appropriate.

15 Marks

28 TUTORIAL QUESTION: BANK RECONCILIATIONS

On 10 January 19X9, Jane Smith received her monthly bank statement for December 19X8. The statement showed the following.

SOUTHERN BANK PLC

J Smith: Statement of Account

Date	Particulars	Debits	Credits	Balance
19X8		£	£	£
Dec 1	Balance			1,862
Dec 5	417864	243		1,619
Dec 5	Dividend		26	1,645
Dec 5	Bank Giro Credit		212	1,857
Dec 8	417866	174		1,683
Dec 10	417867	17		1,666
Dec 11	Sundry Credit		185	1,851
Dec 14	Standing Order	32		1,819
Dec 20	417865	307		1,512
Dec 20	Bank Giro Credit		118	1,630
Dec 21	417868	95		1,535
Dec 21	417870	161		1,374
Dec 24	Bank charges	18		1,356
Dec 27	Bank Giro Credit		47	1,403
Dec 28	Direct Debit	88		1,315
Dec 29	417873	12		1,303
Dec 29	Bank Giro Credit		279	1,582
Dec 31	417871	25		1,557

Her cash book for the corresponding period showed:

CASH BOOK

19X8		£	19X8		Cheque no	£
Dec 1	Balance b/d	1,862	Dec 1	Electricity	864	243
Dec 4	J Shannon	212	Dec 2	P Simpson	865	307
Dec 9	M Lipton	185	Dec 5	D Underhill	866	174
Dec 19	G Hurst	118	Dec 6	A Young	867	17
Dec 26	M Evans	47	Dec 10	T Unwin	868	95
Dec 27	J Smith	279	Dec 14	B Oliver	869	71
Dec 29	V Owen	98	Dec 16	Rent	870	161
Dec 30	K Walters	134	Dec 20	M Peters	871	25
			Dec 21	L Philips	872	37
			Dec 22	W Hamilton	873	12
			Dec 31	Balance c/d		1,793
		2,935				2,935

Required

(a) Bring the cash book balance of £1,793 up to date as at 31 December 19X8.

(b) Draw up a bank reconciliation statement as at 31 December 19X8.

Guidance notes

1   It is extremely important in practice that you are able to prepare a bank reconciliation quickly and accurately. Get into the habit of doing this every month for your own bank account if you do not get a chance to practise at work.

2   The procedure has two steps. First identify corrections and adjustments that need to be made in the cash book. Common mistakes are adding items that should be subtracted or vice versa and taking the opening balance to be positive when it is negative.

3   Secondly identify items reconciling the corrected cash book balance to the bank statement: unpresented cheques are subtracted from the bank balance, and uncleared receipts are added to it.

29   SANDILANDS   *29 mins*

Sandilands Ltd uses a computer package to maintain its accounting records. A printout of its cash book for the month of May 19X3 was extracted on 31 May and is summarised below.

	£		£
Opening balance	546	Payments	335,966
Receipts	336,293	Closing balance	873
	336,839		336,839

The company's chief accountant provides you with the following information.

(a) The company's bank statement for May was received on 1 June and showed an overdrawn balance of £2,954 at the end of May.

(b) Cheques paid to various creditors totalling £7,470 have not yet been presented to the bank.

(c) Cheques received by Sandilands Ltd totalling £6,816 were paid into the bank on 31 May but not credited by the bank until 2 June.

(d) Bank charges of £630 shown on the bank statement have not been entered in the company's cash book.

(e) Three standing orders entered on the bank statement have not been recorded in the company's cash book: a subscription for trade journals of £52, an insurance premium of £360 and a business rates payment of £2,172.

(f) A cheque drawn by Sandilands Ltd for £693 and presented to the bank on 26 May has been incorrectly entered in the cash book as £936.

(g) A cheque for £510 has been charged to the company's bank account in error by the bank. The cheque relates to Sandford plc and should not have appeared on Sandilands Ltd's statement.

(h) A monthly direct debit payable to a leasing company for £1,000 was wrongly paid twice by the bank.

Required

(a) (i) Prepare a corrected cash book calculation for the month of May.

     (ii) Prepare a bank reconciliation statement as at 31 May 19X3.   **12 Marks**

(b) State briefly why organisations prepare bank reconciliation statements on a regular basis.   **4 Marks**

                                    Total Marks = 16

30   MTR LTD (11/96)   *36 mins*

MTR Ltd has recently expanded its activities and its auditors have made suggestions for alterations to its accounting procedures to improve control and facilitate the provision of management information. The directors of MTR Ltd are happy with their current systems which are used to produce annual financial statements, and appear to work satisfactorily. The auditors have suggested performing weekly bank reconciliations rather than the present monthly reconciliation; they have also recommended that MTR Ltd considers setting up an internal audit section.

Required

(a) Explain the differing functions of financial and management accounts.   **6 Marks**

(b) Explain the purposes of both internal and external audit.   **6 Marks**

(c) From the following information, prepare a statement reconciling the present bank balance as shown in the cash book with that shown on the bank statement at 16 November 19X6.

CASH BOOK

Date		£	*Date*		£
10 Nov	Balance b/fwd	5,327	11 Nov	Purchase ledger	1,406
12 Nov	Sales ledger	2,804	12 Nov	PAYE	603
13 Nov	Cash sales	543	14 Nov	VAT	435
15 Nov	Sales ledger	1,480	16 Nov	Cheques cashed	1,342
				Balance c/fwd	6,368
		10,154			10,154

BANK STATEMENT

Date		*Debit* £	*Credit* £	*Balance* £
10 Nov	Balance			6,049
11 Nov	Cheque 101204	420		5,629
12 Nov	Cheque 101206	1,406		4,223
13 Nov	Cheque 101205	302		
	Rates DD	844		3,077
14 Nov	Paid in - cheques		2,804	
	Paid in - cash		543	6,424
15 Nov	Credit transfer		685	7,109
	Bank charges	130		
	Dishonoured cheque	425		
	Cheque 101207	603		5,951
16 Nov	Cheque 101209	1,342		4,609

8 Marks

Total Marks = 20

31   TUTORIAL QUESTION: SALES LEDGER RECONCILIATION

(a) You are an employee of Exelan Ltd and have been asked to help prepare the end of year statements for the period ended 30 November 19X9 by agreeing the figure for the total debtors.

The following figures, relating to the financial year, have been obtained from the books of original entry.

	£
Purchases for the year	361,947
Sales	472,185
Returns inwards	41,226
Returns outwards	16,979
Bad debts written off	1,914
Discounts allowed	2,672
Discounts received	1,864
Cheques paid to creditors	342,791
Cheques received from debtors	429,811
Customer cheques dishonoured	626

You discover that at the close of business on 30 November 19X8 the total of the debtors amounted to £50,241.

Required

Prepare Exelan Ltd's sales ledger control account for the year ended 30 November 19X9.

(b)   To give you some assistance, your rather inexperienced colleague, Peter Johnson, has attempted to extract and total the individual balances in the sales ledger. He provides you with the following listing which he has prepared.

	£
Bury plc	7,500
P Fox & Son (Swindon) Ltd	2,000
Frank Wrendlebury & Co Ltd	4,297
D Richardson & Co Ltd	6,847
Ultra Ltd	783
Lawrenson Ltd	3,765
Walkers plc	4,091
P Fox & Son (Swindon) Ltd	2,000
Whitchurch Ltd	8,112
Ron Bradbury & Co Ltd	5,910
Anderson Ltd	1,442
	46,347

Subsequent to the drawing up of the list, the following errors have so far been found.

(i)   A sales invoice for £267 sent to Whitchurch Ltd had been incorrectly entered in the day book but had not then been posted to the account for Whitchurch Ltd in the sales ledger.

(ii)   One of the errors made by Peter Johnson (you suspect that his list may contain others) was to omit the £2,435 balance of Rectofon Ltd from the list.

(iii) A credit note for £95 sent to Bury plc had been correctly entered in the day book but was entered in the account in the sales ledger as £75.

Required

Prepare a statement reconciling the £46,347 total provided by Peter Johnson with the balance of your own sales ledger control account.

Guidance notes

1   The commonest problem with control account questions is knowing whether the items to be entered are debits and credits. One way of avoiding mistakes is to learn a proforma control account (for example the one shown in our suggested solution). It is better, though, to think logically through the problem. The sales ledger control account *completes the double entry* for sales, discounts allowed, cash from debtors, and so on, and debits and credits will behave accordingly: a sale is entered as a credit in the sales account and therefore a debit in the control account.

2   For part (b), there may be errors other than those you are specifically told about: check the information you are given carefully and assume that the examiner expects you to be on your guard.

3   Remember that the figure for sales in the sales ledger control account derives from totals in the sales day book.

32   HAC (ACC, 11/94)   *27 mins*

The following sales ledger control account has been prepared by an inexperienced member of staff from the accounting records of HAC plc at 30 September 19X4.

SALES LEDGER CONTROL

	£		£
Balance b/fwd	92,580.23	Returns outwards	11,376.19
Sales	318,741.90	Debtor receipts	299,878.43
Discount allowed	12,702.18	Discount received	10,419.76
Decrease in provision for		Bad debts written off	5,318.23
doubtful debts	10,429.61	Balance c/fwd	160,387.70
Purchase ledger contras	49,516.27		
Returns inwards	3,410.12		
	487,380.31		487,380.31

The total of the individual balances in the sales ledger (net of credit balances) has been calculated to be £96,484.43 on 30 September 19X4.

An investigation revealed the following.

(a)   A credit balance of £4,381.22 on an individual account within the sales ledger was included in the calculation of the total of the individual balances as though it were a debit balance.

(b)   One of the pages of the sales daybook had been incorrectly totalled. The total calculated was £2,291.18 more than the correct sum of the individual entries.

(c)   A credit note issued to a customer for £742.37 had been entered in the returns inwards daybook as £472.37.

(d)   No entries had been made in the individual accounts to record:

    (i)   the purchase ledger contras; or
    (ii)   the decrease in the provision for doubtful debts.

(e)   A bad debt of £421.33 written off in 19X2 was recovered in September 19X4: the correct entries have been made in the individual customer account.

Required

(a)   Make any entries that you consider necessary in the sales ledger control account, commencing with the closing balance given, and reconcile the listing of the individual debtor balances to the closing balance shown on the control account (as amended).
               12 Marks

(b)   Explain why control accounts are used.
               3 Marks

Total Marks = 15

33   BC (11/95)   *36 mins*

The assistant accountant of BC Ltd has prepared a sales ledger control account at 30 September 19X5 for you to reconcile with the list of sales ledger balances at that date. The control account balances are:

Debit balances   £226,415   Credit balances   £1,250

The list of balances extracted from the sales ledger totals £225,890. You discover the following.

(a)   The credit balances have been included on the list of debtors as debit balances.

(b)   A sales invoice for £6,400 plus VAT at 17.5% has been recorded in the sales day book as £4,600 plus VAT at 17.5%. It has been entered correctly in the sales ledger.

(c)   Cash discounts allowed amounted to £840 and cash discounts received amounted to £560; the only entry in the control account for discounts is a debit for cash discounts received.

(d)   A dishonoured cheque for £450 from a customer has been recorded correctly in the control account, but no entry has been made in the debtor's personal account.

(e)   A contra entry between the sales and purchase ledgers of £750 has been omitted from the control account.

(f)   The control account contains receipts from cash sales of £860 but does not contain the invoices to which theses receipts refer; no entries have been made in the sales ledger for these invoices or receipts.

(g)   No entries have been made in the control account for bad debts written off (£2,150) and provision for doubtful debts (£2,400). Ignore VAT.

Required

(a)   Correct the sales ledger control account (commencing with the closing balances given).   **9 Marks**

(b)   Reconcile the listing of the individual balances to the revised sales ledger control account balances.   **3 Marks**

(c)   Discuss *four* facilities which a computerised sales ledger system might offer to BC Ltd.   **8 Marks**

Total Marks = 20

34   PQR (specimen paper)   *36 mins*

PQR Ltd has a year end of 31 December. At 30 November 19X3, the following balances exist in the ledger for the VAT, bank and debtors' accounts.

	£
VAT owing to Customs and Excise	3,250
Bank overdraft	6,250
Debtors	127,000

During December 19X3, the following transactions take place.

(a)   Sales of £85,000 plus VAT are made on credit.

(b)   A motor car costing £8,000 plus VAT is bought and paid for by cheque.

(c)   Materials are purchased on credit for £27,000 plus VAT.

(d)   Materials costing £3,000 plus VAT are returned to the supplier and a refund given by cheque.

(e)   Administration expenses of £2,400 plus VAT are incurred and paid for by cheque.

(f)   A VAT refund of £1,567 for the quarter ended 31 October 19X3 is received by cheque from Customs and Excise.

(g)   Debtors pay the balance outstanding at 30 November 19X3 by cheque, deducting £2,000 cash discount.

(h)   Creditors are paid £42,000 by cheque.

VAT is 17½% in all cases.

Required

(a)   Prepare the VAT account for December 19X3, showing the closing balance.

5 Marks

(b)   Calculate the bank balance at 31 December 19X3.   **5 Marks**

(c)   Explain the purpose of the trial balance and describe *four* different types of error which could occur in the trial balance, which would prevent its agreement.

Illustrate your answer using simple examples.   **10 Marks**

Total Marks = 20

35   TUTORIAL QUESTION: ERRORS AND JOURNAL ENTRIES

You work for Perin Products as a bookkeeper and one of your duties is to enter appropriate transactions into the Journal. During the week ended 20 October 19X9 the following details are passed to you for your attention.

October 16   An invoice relating to the sale of £163 of goods had been correctly sent out to D Evans but it is now found that the entry was made in P Evans' account.

October 16   A new machine is purchased on credit from Daley Engineering for £1,260 plus a delivery charge of £30.

October 17   Some office equipment valued at £475 is accepted from J Swanson in repayment of a debt for the same amount.

October 17   The owner of the business, J Perin, takes £60 of goods out of the business for his own use.

October 17   The £102 balance of D Saunder's account is to be written off as a bad debt.

October 18   It comes to light that during the previous week motor vehicle servicing costs of £124 were debited to the Motor Vehicles Account.

October 18   A payment by cheque to A Brigham for £20 made earlier in the week was debited to the Bank Account and credited to A Brigham.

October 19   It is found that when a credit note for £89 was previously issued to N Quinn, it had been entered in the relevant day book as £98.

October 19   On 30 September, some office equipment costing £610 had been purchased from Boxted Supplies Ltd. Unfortunately, the equipment is unsuitable and has been returned, a full allowance now being given by Boxted Supplies Ltd.

October 20   It is discovered that an invoice for £425 relating to goods received from EFI Ltd on 30 September was filed away and not entered anywhere in the books of Perin Products.

Required

Show the journal entries that you would have made during the week. Narratives and folio numbers are not required.

Guidance notes

1   The purchase on credit of machinery on 16 October would be recorded in the purchase day book and so need not be recorded in the journal. Similarly, the return of goods to Boxted Supplies Ltd should have been recorded in the purchase returns day book - but if no such book is kept, then a journal entry would be required, as in our solution. The EFI Ltd invoice should be posted in the normal way and so no journal is required.

2   You may be familiar with computerised accounting systems where the sales and purchase ledgers are integrated with the nominal ledger. In such a system, individual sales and purchase ledger accounts form part of the double entry system instead of being purely memorandum accounts, as in traditional systems. The ledger account totals can be extracted quickly and easily for accounts purposes and so no separate control account is needed.

3   It is therefore unnecessary in an integrated system to make the traditional distinction between errors which affect the ledger only and errors which affect the control account. However, it is important to remember that the traditional use of control accounts is still widespread. If you choose to write out your journals as if posting to an integrated ledger, you should make this perfectly clear.

4   Answers are provided for both systems in our suggested solution.

36   **TUTORIAL QUESTION: SUSPENSE ACCOUNTS**

A trial balance has an excess of debits over credits of £14,000 and a suspense account has been opened to make it balance. It is later discovered that:

(a)   the discounts allowed balance of £3,000 and the discounts received balance of £7,000 have both been entered on the wrong side of the trial balance;

(b)   the creditors control account balance of £233,786 had been included in the trial balance as £237,386;

(c)   an item of £500 had been omitted from the sales records (ie from the sales day book);

(d) the balance on the current account with the senior partner's wife had been omitted from the trial balance. This item when corrected removes the suspense account altogether.

Required

Open the suspense account and record the necessary corrections in it. Show in the account the double entry for each item entered.

Guidance notes

1   Incompetent bookkeepers and their suspense accounts are common features in examination questions and often provide a stern test of your understanding of double entry. The trick, as usual, is to think logically and take a methodical approach. The approach suggested below may seem long-winded, but once mastered it is very reliable.

2   First work out, in terms of debits and credits, what postings were actually made.

3   Then work out, in terms of debits and credits, what postings should have been made.

4   Now decide what entries need to be made to correct all the balances on any accounts affected. These entries are made in the accounts concerned.

5   Finally complete the double entry by summing all the entries made at Step **4** and posting the complementary net debit or credit to the suspense account. Then start again from Step **2** for the next transaction.

It is vital to remember that it is the Step **5** entry that goes to the appropriate side of the suspense account, not the Step **4** entries.

6   If the result of netting off the entries at Step **4** is nil there is no entry in the suspense account.

7   Commonly, suspense account balances are made up of transposition errors, errors of omission (single entry), errors of commission (posting a debit as a credit or vice versa) and items deliberately posted to suspense because they could not be identified at the time.

37   RST   *31 mins*

The draft final accounts of RST Limited for the year ended 30 April 19X5 showed a net profit for the year after tax of £78,263.

During the subsequent audit, the following errors and omissions were discovered. At the draft stage a suspense account had been opened to record the net difference.

(a) Trade debtors were shown as £55,210. However:
   (i)   bad debts of £610 had not been written off;
   (ii) the existing provision for doubtful debtors, £1,300, should have been adjusted to 2% of debtors;
   (iii) a provision of 2% for discounts on debtors should have been raised.

(b) Rates of £491 which had been prepaid at 30 April 19X4 had not been brought down on the rates account as an opening balance.

(c) A vehicle held as a fixed asset, which had originally cost £8,100 and for which £5,280 had been provided as depreciation, had been sold for £1,350. The proceeds had been correctly debited to bank but had been credited to sales. No transfers had been made to disposals account.

(d) Credit purchases of £1,762 had been correctly debited to purchases account but had been credited to the supplier's account as £1,672.

(e) A piece of equipment costing £9,800 and acquired on 1 May 19X4 for use in the business had been debited to purchases account. (The company depreciates equipment at 20% per annum on cost.)

(f) Items valued at £2,171 had been completely omitted from the closing stock figure.

(g) At 30 April 19X5 an accrual of £543 for electricity charges and an insurance prepayment of £162 had been omitted.

(h) The credit side of the wages account had been under-added by £100 before the balance on the account had been determined.

Required

Using relevant information from that given above, you are required to do the following.

(a) Prepare a statement correcting the draft net profit after tax.   **13 Marks**

(b) Post and balance the suspense account. (*Note.* The opening balance of this account has not been given and must be derived.)   **4 Marks**

Total Marks = 17

38   TD (5/96)   *36 mins*

At the year end of TD, an imbalance in the trial balance was revealed which resulted in the creation of a suspense account with a credit balance of £1,040.

Investigations revealed the following errors.

(i)   A sale of goods on credit for £1,000 had been omitted from the sales account.

(ii)   Delivery and installation costs of £240 on a new item of plant had been recorded as a revenue expense.

(iii) Cash discount of £150 on paying a creditor, JW, had been taken, even though the payment was made outside the time limit.

(iv) Stock of stationery at the end of the period of £240 had been ignored.

(v)   A purchase of raw materials of £350 had been recorded in the purchases account as £850.

(vi) The purchase returns day book included a sales credit note for £230 which had been entered correctly in the account of the debtor concerned, but included with purchase returns in the nominal ledger.

Required

(a) Prepare journal entries to correct *each* of the above errors. Narratives are *not* required.   **12 Marks**

(b) Open a suspense account and show the corrections to be made.   **3 Marks**

(c) Prior to the discovery of the errors, TD's gross profit for the year was calculated at £35,750 and the net profit for the year at £18,500.

Calculate the revised gross and net profit figures after the correction of the errors.   **5 Marks**

Total Marks = 20

39   TUTORIAL QUESTION: USING COMPUTERS AND SOFTWARE

PCs are used by many organisations of varying sizes either to prepare their accounts or to assist the managers of an organisation to control its activities.

(a) Describe how a PC accounting package may be used to deal with accounting transactions.

(b) What are the advantages of using such accounting packages instead of a manual system?

(c) Spreadsheets and databases are also commonly used by accountants, but what is the difference between a database and a spreadsheet?

Guidance notes

1   Questions about computers in accounting are likely to be part of a larger question on a specific aspect of accounting. You must, therefore, be ready to apply the knowledge that you are here invited to air in general terms.

2   Note that you are not asked how computers work when they are operating accounting packages. You are expected to write about the practicalities of using packages.

3   Spreadsheets and databases are not accounting packages in themselves, even though they are used by accountants.

40   INTERLOCKING AND INTEGRATED (ACC, 5/91)   *27 mins*

(a) Contrast the classification of costs which is used for cost accounting purposes with that used for financial accounting purposes.   **6 Marks**

(b) Nowadays, all but the smallest organisations use computerised accounting packages. In view of this, critically evaluate the importance of interlocking systems and explain the disadvantages of using integrated systems.   **9 Marks**

Total Marks = 15

41   ASSETS AND STOCKS (ACC, 5/92)   *27 mins*

(a) (i)   What information should be recorded in respect of each item of plant in a fixed asset register?

(ii) Explain how the use of a computer database can improve efficiency in accounting for, and controlling, an organisation's fixed assets.   **9 Marks**

(b) The matching concept and the cost concept are applied by accountants when preparing accounts. Explain the application of each of these concepts to accounting for stocks.   **6 Marks**

Total Marks = 15

42   SALES LEDGER PACKAGE (ACC, 11/93)   *27 mins*

(a) Explain how the use of a PC sales ledger accounting package could benefit a small organisation in the control of its debtors.   **7 Marks**

(b) What is a spreadsheet? Explain briefly one cost accounting use of a PC spreadsheet package.   **8 Marks**

Total Marks = 15

43   SPREADSHEETS   *18 mins*

'The increasing use of spreadsheets will make accounting out of date.'

Required

Briefly explain the usefulness of spreadsheets to accountants, and comment on the above statement.   **10 Marks**

DO YOU KNOW? - FINAL ACCOUNTS AND AUDIT

- *Check that you know the following basic points before you attempt any questions. If in doubt, you should go back to your BPP Study Text and revise first.*

- Trading accounts, profit and loss accounts and balance sheets have standard formats depending on the type of business. These must be committed to memory.

- Sole traders' accounts are not (strictly speaking) governed by legislation or accounting standards, but accountants should always follows best practice when preparing accounts of any kind.

- In tackling an *incomplete records* question you should take the following steps.

  o Prepare an opening statement of affairs if no balance sheet is given in the question.

  o Write up or complete any bank account transactions and write up the cash receipts and payments account. There will usually be a balancing figure on the cash account, usually drawings, bankings or cash sales.

  o Write up or complete the debtors and creditors control account. This will give you sales and purchases.

  o Make any adjustments for accruals and prepayments. Write up the trading account, the profit and loss account and the balance sheet.

- Bodies such as *clubs and societies* do not set out primarily to make a profit, therefore it is inappropriate to prepare a profit and loss account. Instead an income and expenditure account is prepared.

- There is no capital account in the balance sheet, instead there is an accumulated fund (= net assets).

- *Limited companies* also have special features. Their accounts include certain items that are not found in the accounts of an unincorporated business such as *dividends, share capital and debentures*. There are specialised accounting transactions associated with these items.

- The accounting records and financial statements of a limited company are strictly regulated by statute.

- Manufacturing accounts are prepared for internal management use only. Their purpose is to distinguish between the costs and profitability associated with manufacturing operations and those associated with trading (which are shown in the trading account).

- Cash flow statements concentrate on the sources and uses of cash, are a useful indicator of a company's liquidity and solvency, and have replaced funds flow statements.

- It is important that you are in a position to answer a written question discussing the advantages and disadvantages of cash flow statements.

- While a detailed knowledge of the format of FRS 1 *Cash flow statements* is not required, it will help to structure your answer if you are aware of the sub-divisions used.

- There are two main types of audit: internal and external

  o *External auditors* report to the *members* of a company on whether the accounts give a true and fair view.

  o *Internal auditors* are employees of the company and report to *management* on matters fixed by management.

- *Key questions*

  Tutorial questions 44, 48, 51, 55, 59
  49   *Happy Tickers*
  54   *JB*
  58   *DWS*
  62   *FPC*
  66   *SH Ltd*
  69   *GTZ*

---

44   TUTORIAL QUESTION: ACCOUNTS PREPARATION

The following trial balance has been extracted from the ledger of Mr Yousef, a sole trader.

TRIAL BALANCE AS AT 31 MAY 19X6

	Dr £	Cr £
Sales		138,078
Purchases	82,350	
Carriage	5,144	
Drawings	7,800	
Rent, rates and insurance	6,622	
Postage and stationery	3,001	
Advertising	1,330	
Salaries and wages	26,420	
Bad debts	877	
Provision for doubtful debts		130
Debtors	12,120	
Creditors		6,471
Cash on hand	177	
Cash at bank	1,002	
Stock as at 1 June 19X5	11,927	
Equipment		
At cost	58,000	
Accumulated depreciation		19,000
Capital		53,091
	216,770	216,770

The following additional information as at 31 May 19X6 is available.

(a) Rent is accrued by £210.
(b) Rates have been prepaid by £880.
(c) £2,211 of carriage represents carriage inwards on purchases.
(d) Equipment is to be depreciated at 15% per annum using the straight line method.
(e) The provision for bad debts to be increased by £40.
(f) Stock at the close of business has been valued at £13,551.

Required

Prepare a trading and profit and loss account for the year ended 31 May 19X6 and a balance sheet as at that date.

Guidance notes

1   Presentation is always important, but especially so in accounts preparation questions. It is best to draw up a proforma profit and loss account and balance sheet using the headings given to you in the trial balance, and allowing a whole side of paper for each. Do not enter any numbers at this stage.

2   Now work through all of the additional information that you are given and perform any calculations that are required. For example the information in (a) is the only additional information you are given about stock, so you can go ahead and enter the figures for opening stock in your proforma profit and loss account and for closing stock in the P & L and balance sheet. Other calculations (for example the depreciation provision) can best be done in a separate working. In other cases you may be able to do your workings on the face of your proforma P & L or balance sheet (for example 'Provision for bad debts (130 + 40)). When you check your own answers you will see a variety of such presentation techniques demonstrated in our suggested solutions to the questions in this section and you should try to emulate them.

3   The golden rule while you are doing your calculations is to keep the double entry going. The depreciation provision affects fixed assets in the balance sheet and the depreciation charge in the P & L. Accruals affect the relevant P & L account *and* the accruals provision in the balance sheet. Make *both* entries as soon as you have the relevant figures.

4   Finally, insert any remaining figures, taking them straight from the trial balance, and add up your profit and loss account and balance sheet. If it does not balance you have made a mistake. Work out the difference and see if it matches any of the figures you have been given

or have calculated - this should enable you to correct your mistake. If not divide the difference by two and see if the resulting figure matches another one (this will mean that you have treated a debit as a credit or vice versa). If this fails it is probably not worth spending more time on the question, unless you have plenty of spare time left. Assuming time is short, just leave a note ('Difference: £X') to show the examiner that you are aware that there is still a problem and get on with the next question.

45 TUTORIAL QUESTION: IDENTIFY FAULTS

Jenny Jacques is the proprietor of 'The Copper Kettle'. She has presented you with the following financial statements. These contain a number of faults.

JENNY JACQUES
FINAL ACCOUNTS AS AT 31 MAY 19X8

	£	£
Sales		127,000
Add return outwards		3,600
		130,600
Rents received		2,500
		133,100
Less cost of goods sold:		
Stock at 31 May 19X8	7,450	
Purchases	111,090	
Returns inwards	2,140	
Discounts received	11,800	
	132,480	
Less stock at 31 May 19X7	6,780	
		125,700
Gross profit		7,400
Less operating expenses:		
Selling and distribution	11,800	
Drawings	10,060	
Administration	4,670	
		26,530
Net profit		33,930

BALANCE SHEET FOR 31 MAY 19X8

	£	£	£
Fixed assets			
Equipment at cost			28,500
Stock at cost			6,780
			38,280
Accumulated depreciation			(14,250)
			21,030
Current assets			
Cash on hand		130	
Trade debtors		11,090	
Accrued expenses		230	
Bank overdraft		1,050	
		12,500	
Current liabilities			
Trade creditors	7,530		
Prepaid expenses	140		
		7,670	
Working capital			20,170
Net assets			41,200
Financed by capital			
As at 1 June 19X7			18,440
Add net profit			33,930
			52,370
Difference			11,170
			41,200

Required

Identify as many of the faults in the above financial statements as you can.

Guidance note

We identify and explain sixteen faults in our answer. The best way to find them is to write out your own version of the financial statements in good form. If your version corresponds exactly with the one shown in our solution, you have found all the mistakes.

46 GBA (11/95)   *54 mins*

GBA is a sole trader, supplying building materials to local builders. He prepares his accounts to 30 June each year. At 30 June 19X5, his trial balance was as follows.

	Dr £	Cr £
Capital at 1 July 19X4		55,550
Purchases and sales	324,500	625,000
Returns	2,300	1,700
Discounts	1,500	2,500
Stock of building materials at 1 July 19X4	98,200	
Packing materials purchased	12,900	
Distribution costs	17,000	
Rent, rates and insurance	5,100	
Telephone	3,200	
Car expenses	2,400	
Wages	71,700	
Provision for doubtful debts at 1 July 19X4		1,000
Heat and light	1,850	
Sundry expenses	6,700	
Delivery vehicles - cost	112,500	
Delivery vehicles - depreciation at 1 July 19X4		35,000
Equipment - cost	15,000	
Equipment - depreciation at 1 July 19X4		5,000
Debtors and creditors	95,000	82,000
Loan		10,000
Loan repayments	6,400	
Bank deposit account	15,000	
Bank current account	26,500	
	817,750	817,750

The following additional information at 30 June 19X5 is available.

(a) Closing stocks of building materials   £75,300
     Closing stocks of packing materials   £700

There was also an unpaid invoice of £200 for packing materials received and consumed during the year.

(b) Prepayments

     Rent, rates and insurance   £450

(c) Accrued expenses

     Heat and light   £400
     Telephone   £500

(d) Wages includes £23,800 cash withdrawn by GBA.

(e) Debtors have been analysed as follows.

	£
Current month	60,000
30 to 60 days	20,000
60 to 90 days	12,000
over 90 days	3,000

Provision is to be made for doubtful debts as follows.

30 to 60 days	1%
60 to 90 days	2.5%
over 90 days	5% (after writing off £600)

(f)   Sundry expenses includes £3,500 for GBA's personal tax bill.

(g)   The loan was taken out some years ago, and is due for repayment on 31 March 19X6. The figure shown in the trial balance for 'loan repayments' includes interest of £800 for the year.

(h)   The bank deposit account was opened on 1 January 19X5 as a short-term investment; interest is credited at 31 December annually; the average rate of interest since opening the account has been 6% per annum.

(i)   At 1 July 19X4, GBA decided to bring one of his family cars, valued at £8,000, into the business. No entries have been made in the business books for its introduction.

(j)   Depreciation is to be provided as follows.

20% on cost for delivery vehicles
25% on the reducing balance for the car
25% on the reducing balance for equipment

Required

(a)   Prepare a trading and profit and loss account for the year ended 30 June 19X5.

12 Marks

(b)   Prepare a balance sheet at 30 June 19X5.   **10 Marks**

(c)   Explain to GBA why *four* of the transactions which have occurred in his business during the year have affected his bank balance but have not affected the calculation of his profit for the year.   **8 Marks**

Total Marks = 30

47   PLJ (5/97)   *54 mins*

PLJ has been in business for some years and has kept her drawings slightly below the level of profits each year. She has never made a loss, and therefore feels that her business is growing steadily. You act as her accountant, and she has passed you the following list of balances at 30 April 19X7.

	£'000
Capital at 1 May 19X6	228
Drawings	14
Plant at cost	83
Plant depreciation at 1 May 19X6	13
Office equipment at cost	31
Office equipment depreciation at 1 May 19X6	8
Debtors	198
Creditors	52
Sales	813
Purchases	516
Returns inwards	47
Discounts allowed	4
Provision for doubtful debts at 1 May 19X6	23
Administration costs	38
Salaries	44
Research costs	26
Loan to a friend, repayable in 6 months	25
Bank	50
Bad debts written off	77

You ascertain that stock at 1 May 19X6 was £84,000 and stock at 30 April 19X7 was £74,000. On 1 November 19X6, she brought her personal computer, valued at £2,000, from home into the office; no entries have been made for this.

You are also given the following information at 30 April 19X7.

(a)   Depreciation on plant is charged at 10% per annum on cost.

Depreciation on office equipment is charged at 20% per annum on the net book value at the year end.

(b) Administration costs includes insurance prepaid of £3,000.

(c) Salaries accrued amount to £2,000.

(d) The research costs are all in relation to pure research.

(e) It is agreed that the provision for doubtful debts figure is to remain at £23,000.

Required

(a) Prepare a trial balance at 30 April 19X7, after adjusting for the computer which PLJ has brought from home, but prior to making any other adjustments.   **6 Marks**

(b) Prepare a trading and profit and loss account for the year ended 30 April 19X7.
                                                                                7 Marks

(c) Prepare a balance sheet at 30 April 19X7.   **10 Marks**

(d) Explain to PLJ why her assumption that the business is growing steadily may be incorrect.

In your answer, explain the theory of capital maintenance and explain how the historical cost concept can affect this theory.   **7 Marks**

                                                                   Total Marks = 30

48   TUTORIAL QUESTION: INCOME AND EXPENDITURE ACCOUNTS

The HB tennis club was formed on 1 April 19X0 and has the following receipts and payments account for the six months ended 30 September 19X0.

	£		£
Receipts		*Payments*	
Subscriptions	12,600	Purchase of equipment	4,080
Tournament fees	465	Groundsman's wages	4,520
Bank interest	43	Rent and business rates	636
Sale of club ties	373	Heating and lighting	674
Life membership fees	4,200	Postage and stationery	41
		Court maintenance	1,000
		Tournament prizes	132
		Purchase of club ties	450
		Balance c/d	6,148
	17,681		17,681

Notes

(a) The annual subscription fee is £300. On 30 September there were still five members who had not paid their annual subscription, but this money was received on 4 October 19X0.

(b) The equipment is expected to be used by the club for five years, after which time it will need to be replaced. Its estimated scrap value at that time is £50.

(c) During the six months, the club purchased 100 ties printed with its own design. Forty of these ties remained unsold at 30 September 19X0.

(d) The club had paid business rates in advance on 30 September 19X0 of £68.

(e) The club treasurer estimates that the following amounts should be accrued for expenses.

	£
Groundsman's wages	40
Postage and stationery	12
Heating and lighting	53

(f) The life membership fees received relate to payments made by four families. The scheme allows families to pay £1,050 which entitles them to membership for life without further payment. It has been agreed that such receipts would be credited to income and expenditure in equal instalments over ten years.

Required

(a) Prepare the club's Income and Expenditure account for the six months ended 30 September 19X0.

(b) Prepare the club's balance sheet at 30 September 19X0.

Guidance notes

1   The only real difference between an income and expenditure account and a profit and loss account is the format. Group together all the items of income under a heading 'Income' and leave a line for the total. Then do the same for expenditure. The net figure is called a 'surplus' and it is transferred to an accumulated fund which replaces the 'retained profits' on the balance sheet.

2   Do not forget that in this question you are preparing accounts for six months, whereas much of the information given relates to a full year.

3   Subscriptions will appear in the income and expenditure account, and there will also be headings under current assets for subscriptions due and under current liabilities for subscriptions paid in advance. Be especially careful here to think through the implications of the fact that you are preparing accounts for six months.

49   HAPPY TICKERS   *45 mins*

The accounting records of the Happy Tickers Sports and Social Club are in a mess. You manage to find the following information to help you prepare the accounts for the year to 31 December 19Y0.

SUMMARISED BALANCE SHEET 31 DECEMBER 19X9

	£		£
Half-share in motorised roller	600	Insurance (3 months)	150
		Subscriptions 19Y0	120
New sports equipment unsold	1,000	Life subscriptions	1,400
			1,670
Used sports equipment at valuation	700	Accumulated fund	2,900
Rent (2 months)	200		
Subscriptions 19X9	60		
Cafe stocks	800		
Cash and bank	1,210		
	4,570		4,570

Receipts in year to 31 December 19Y0

	£
Subscriptions - 19X9	40
- 19Y0	1,100
- 19Y1	80
- life	200
From sales of new sports equipment	900
From sales of used sports equipment	14
Cafe takings	4,660
	6,994

Payments in the year to 31 December 19Y0

	£
Rent (for 12 months)	1,200
Insurance (for 18 months)	900
To suppliers of sports equipment	1,000
To cafe suppliers	1,900
Wages of cafe manager	2,000
Total cost of repairing motorised roller	450
	7,450

Notes

(a) Ownership and all expenses of the motorised roller are agreed to be shared equally with the Carefree Conveyancers Sports and Social Club which occupies a nearby site. The roller cost a total of £2,000 on 1 January 19X6 and had an estimated life of 10 years.

(b) Life subscriptions are brought into income equally over 10 years, in a scheme begun in 19X5. Since the scheme began the cost of £200 per person has been constant. Prior to 31 December 19X9 10 life subscriptions had been received.

(c) Four more annual subscriptions of £20 each had been promised relating to 19Y0, but not yet received. Annual subscriptions promised but unpaid are carried forward for a maximum of 12 months.

(d) New sports equipment is sold to members at cost plus 50%. Used equipment is sold off to members at book valuation. Half the sports equipment bought in the year (all from a cash and carry supplier) has been used within the club, and half made available for sale, new, to members. The 'used equipment at valuation' figure in the 31 December 19Y0 balance sheet is to remain at £700.

(e) Closing cafe stocks are £850, and £80 is owed to suppliers at 31 December 19Y0.

Required

(a) Calculate profit on cafe operations and profit on sale of sports equipment. **6 Marks**

(b) Prepare statement of subscription income for 19Y0. **4 Marks**

(c) Prepare income and expenditure statement for the year to 31 December 19Y0, and balance sheet as at 31 December 19Y0. **11 Marks**

(d) Why do life subscriptions appear as a liability? **4 Marks**

Total Marks = 25

---

50 RACKETS   *27 mins*

You have been appointed the bookkeeper of a tennis club called Rackets Unlimited. The club began on 1 July 19W9, and no accounts have yet been prepared. The club has three ways of receiving subscriptions,

(a) £10 per year

(b) If two years' subscriptions are paid at once £1 may be deducted from the second year. If three year's subscriptions are paid at once, £2 may also be deducted from the third year.

(c) If 10 years' subscriptions are paid at once no deductions are allowed, but members are regarded as members for life.

You have completed the following table of subscription receipts.

Member	Relevant to membership year ended 30.6.X0 Date received	Amount £	Relevant to membership year ended 30.6.X1 Date received	Amount £	Relevant to membership year ended 30.6.X2 Date received	Amount £
A	July 'W9	10				
B	July 'W9	10	July 'X0	10		
C	July 'W9	10	June 'X0	10	July 'X1	10
D	Sept 'W9	10	Sept 'X0	27		
E	Oct 'W9	27				
F	Oct 'W9	10	July 'X0	10	June 'X1	27
G	Oct 'W9	100				
H	Oct 'W9	10	June 'X0	10	June 'X1	100
I	Oct 'W9	10	June 'X0	19		
J			July ' X1	10		
K			July 'X0	27		
L	Dec 'W9	10			June 'X1	10
M	July 'X0	19				
N			July 'X1	100		

The club does not intend to accrue for any income not received by the date of preparation of financial statements.

Required

(a) To assist in the preparation of some accounts, complete a table with the following headings:

Member	Income year to 30.6.X0	Income year to 30.6.X1	Balance c/f at 30.6.X1 Dr	Cr

13 Marks

(b) State *two* comments about your table which you think might be helpful to the club committee.   **2 Marks**

Total Marks = 15

51   TUTORIAL QUESTION: INCOMPLETE RECORDS

Miss Anne Teek runs a market stall selling old pictures, china, copper goods and curios of all descriptions. Most of her sales are for cash although regular customers are allowed credit. No double entry accounting records have been kept, but the following information is available.

SUMMARY OF NET ASSETS AT 31 MARCH 19X8

	£	£
Motor van		
Cost	3,000	
Depreciation	2,500	
Net book value		500
Current assets		
Stock	500	
Debtors	170	
Cash at bank	2,800	
Cash in hand	55	
	3,525	
Less current liabilities		
Creditors	230	
Net current assets		3,295
		3,795

Additional information

(a) Anne bought a new motor van in January 19X9 receiving a part exchange allowance of £1,800 for her old van. A full year's depreciation is to be provided on the new van, calculated at 20% on cost.

(b) Anne has taken £50 cash per week for her personal use. She also estimates that petrol for the van, paid in cash, averages £10 per week.

(c) Other items paid in cash were as follows.

Sundry expenses	£24
Repairs to stall canopy	£201

(d) Anne makes a gross profit of 40% on selling prices. She is certain that no goods have been stolen but remembers that she appropriated a set of glasses and some china for her own use. These items had a total selling price of £300.

(e) Trade debtors and creditors at 31 March 19X9 are £320 and £233 respectively, and cash in hand amounts to £39. No stock count has been made and there are no accrued or prepaid expenses.

A summary of bank statements for the twelve months in question shows the following.

Credits	£
Cash banked (all cash sales)	7,521
Cheques banked (all credit sales)	1,500
Dividend income	210
	9,231

	£
Debits	
Purchase of motor van	3,200
Road fund licence	80
Insurance on van	323
Creditors for purchases	7,777
Rent	970
Sundry	31
Accountancy fees (re current work)	75
Bank overdraft interest (six months to 1 October 19X8)	20
Returned cheque (bad debt)	29
	12,505

The bank statement for 1 April 19X9 shows an interest charge of £27.

Required

Prepare Anne's trading and profit and loss account for the year to 31 March 19X9, and a balance sheet as at that date.

(Assume a 52 week year.)

Guidance notes

1   The opening balance sheet is given here and so there is no need to reconstruct it. Otherwise this should always be your first step in incomplete records questions.

2   The next step is to open up four accounts for the trading account, debtors, creditors and cash (a two column cash book).

3   Enter the opening balances.

4   Work through the additional information making entries in your four accounts as appropriate, and being sure to keep the double entry going.

5   Look for the balancing figures.

6   Complete the P & L account and balance sheet.

52   SOLE TRADER 'T' (ACC, 5/91)   *27 mins*

The following information relates to T, a sole trader.

During the year ended 30 April 19X1 he sold goods to the value of £125,000. During the year, all goods were sold at a profit mark-up on cost of 25%.

During the year his administration costs amounted to £7,500.

At 30 April 19X1 his closing stock represented 36.5 days sales and this was twice as much as his opening stock. His debtors payment period was 50 days and his creditors represented 30 days' purchases.

The ratio of his current assets to liabilities was 1.4: 1.0.

The fixed assets were equal to 30% of his capital employed.

Required

Prepare T's profit and loss account for the year ended 30 April 19X1 and his balance sheet at that date, in as much detail as possible from the above information.

(Where necessary, round your workings to the nearest £.)

15 Marks

53   JAY (ACC, 5/94)   *45 mins*

J had the following assets and liabilities on 1 October 19X2.

	£
Plant and equipment	6,420
Motor vehicles	4,200
Stock of goods for resale	890
Trade creditors	470
Trade debtors	1,260
Balance at bank	3,520
Cash in hand	80
Accrued electricity	30
Prepaid business rates	1,300

J's summarised cashbook for the year ended 30 September 19X3 was as follows.

	Cash £	Bank £		Cash £	Bank £
Balance b/f	80	3,520	Electricity		270
Trade debtors		29,640	Postage/stationery		65
Sales	3,630		Business rates		2,800
Plant disposal		1,735	Wages		1,750
Bank	3,000		Bank charges		120
			Rent		2,400
			Purchases	6,460	
			Trade creditors		12,740
			Van		1,405
			Vehicle expenses		980
			Drawings		6,000
			Cash		3,000
			Balance b/f	250	3,365
	6,710	34,895		6,710	34,895

Other information

(a)   The plant disposal occurred on 1 August 19X3. On 1 October 19X2 the net book value of the plant disposed of was £1,420

(b)   The amount entered in the cashbook for business rates is made up of two equal payments of £1,400. These occurred on 1 March 19X3 and 1 September 19X3 and were made in respect of the six-month periods ending 30 September 19X3 and 31 March 19X4.

(c)   The amount entered in the cashbook for the van relates to an acquisition which occurred on 1 April 19X3. The value shown includes

	£
Twelve months' road fund licence (annual vehicle tax)	110
Petrol	20
Twelve-month maintenance warranty	200

(d)   Wages owing on 30 September 19X3 are estimated to be £180.

(e)   Closing stock on 30 September 19X3, valued at cost, amounted to £775.

(f)   Electricity owing on 30 September 19X3 amounted to £345.

(g)   A full year's depreciation is to be provided on all assets held on 30 September 19X3 at the following rates, using the reducing balance method.

Plant and equipment	15%
Motor vehicle	25%

(h)   On 30 September 19X3 trade debtors amounted to £1,330 and trade creditors were £265.

Required

(a)   Prepare J's trading and profit and loss account for the year ended 30 September 19X3, in vertical form.   **10 Marks**

(b)   Calculate J's capital at 1 October 19X2.   **3 Marks**

(c)   Prepare J's balance sheet at 30 September 19X3, in vertical form.   **8 Marks**

(d)   When preparing the final accounts of any business, accounting policies are used to ensure consistency from one period to another.

Identify *three* accounting policies which have been adopted by J, and explain how one of these has affected the preparation of the final accounts.   **4 Marks**

Total Marks = 25

---

54   JB (11/96)   *54 mins*

On 31 December 19X5 the accounting records of JB were partly destroyed by fire. Her accountant has provided the following list of assets, liabilities and capital at 31 December 19X4.

	£
Plant and machinery	128,000
Office equipment	45,000
Stocks	30,500
Debtors and prepayments	35,000
Creditors and accruals	17,600
Bank overdraft	8,850
Loan (interest 10% per annum)	95,000
Capital	117,050

A summary of her receipts and payments during 19X5 can be extracted from the bank statements, as follows.

		£
Receipts:	Capital paid in	22,000
	Received from debtors	427,500
Payments:	Cash withdrawn	22,450
	Loan repayments	20,000
	Paid to creditors	175,600
	Rent paid	22,000
	Wages	90,000
	General expenses paid	12,500

The following additional information is obtained.

(a)   At 31 December 19X4, the debtors figure included £2,500 for rent paid in advance, and the creditors figure included £4,300 for wages accrued for the last week of 19X4.

(b)   The plant and machinery had been purchased for £200,000 in 19X3, and was being depreciated at 20% per annum on the reducing balance basis.

The office equipment was bought during 19X4 and was being depreciated over 10 years on the straight-line basis, with a full year's depreciation in the year of purchase.

(c)   During 19X5, JB transferred a private motor vehicle worth £5,000 to her business. It is to be depreciated over 4 years on the straight-line basis, with a full year's depreciation in the year of acquisition.

(d)   Of the cash withdrawn from the bank during 19X5, £6,750 was for wages, £4,200 was for cash payments to suppliers, £2,600 was for printing of advertising leaflets (of which half are still to be distributed), and the remainder was taken by JB for her own use.

(e)   The bank balance at 31 December 19X5, according to the bank statement, after adjusting for unpresented cheques, was £106,700. Any difference is assumed to be cash sales banked, after deducting £30 per week wages paid to JB's daughter, who assists in the office.

(f)   The loan repayments from the bank account include interest of £9,500.

(g)   Other balances at 31 December 19X5 are:

	£
Stock	27,850
Rent paid in advance	2,700
Wages owing	5,250
Creditors for supplies	12,200
Debtors	22,300

(h) It is subsequently discovered that a debtor owing £16,000 has gone into liquidation, and a dividend of 20p in the £ is expected.

Required

(a) Prepare the trading and profit and loss account for JB for the year ended 31 December 19X5. **15 Marks**

(b) Prepare a balance sheet for JB at 31 December 19X5. **10 Marks**

(c) JB comments that, as you have managed to prepare these accounts without the need for her usual books and ledgers, then perhaps she does not need to maintain them in the future.

Briefly explain the benefits of maintaining a double-entry book-keeping system. **5 Marks**

Total Marks = 30

55 TUTORIAL QUESTION: COMPANY ACCOUNTS

The trial balance of Toby Ltd at 31 December 19X8 is as follows:

	£	£
Share capital - £1 ordinary shares		10,000
Profit and loss account		19,000
Sales and purchases	61,000	100,000
Sales returns and purchase returns	2,000	4,000
Sales and purchase ledger control accounts	20,000	7,000
Land and buildings (at cost)	40,000	
Plant (at cost, and depreciation to 1 January 19X8)	50,000	22,000
Debentures (10% pa interest)		30,000
Opening stock	15,000	
Operating expenses	9,000	
Administration expenses	7,000	
Selling expenses	6,000	
Bank		8,000
Suspense account		10,000
	210,000	210,000

Notes

(a) 5,000 new shares were issued during the year at £1.60 per share. The proceeds have been credited to the suspense account.

(b) Sales returns of £1,000 have been entered in the sales day book as if they were sales.

(c) The bookkeeper has included the opening provision for doubtful debts of £800 in the selling expenses account in the trial balance. The provision is required to be 5% of debtors.

(d) A standing order payment of £1,000 for rates paid in December has not been entered. This payment covered the half-year to 31 March 19X9.

(e) Closing stock is £18,000.

(f) No debenture interest has been paid.

(g) The remaining balance on the suspense account after the above represents the sales proceeds of a fully depreciated item of plant, costing £10,000. No other entries (except bank) have been made concerning this disposal.

(h) Depreciation at 10% on cost should be provided on the plant.

Required

Prepare a trading, profit and loss account for the year, and balance sheet as at 31 December 19X8, in good order, taking account of the above notes.

Guidance notes

1   Company accounts questions are the commonest type of accounts preparation questions in the examination, so you can expect to have to deal with things like debentures, share capital, share premiums and so on as a matter of course. Otherwise the techniques are no different from any other accounts preparation question.

2   Do not charge depreciation on plant that has been disposed of: now you have been told, this sounds foolish, but it is an easy error to make. Also don't forget that the bad debt expense is part of selling expenses.

56   ABC (ACC, 11/94)   *45 mins*

ABC Ltd has extracted the following trial balance from its ledgers at its year end - 31 October 19X4.

	£	£
Premises at cost	60,000	
Equipment at cost	23,400	
Vehicles at cost	12,800	
Stock (1 November 19X3)	4,950	
Debtors and creditors	12,595	8,742
Ordinary share capital		50,000
Sales		123,740
Postage, stationery etc	1,249	
Returns inwards	4,243	
Purchases	76,297	
Carriage outwards	1,325	
Wages and salaries	28,291	
Provision for bad and doubtful debts		748
Provision for depreciation		
Premises		24,000
Equipment		5,840
Vehicles		6,300
Business rates	12,240	
Lighting and heating	3,624	
Bank balance	1,236	
Profit and loss account		22,880
	242,250	242,250

Notes

(a)   Stock held on 31 October 19X4, valued at cost, amounted to £6,492. However, some of these items (cost value £2,089) are reported to be obsolete; their scrap value is £545.

(b)   Business rates include £4,500 paid on 1 October 19X4 for the six months ending 31 March 19X5.

(c)   Wages owing on 31 October 19X4 were £624.

(d)   Lighting and heating owing on 31 October 19X4 is estimated to be £393.

(e)   An aged debtor analysis of ABC Ltd's sales ledger balances is shown below.

Total	Current	30 days	60 days	90 days	90+ days
£	£	£	£	£	£
12,595	6,500	3,440	1,355	800	500

It is company policy to write off all debts more than 90 days old as bad debts and to provide for doubtful debts on the basis of the aged balance as follows.

	%
Current	3
30 days	10
60 days	20
90 days	50

(f) It is company policy to provide a full year's depreciation on all fixed assets held at the end of each year using the following methods and rates.

Premises	4% per annum on cost
Equipment	15% per annum on cost
Vehicles	25% per annum reducing balance

Required

(a) Prepare a draft trading and profit and loss account for ABC Ltd for the year ended 31 October 19X4, in vertical format (ignore taxation). **8 Marks**

(b) Prepare a draft balance sheet at 31 October 19X4, in vertical format. **7 Marks**

(c) The managing director is disappointed by the results shown in the draft profit and loss account and has suggested the following adjustments:

    (i) that the provision for bad and doubtful debts be eliminated;
    (ii) that depreciation need not be provided.

Comment on these suggestions, having regard to appropriate accounting concepts.

10 Marks
Total Marks = 25

57 JAYKAY (ACC, 5/93)   *49 mins*

The following trial balance has been extracted from the ledgers of JK Ltd at 31 March 19X3.

	£	£
Sales (all on credit)		647,400
Stock (1 April 19X2)	15,400	
Trade debtors and creditors	82,851	41,936
Purchases (all on credit)	321,874	
Carriage in	13,256	
Carriage out	32,460	
Electricity	6,994	
Business rates	8,940	
Wages and salaries	138,292	
Postages and stationery	6,984	
Rent	14,600	
VAT control		16,382
PAYE control		4,736
Motor vehicles: at cost	49,400	
depreciation		21,240
Bank deposit account	90,000	
Bank current account	77,240	
Ordinary shares of £1 each		50,000
Profit and loss: unappropriated profit		76,597
	858,291	858,291

The following notes are also relevant.

(a) Stock at 31 March 19X3, valued at cost, was £19,473.

(b) Prepaid rent amounted to £2,800.

(c) Accruals are estimated as follows.

	£
Electricity	946
Wages and salaries	2,464

(d) Depreciation on motor vehicles is to be provided at 25% per annum using the reducing balance method.

(e) Accrued interest on the bank deposit account amounts to £7,200.

(f) A provision for corporation tax of £30,000 is to be made on the profits of the year.

(g) No interim dividend was paid but the directors propose a final dividend of £0.05 per share.

Required

(a) Prepare JK Ltd's trading, profit and loss and appropriation account for the year ended 31 March 19X3, in vertical format. **10 Marks**

(b) Prepare JK Ltd's balance sheet at 31 March 19X3, in vertical format. **7 Marks**

(c) Calculate and comment briefly on the debtors' and creditors' payment periods and the stockholding period of JK Ltd. **10 Marks**

Total Marks = 27

58   DWS (5/95)   *54 mins*

DWS Ltd prepares its accounts to 30 September each year. At 30 September 19X4 its trial balance was as follows.

	Debit £	*Credit* £
Plant and machinery		
Cost	125,000	
Depreciation at 1 October 19X3		28,000
Office equipment		
Cost	45,000	
Depreciation at 1 October 19X3		15,000
Stocks at 1 October 19X3	31,000	
Purchases and sales	115,000	188,000
Returns inwards and outwards	8,000	6,000
Selling expenses	12,000	
Heat and light	8,000	
Wages and salaries	14,000	
Directors' fees	5,000	
Printing and stationery	6,000	
Telephone and fax	6,000	
Rent, rates and insurances	4,000	
Trade debtors and creditors	35,000	33,000
Provision for doubtful debts at 1 October 19X3		4,000
Bank	3,000	
Petty cash	1,000	
Interim dividend paid	2,000	
Ordinary shares of 50p each		100,000
Share premium account		8,000
General reserve		7,000
Profit and loss account balance at 1 October 19X3		34,000
Suspense account	3,000	
	423,000	423,000

The following additional information at 30 September 19X4 is available.

(a) Closing stocks of goods for resale £53,000

(b) Prepayments

Telephone and fax rental	£1,000
Rates and insurance	£1,000

(c) Accruals

Wages and salaries	£1,500
Directors' fees	2% of net turnover
Auditor's fees	£3,500

(d) Specific bad debts to be written off amount to £3,000.

(e)   Provision for doubtful debts is to be amended to 5% of debtors, after adjusting for bad debts written off.

(f)   The following bookkeeping errors are discovered.

    (i)   The purchase of an item of stock has been debited to the office equipment account - cost £1,200.

    (ii)   The payment of £1,300 to a creditor has been recorded by debiting the bank account and crediting the creditor's account.

Any remaining balance on the suspense account is to be added to prepayments or accruals, as appropriate, on the balance sheet.

(g)   The figure in the trial balance for the bank balance is the balance appearing in the cash book, prior to the reconciliation with the bank statement. Upon reconciliation, it is discovered that:

    (i)   unpresented cheques amount to £3,000;
    (ii)   bank charges not entered in the ledgers amount to £4,000.

(h)   Depreciation of fixed assets is to be provided as follows.

Plant and machinery	10% on cost
Office equipment	$33^{1}/_{3}$ % on the reducing balance at the end of the year

(i)   A final dividend of 1.5p per share is to be proposed.

(j)   £10,000 is to be transferred to general reserves.

(k)   Provision of £1,000 for corporation tax is to be made.

Required

(a)   Prepare a trading and profit and loss account for the year ended 30 September 19X4.

12 Marks

(b)   Prepare a balance sheet at 30 September 19X4.   **8 Marks**

(c)   Calculate *two* liquidity ratios.   **4 Marks**

(d)   Explain the meaning of the two ratios you have calculated and discuss any further information which might be needed in order to assess liquidity more accurately.

6 Marks

Total Marks = 30

59   TUTORIAL QUESTION: MANUFACTURING ACCOUNTS

From the information given below you are required to prepare the manufacturing, trading and profit and loss account of Abcoll Ltd for the year ended 31 December 19X5.

Balances at 31 December 19X4

	£
Authorised and issued share capital	
Ordinary shares of £1 each fully paid	100,000
Reserves	1,000
Creditors	57,400
Fixed assets (cost £60,000)	39,000
Stocks	
Raw materials	25,000
Work in progress, valued at prime cost	5,800
Finished goods	51,000
Debtors	35,000
Cash at bank	2,000
Administration expenses prepaid	600

The following transactions occurred during 19X5.

Invoiced sales, less returns	243,000
Cash received from debtors	234,700
Discounts allowed	5,400
Bad debts written off	1,100
Invoiced purchases of raw materials, less returns	80,000
Payments to creditors	82,500
Discounts received	1,700
Factory wages paid	33,300
Manufacturing expenses paid	61,900
Administration expenses paid	16,200
Selling and distribution expenses paid	16,800
Payment for purchase of fixed assets	30,000

Balances at 31 December 19X5

	£
Fixed assets (cost £90,000)	60,000
Stocks	
Raw materials	24,000
Work in progress	5,000
Finished goods	52,000
Administration expenses accrued	1,100
Factory wages accrued	700
Selling and distribution expenses prepaid	1,200

The following information is given.

(a) Depreciation of fixed assets is to be apportioned between manufacturing, administration and selling in the proportions of 7: 2: 1.

(b) Discounts allowed and bad debts written off are to be regarded as selling and distribution expenses.

(c) Discounts received are to be credited to administration expenses.

(d) Taxation is to be ignored.

Guidance notes

1 A manufacturing account is a detailed breakdown of what would be the 'Purchases' line in cost of sales in a non-manufacturing organisation. Your aim is to set out how raw materials, work in progress, direct wages and indirect factory expenses are gathered together to arrive at the 'Factory cost of finished goods produced'.

2 Most of the figures can be taken straight from the figures given, but don't forget accruals and depreciation.

3 Once you have the figure for finished goods produced you can prepare the trading and profit and loss account in the normal way.

4 Beware! You do not need all of the figures you are given in this question.

---

60   FACTORY (ACC, 11/93)   *49 mins*

The following balances have been extracted from the trial balance of ABC Limited, a manufacturing company, at 31 October 19X3:

	£
Raw material stock (1 November 19X2)	12,987
Purchase of raw materials	133,759
Direct labour	68,471
Rent and business rates	15,800
Factory power	22,436
Salaries	38,850
Factory indirect wages	26,793
Depreciation charge for the year	
Buildings	4,000
Equipment	15,980
Motor vehicles	7,620
Carriage inwards on raw materials	982
Sales	459,870
Discount allowed	1,458
Discount received	2,131
Heat and light	10,940
Postage and stationery	3,560
Work-in-progress (1 November 19X2)	15,468
Carriage outwards	1,103
Dividends paid	2,500
Debenture interest paid	4,000
Stock of finished goods (1 November 19X2)	12,903
Royalties paid	14,500

Notes

1 The balance on the rent and business rates account includes a payment of £6,000 made during September 19X3 for the six months ending 31 March 19X4.

2 Direct wages outstanding at 31 October 19X3 amounted to £2,350.

3 Factory power outstanding on 31 October 19X3 is estimated to £3,460.

4 The company manufactures two products - Alpha and Beta. Equal quantities of Alpha and Beta were *made and sold* during the year ended 31 October 19X3. The selling price of Alpha and Beta is the same.

5 Although Alpha and Beta are made from the same raw material by the same grade of labour, Alpha uses twice as much direct labour as Beta, but Beta requires three times as much direct material as Alpha.

6 The royalty payments relate only to Alpha.

7 Factory indirect wages and salaries are to be shared between the products in proportion to each product's share of direct wages.

8 All other factory costs are to be divided equally between each product.

9 Some of the costs shown above relate to both the factory and the administration function of the company. They should be apportioned as shown in the following table.

	Factory	*Administration*
Rent and business rates	80%	20%
Salaries	40%	60%
Depreciation - Buildings	60%	40%
Depreciation - Equipment	70%	30%
Depreciation - Motor vehicles	40%	60%
Heat and light	50%	50%
Postage and stationery	0%	100%

10 Opening stocks and work-in-progress were analysed between the products as follows.

	Alpha	*Beta*
	£	£
Work-in-progress	7,530	7,938
Finished goods	6,362	6,541

11 Stocks and work-in-progress at 31 October 19X3 were as follows.

	£
Raw materials	3,728

	Alpha £	Beta £
Work-in-progress	5,820	6,187
Finished goods	5,239	4,792

12 The debenture interest paid relates to an 8% debenture issued five years ago. The nominal value of the debenture is £100,000.

13 A provision for corporation tax is to be made in the sum of £24,000.

14 The directors propose a final dividend of £12,500.

Required

(a) Prepare a vertical, columnar manufacturing account for ABC Limited for the year ended 31 October 19X3, showing clearly the costs of manufacture for each of the company's products and in total. **14 Marks**

(b) Prepare a vertical, columnar trading account for ABC Limited for the year ended 31 October 19X3, showing clearly the gross profit attributed to each of the company's products and in total. **5 Marks**

(c) Prepare a vertical profit and loss and appropriation account for ABC Limited for the year ended 31 October 19X3. **8 Marks**

Total Marks = 27

61 **MANUFACTURING (specimen paper)** *54 mins*

ABC Ltd prepares its accounts to 31 October each year. Its trial balance at 31 October 19X3 was as follows.

	Dr £'000	Cr £'000
Premises - cost	600	
Manufacturing plant - cost	350	
Office equipment - cost	125	
Accumulated depreciation at 1 November 19X2		
Premises		195
Manufacturing plant		140
Office equipment		35
Stocks at 1 November 19X2		
Raw materials	27	
Work in progress	18	
Finished goods	255	
Sales of finished goods		2,350
Purchases of raw materials	826	
Returns inwards and outwards	38	18
Direct wages	575	
Heat, light and power	242	
Salaries	122	
Printing, postage and stationery	32	
Rent, rates and insurances	114	
Loan interest payable	12	
Loan		250
Trade debtors and creditors	287	75
Provision for doubtful debts		11
VAT account		26
Interim dividend paid	10	
Ordinary shares of £1 each		500
Share premium account		100
Profit and loss account balance		442
Bank balance	509	
	4,142	4,142

The following additional information at 31 October 19X3 is available.

(a) *Closing stocks*

Raw materials	£24,000
Work-in-progress	£19,000
Finished goods	£147,000

(b) *Prepayments*

Rates	£17,000
Insurances	£4,000

(c) *Accruals*

Direct wages	£15,000
Salaries	£8,000

(d) Salaries are to be apportioned as follows.

Manufacturing	20%
Administration	80%

(e) Specific bad debts to be written off amount to £47,000, including VAT at 17½%. The company maintains a separate bad debts account. The debts have all been outstanding for more than six months.

(f) The provision for doubtful debts is to be amended to 2½% of debtors, after adjusting for bad debts written off.

(g) Depreciation of fixed assets is to be provided as follows.

Premises	2% on cost
Plant	10% on cost
Office equipment	20% on reducing balance

25% of premises depreciation is to be apportioned to the manufacturing account.

(h) The loan was taken out on 1 November 19X2, and the capital is to be repaid as follows.

1 January 19X4	£100,000
1 January 19X5	£100,000
1 January 19X6	£50,000

Interest is to be charged on the outstanding capital at 20% per annum.

(i) Other expenses are to be apportioned as follows.

Heat, light and power	½ manufacturing ½ selling and administration
Rent, rates and insurances	$1/_3$ manufacturing $2/_3$ administration

(j) One line of finished goods stock, currently recorded at £8,000, has a net realisable value of £3,000.

(k) A final dividend of 10p per share is to be proposed.

(l) A provision for corporation tax of £35,000 is to be made on the profits of the year.

Required

(a) Prepare a manufacturing account for the year ended 31 October 19X3.   **8 Marks**

(b) Prepare a trading and profit and loss account for the year ended 31 October 19X3.
12 Marks

(c) Prepare a balance sheet at 31 October 19X3.   **10 Marks**

The accounts are to be presented in vertical format, but not in a format for publication.

Total Marks = 30

62 FPC (5/96)

FPC Ltd is a manufacturing company which sells its goods to wholesalers. Its trial balance at 31 March 19X6 was as follows.

	Dr £	Cr £
Issued share capital, £1 ordinary shares		750,000
10% debentures, repayable 20Y5		200,000
Profit and loss account at 1 April 19X5		98,000
Premises: at cost	900,000	
provision for depreciation at 1 April 19X5		360,000
Plant: at cost	150,000	
provision for depreciation at 1 April 19X5		75,000
Sales		2,960,000
Raw materials purchased	1,500,000	
Carriage outwards	10,000	
Carriage inwards	15,000	
Returns outwards		22,000
Returns inwards	14,000	
Debtors	220,000	
Creditors		300,000
Bank balance	500,000	
Stock at 1 April 19X5		
Raw materials	60,000	
Work in progress	30,000	
Finished goods	70,000	
Direct labour	600,000	
Discounts allowed	4,000	
Discounts received		2,500
Rent and rates	120,000	
Insurance	100,000	
Factory supervisors' salaries	150,000	
Office wages and salaries	175,000	
Sales officers' commission	113,500	
Administration expenses	45,000	
Value added tax account		8,500
Provision for doubtful debts at 1 April 19X5		7,000
Bad debts written off	6,500	
	4,783,000	4,783,000

The following additional information at 31 March 19X6 is available.

(a) Closing stocks
      Raw materials   £80,000
      Work in progress £42,500
      Finished goods   £100,000

(b) Rent and rates prepaid amount to £10,000
     Insurance prepaid amounts to £20,000

     20% of rent, rates and insurance is to be regarded as factory cost.

(c) Direct labour accrued amounts to £17,500.

(d) Included in the above trial balance are finished goods sold on a 'sale or return' basis, which must be accepted or rejected by 15 April 19X6. Their selling price is £35,000 and their cost price is £27,000. VAT is not applicable on these goods.

(e) The premises are to be depreciated at 2% per annum, straight line.
     The plant is to be depreciated at 10% per annum straight line.

     25% of premises depreciation is to be regarded as factory cost.
     75% of plant depreciation is to be regarded as factory cost.

(f) The provision for doubtful debts is to be amended to 5% of debtors.

(g) Sales officers' commission for the year is to be 5% of net sales.

(h)   Administration expenses includes stationery which has been recorded at its total invoice value of £9,400, including VAT at 17.5%. The VAT is reclaimable.

(i)   The debentures were issued on 1 October 19X5. Interest is due on 1 April and 1 October annually in arrears.

(j)   Corporation tax of £22,000 is to be provided for the year.

(k)   A dividend of 3p per share is proposed.

Required

(a)   Prepare a manufacturing account for the year ended 31 March 19X6.   **9 Marks**

(b)   Prepare a trading and profit and loss account appropriation account for the year ended 31 March 19X6. *Note.* A balance sheet is *not* required.   **12 Marks**

(c)   For *each* of the following items which appear in the accounts of FPC Ltd, explain how the accounting concept stated against each one affects its treatment.

(i)	Stocks of raw materials	-	the consistency concept
(ii)	Goods on sale or return	-	the matching concept and the realisation concept
(iii)	Provision for doubtful debts	-	the prudence concept **9 Marks**

Total Marks = 30

63   TUTORIAL QUESTION: RATIOS AND CASH FLOWS

Dozy's balance sheets at 31 December 19X0 and 31 December 19X1 are given below. Dozy uses the historical cost convention.

	19X0		19X1	
	£'000	£'000	£'000	£'000
Fixed assets - cost	100		150	
- depreciation	20		30	
Net book value		80		120
Stock	30		30	
Debtors	50		60	
Cash	5		10	
		85		100
Creditors		(90)		(80)
		75		140
Long term loan (10%)		–		60
		75		80
Capital		10		10
Profits brought forward		50		65
Net profit for the year		15		5
Owner's equity		75		80

Note. Dozy made no drawings during the year, and paid no tax. No fixed assets were sold or otherwise disposed of.

Required

(a)   Calculate from the information provided the following ratios for both 19X0 and 19X1.

   (i)   Return on owner's equity.
   (ii)   Return on capital employed.
   (iii) Current ratio.
   (iv)   Gearing ratio.
   (v)   Debtors' turnover period if sales in 19X0 were £500 and in 19X1 were £700.
   (vi)   Stock turnover if *gross* profit on sales were 30%.

   Comment briefly on the results.

(b)   (i)   What are the aims of a cash flow statement?
      (ii)   What are the main constituents of a cash flow statement?

Guidance notes

1   You *must* know how to calculate ratios: you are throwing away extremely easy marks if you don't. Practice on every set of accounts you can get your hands on.

2   Marks are generally awarded for sensible comments of any kind, though students are sometimes too timid to make them. Be brave! Our suggested solution may not be any more valid than your own interpretation in this sort of question.

3   The ASB has recently (October 1996) revised FRS 1 *Cash flow statements*. You do not need to know the format for this paper.

64   VICTOR   *43 mins*

Given below are the balance sheets of Victor plc for 19X6 and 19X7, together with the profit and loss statement for 19X7.

BALANCE SHEETS OF VICTOR PLC AT 31 DECEMBER

	19X6		*19X7*	
	£'000	£'000	£'000	£'000
Fixed assets				
Goodwill at cost less amortisation		110		100
Land at cost		140		230
Buildings at cost	168		258	
Less provision for depreciation	22		28	
		146		230
Motor vehicles at cost	162		189	
Less provision for depreciation	46		41	
		116		148
		512		708
Current assets				
Stocks	76		100	
Debtors	60		64	
Prepaid expenses	6		5	
Bank	10		0	
	152		169	
Current liabilities				
Creditors	99		79	
Accrued wages	5		6	
Corporation tax payable	60		70	
Bank overdraft	0		24	
	164		179	
Net current liabilities		12		10
		500		698
Long-term liabilities				
Debentures		60		100
		440		598
Called up share capital (£1 shares)		300		360
Share premium account		0		48
General reserve		44		60
Retained profits		96		130
		440		598

PROFIT AND LOSS STATEMENT
FOR THE YEAR ENDED 31 DECEMBER 19X7

	£'000	£'000
Sales revenue		670
Less cost of sales		323
Gross operating profit		347
Profit on disposal of motor vehicles		7
		354
Expenses		
Wages	112	
Office expenses	27	
Selling expenses	9	
Depreciation of:		
motor vehicles	22	
buildings	6	
Interest	18	
Amortisation of goodwill	10	
		204
Net profit before taxation		150
Less corporation tax		70
Net profit after taxation		80

Additional information is provided as follows.

(a)   During 19X7, motor vehicles costing £42,000 and depreciated by £27,000 were sold. New motor vehicles costing £69,000 were purchased in the year.

(b)   A dividend of £30,000 was paid out in June 19X7.

(c)   Corporation tax paid in 19X7 amounted to £60,000.

Required

Prepare a cash flow statement for the year ended 31 December 19X7.

24 Marks

65   **GH (5/95)**   *36 mins*

GH has the following balance sheet at 30 April 19X5, with corresponding figures for the previous year.

	19X5		19X4	
	£	£	£	£
Fixed assets		277,000		206,000
Current assets				
Stocks	46,000		42,000	
Debtors	37,500		36,000	
Cash and bank	12,500		54,000	
	96,000		132,000	
Current liabilities				
Creditors	16,000		23,000	
		80,000		109,000
		357,000		315,000
Long-term liabilities		10,000		50,000
		347,000		265,000
Financed by				
Capital at start		265,000		214,000
Capital introduced		20,000		-
Net profit for the year		92,000		78,000
		377,000		292,000
Drawings		30,000		27,000
		347,000		265,000

The following information concerning the year to 30 April 19X5 is also available.

(a) Fixed assets were sold for £30,000. Their original cost had been £48,000 and depreciation of £12,000 had been charged in previous years.

(b) Fixed assets costing £120,000 were purchased during the year.

Required

(a) Prepare a cash flow statement for the year to 30 April 19X5, in a format which shows the increase or decrease in cash balances. State any assumptions which you make.   **14 Marks**

(b) Briefly describe the accounting information requirements of *four* different user groups.   **6 Marks**

Total Marks = 20

66   SH LTD (11/96)   *36 mins*

You are presented with the following information relating to SH Ltd:

PROFIT AND LOSS ACCOUNT FOR THE YEAR ENDED 30 JUNE 19X6

	£'000
Gross profit	980
Trading expenses	475
Depreciation	255
Net profit	250
Dividends	80
Retained profit for the year	170

BALANCE SHEETS AT 30 JUNE

	19X5	19X6
	£'000	£'000
Fixed assets at cost	3,000	3,500
Less accumulated depreciation	2,100	2,300
Net book value	900	1,200
Current assets		
Stocks	825	1,175
Debtors	5,200	5,065
Bank and cash	2,350	2,160
	8,375	8,400
Less current liabilities		
Creditors	5,000	4,350
Dividends	75	80
	5,075	4,430
Net current assets	3,300	3,970
Total net assets	4,200	5,170
Financed by:		
Ordinary shares of £1 each	2,800	3,200
Share premium	–	400
Profit and loss account	1,400	1,570
	4,200	5,170

During the year ended 30 June 19X6, fixed assets which had cost £230,000 were sold for £145,000. The loss on this disposal had been included in trading expenses in the profit and loss account.

Required

(a) Produce a cashflow statement for the year ended 30 June 19X6, which reconciles the profit with the change in cash balances.   **14 Marks**

(b) Discuss the liquidity of SH Limited, using *two* ratios to assist you.   **6 Marks**

Total Marks = 20

67 CONTROLS (specimen paper)

36 mins

You have recently been appointed to the position of accounts supervisor in your company. A computerised accounting system is used to maintain the purchase ledger.

Invoices and credit notes are input immediately they arrive, and cheques are produced automatically at the end of each month, for the outstanding balance on each creditor's account.

If an invoice is received for which there is no account on the file, an account is set up automatically by the computer, and is allocated a unique number.

You can see that there are several controls which need to be implemented in order to prevent payment being made to suppliers who are not entitled to such payment.

Required

(a) Describe *six* controls over the accounting documents and records which would help to prevent errors or fraud in the operation of the computerised purchase ledger.

12 Marks

(b) Discuss the main reasons for the existence of accounting controls. **8 Marks**

Total Marks = 20

68 EXTERNAL AND INTERNAL AUDIT (FAC, 5/93)

27 mins

The managing director of Q plc has complained that the company pays far more for its annual external audit than it costs to run the internal audit department and yet the internal audit department seems to provide senior management with much more useful information.

Required

(a) Explain why the managing director might feel that the internal audit function is more useful than external audit. **8 Marks**

(b) Suggest ways in which the internal audit department could assist the external auditor, thereby reducing the external audit fee. **7 Marks**

Total Marks = 15

69 GTZ (5/96)

36 mins

You are assistant accountant with GTZ Ltd, which is a small commercial organisation. You have recently encountered several problems which have highlighted weaknesses in the accounting system. As a result, you propose to suggest some improvements in the controls exercised by the accounting staff, and to discuss these improvements with the company's auditor.

Required

(a) For *each* of the following problems, suggest controls which could be introduced which would help to improve the reliability of the accounting system

   (i) A supplier refusing to supply further goods until payment has been made for an invoice issued six months ago, of which GTZ has no record

   (ii) A debtor's ledger account being credited with a credit note which was never issued

   (iii) A cheque from a regular cash sale customer being returned by the bank and being filed in the cashier's drawer without any ledger entries being made

   (iv) A refund being given from petty cash to a customer already refunded by cheque **8 Marks**

(b) You are given the following details regarding stock movements during April 19X6.

1 April	100 units on hand, valued at £10 each
8 April	Stock sold for £360, with a mark-up of 50%
18 April	38 units purchased for £480 less trade discount of 5%
20 April	50 units sold
23 April	35 units sold
28 April	20 units purchased for £260

Required

Prepare a stock record card using both the FIFO (First In First Out) and AVCO (Average Cost) methods, in order to determine the quantity and value of closing stock at 30 April 19X6.   **10 Marks**

(c) If the physical stock check carried out at 30 April revealed a closing stock quantity of 50 units, suggest *two* possible reasons for the discrepancy.   **2 Marks**

Total Marks = 20

DO YOU KNOW? - INTERPRETATION OF ACCOUNTS

- *Check that you know the following basic points before you attempt any questions. If in doubt, you should go back to your BPP Study Text and revise first.*

- The profit and loss account and balance sheet provide useful information about the condition of a business. Ratios can be calculated and trends identified so that different businesses can be compared or the performance of a business over time can be judged.

- Ratios are often classified as follows.

  - *Liquidity ratios* (current ratio, acid test ratio, turnover periods)
  - *Gearing ratios* (debt:equity, interest cover, dividend cover)
  - *Profitability ratios* (ROCE, ROOE, asset turnover, profit margins)
  - *Investors' ratios (dividend yield, P/E ratio, earnings per share)*

- Additional information may be gleaned from funds flow statements or cash flow statements. These are intended to reveal how a business obtains its funds and how it uses them.

- The interpretation of financial statements requires a large measure of common sense. For example:

  - you should not expect a firm of solicitors (say) to have substantial plant and machinery;

  - you should not expect a chain of supermarkets to make many sales on credit; you should expect it to turn over its (perishable) stock quickly;

  - you should expect a business that 'piles 'em high and sells 'em cheap' to have a low gross profit margin;

  - you should expect a more upmarket organisation to have higher selling and administrative costs, reflecting the level of service given to customers.

- The limitations of ratio analysis are as follows.

  - Comparative information is not always available.

  - They sometimes use out of date information.

  - Interpretation requires thought and analysis. Ratios should not be considered in isolation.

  - The exercise is subjective and results can therefore be manipulated.

  - Ratios are not defined in standard form.

  - Companies may not always use the same accounting policies so the figures behind the ratios may not be comparable.

- Your syllabus requires you to have an appreciation of the types of headings which appear in company accounts and the general contents of each heading. This is to enable candidates to look at a set of company accounts and gain a general understanding of the picture it portrays.

Key questions

70   TUTORIAL QUESTION: RATIOS

The following are the summarised accounts for Carrow Ltd, a company with an accounting year ending on 30 September.

SUMMARISED BALANCE SHEETS AS AT 30 SEPTEMBER

	19X6 £'000	£'000	19X7 £'000	£'000
Tangible fixed assets (at cost less depreciation)		4,995		12,700
Current assets				
Stocks	40,145		50,455	
Debtors	40,210		43,370	
Cash at bank	12,092		5,790	
	92,447		99,615	
Creditors: amounts falling due within one year				
Trade creditors	32,604		37,230	
Taxation	2,473		3,260	
Proposed dividend	1,785		1,985	
	36,862		42,475	
Net current assets		55,585		57,140
Total assets less current liabilities		60,580		69,840
Creditors: amounts falling due after more than one year				
10% debenture 20Y6/20Z0		(19,840)		(19,840)
		40,740		50,000
Capital and reserves				
Called-up share capital of £0.25 per share		9,920		9,920
Profit and loss account		30,820		40,080
		40,740		50,000

SUMMARISED PROFIT AND LOSS ACCOUNTS
FOR THE YEAR ENDED 30 SEPTEMBER

	19X6 £'000	19X7 £'000
Turnover	486,300	583,900
Operating profit	17,238	20,670
Interest payable	1,984	1,984
Profit on ordinary activities before taxation	15,254	18,686
Tax on profit on ordinary activities	5,734	7,026
Profit for the financial year	9,520	11,660
Dividends	2,240	2,400
Retained profit for the year	7,280	9,260
Retained profits brought forward	23,540	30,820
Retained profits carried forward	30,820	40,080

Required

Calculate, for each year, two ratios for each of the following user groups, which are of particular significance to them.

(a)   Shareholders
(b)   Trade creditors
(c)   Internal management

Guidance notes

1   This tutorial question simply asks for calculations. In an examination you would almost certainly be asked to comment on any changes revealed by your ratios.

2   You should target your answer to the requirement of the question. For example, shareholders are unlikely to be particularly interested in the current or quick ratio.

3   Do not simply show numbers in your calculations; show in words how the ratio is calculated. Remember that there are sometimes different ways of calculating a ratio; if the examiner understands the method you have used, he is more likely to give you credit if you make an arithmetical mistake.

71   ARH (5/96)   *36 mins*

ARH plc has the following results for the last two years of trading.

ARH PLC
TRADING AND PROFIT AND LOSS ACCOUNT FOR THE YEAR ENDED

	31.12.X4	*31.12.X5*
	£'000	£'000
Sales	14,400	17,000
Less cost of sales	11,800	12,600
Gross profit	2,600	4,400
Less expenses	1,200	2,000
Net profit for the year	1,400	2,400
Dividends proposed	520	780
Retained profit for the year	880	1,620

ARH PLC
BALANCE SHEET

	31 December 19X4		*31 December 19X5*	
	£'000	£'000	£'000	£'000
Fixed assts		2,500		4,000
Current assets				
Stocks	1,300		2,000	
Debtors	2,000		1,600	
Bank balances	2,400		820	
	5,700		4,420	
Less current liabilities				
Creditors	1,500		2,700	
Net current assets		4,200		1,720
		6,700		5,720
Less long term liabilities				
10% debentures		2,600		-
		4,100		5,720
Financed by:				
2.4 million ordinary shares of £1 each		2,400		2,400
Revaluation reserves		500		500
Retained profits		1,200		2,820
		4,100		5,720

Required

(a) Calculate *three* profitability ratios for *each* year and briefly discuss your results.

6 Marks

(b) Compare the profitability of the second year with the decrease in bank balances *and* discuss possible reasons for this decrease. Include liquidity ratios of your choice to illustrate your comparison.   **10 Marks**

(c) Explain what is meant by the accounting term *reserves*. Explain how the item *revaluation reserves* in the above balance sheet might have arisen.   **4 Marks**

Total Marks = 20

72   JK (specimen paper)   *36 mins*

You are considering the purchase of a small business, JK, and have managed to obtain a copy of its accounts for the last complete accounting year to 30 September 19X3. These appear as follows.

TRADING AND PROFIT AND LOSS ACCOUNT
FOR THE YEAR TO 30 SEPTEMBER 19X3

	£	£
Sales		385,200
Less cost of goods sold		
Opening stocks	93,250	
Purchases	174,340	
Closing stocks	(84,630)	
		182,960
Gross profit		202,240
Less expenses		
Selling and delivery costs	83,500	
Administration costs	51,420	
Depreciation	36,760	
		171,680
Net profit		30,560

BALANCE SHEET AT 30 SEPTEMBER 19X3

	£	£
Fixed assets		
Assets at cost	235,070	
less: Depreciation to date	(88,030)	
		147,040
Current assets		
Stocks	84,630	
Debtors and prepayments	36,825	
Bank and cash	9,120	
	130,575	
Current liabilities		
Creditors and accruals	(62,385)	
		68,190
		215,230
Financed by:		
Capital at 1 October 19X3		197,075
Net profit for the year		30,560
Proprietor's drawings		(12,405)
		215,230

You discover that JK has adopted the following treatment of certain items in the accounts.

(a) In previous years, depreciation has been provided on the straight-line basis over 10 years, but in the year shown above, the reducing balance basis has been used, at a rate of 20% per annum, as there was sufficient profit to absorb a high charge this year.

(b) The debtors figure includes several debts which have been outstanding for some time, despite repeated reminders to the customers concerned.

(c) No allowance has been made in the accounts for expenses incurred for which invoices have not been received at the year end.

Required

(a) Calculate the following accounting ratios from the accounts as presented above:

    (i)   net profit percentage;
    (ii)   return on capital employed;
    (iii) current ratio;
    (iv) quick (acid test) ratio.   **8 Marks**

(b) State the fundamental accounting concept which governs each of these three treatments:

    (i)   depreciation of fixed assets;
    (ii)   outstanding debtors;
    (iii) expenses incurred not yet invoiced;

and discuss the effects which each treatment will have had on the ratios you have calculated. **12 Marks**

Total Marks = 20

73   MBC (11/95) *36 mins*

The following figures have been extracted from the published accounts of MBC plc, at 31 October 19X5.

	£m
Ordinary share capital	30
Share premium	3
Reserves	5
	38
6% debentures	10
	48

The net profit (after tax of £1m) for the year to 31 October 19X5, was £4m and dividends amounted to £0.5m. The company is considering raising a further £10m in the next financial year to finance research and development.

Required

(a)   State the formula for, and calculate, the company's gearing ratio. **2 Marks**

(b)   State the formula for, and calculate, the company's return on capital employed (ROCE). **3 Marks**

(c)   Discuss the different effects on gearing and ROCE of raising the additional £10m by the issue of shares or by the issue of debentures. **8 Marks**

(d)   Briefly describe the various kinds of research and development, and explain the accounting concepts which govern the treatment of such expenditure in the accounts. **7 Marks**

Total Marks = 20

74   R LTD (5/97) *36 mins*

The directors of R Ltd are hoping to negotiate an overdraft to provide working capital for a proposed expansion of business. The bank manager has called for accounts for the last three years and the directors have produced the following extracts.

BALANCE SHEETS AT 31 DECEMBER

	19X4		19X5		19X6	
	£'000	£'000	£'000	£'000	£'000	£'000
Fixed assets		147		163		153
Current assets						
Stocks	27		40		46	
Debtors	40		45		52	
Bank	6		15		8	
	73		100		106	
Less: current liabilities						
(including tax and dividends)	33		45		43	
		40		55		63
		187		218		216
Credit sales		360		375		390
Credit purchases		230		250		280
Net profit before tax		32		46		14

The bank manager has obtained the following additional information.

(a)   The company commenced on 1 January 19X4 with an issued capital of 100,000 £1 ordinary shares issued at a premium of 60p each.

(b)   Corporation tax amounted to £5,000 in 19X5 and £6,000 in 19X6. There was no corporation tax for 19X4.

(c) Dividends were declared of 5p per share in 19X4, and 10p per share in each of 19X5 and 19X6.

(d) £18,000 was transferred to General Reserves in 19X5.

Required

(a) Draw up appropriation accounts for *each* of the *three* years.   **6 Marks**

(b) Draw up the capital section of the balance sheet for *each* of the *three* years.   **4 Marks**

(c) State the formula for, and calculate, for *each* of the *three* years:

    (i)   debtors' collection periods,   **3 Marks**
    (ii)   creditors' payment periods.   **3 Marks**
    (iii)   Comment briefly on how your results might affect the proposed overdraft.

                                             4 Marks

                                       Total Marks = 20

75   MULTIPLE CHOICE QUESTIONS: SELECTION 1   *36 mins*

1   Hengist, a sole trader, has calculated that his cost of sales for the year is £144,000. His sales figure for the year includes an amount of £2,016 being the amount paid by Hengist himself into the business bank account for goods withdrawn for private use. The figure of £2,016 was calculated by adding a mark-up of 12% to the cost of the goods. His gross profit percentage on all other goods sold was 20%.

    What is the total figure of sales for the year?

    A   £172,656
    B   £177,750
    C   £179,766
    D   £180,000

2   Horsa's sales follow a seasonal pattern. Monthly sales in the final quarter of the year are twice as high as during other periods. He also benefits from a higher mark-up during the final quarter: an average of 25% on cost compared with 20% during the rest of the year.

    Horsa's sales in 19X9 totalled £210,000. What was the amount of his gross profit?

    A   £36,750
    B   £37,800
    C   £39,667
    D   £46,200

3   The bookkeeper of Leggit Ltd has disappeared. There is no cash in the till and theft is suspected. It is known that the cash balance at the beginning of the year was £240. Since then, total sales have amounted to £41,250. Credit customers owed £2,100 at the beginning of the year and owe £875 now. Cheques banked from credit customers have totalled £24,290. Expenses paid from the till receipts amount to £1,850 and cash receipts of £9,300 have been lodged in the bank.

    How much has the bookkeeper stolen during the period?

    A   £7,275
    B   £9,125
    C   £12,155
    D   £16,575

4   A club takes credit for subscriptions when they become due. On 1 January 19X5 arrears of subscriptions amounted to £38 and subscriptions paid in advance were £72. On 31 December 19X5 the amounts were £48 and £80 respectively. Subscription receipts during the year were £790.

    In the income and expenditure account for 19X5 the income from subscriptions would be shown as:

    A   £748
    B   £788
    C   £790
    D   £792

5   A club takes no credit for subscriptions due until they are received. On 1 January 19X5 arrears of subscriptions amounted to £24 and subscriptions paid in advance were £14. On 31 December 19X5 the amounts were £42 and £58 respectively. Subscription receipts during the year were £1,024.

In the income and expenditure account for 19X5 the income from subscriptions would be shown as:

A   £956
B   £980
C   £998
D   £1,050

6   For many years, life membership of the Tipton Poetry Association cost £100, but with effect from 1 January 19X5 the rate has been increased to £120. The balance on the life membership fund at 31 December 19X4 was £3,780 and membership details at that date were as follows:

	No of members
Joined more than 19 years ago	32
Joined within the last 19 years	64
	96

The Association's accounting policy is to release life subscriptions to income over a period of 20 years beginning with the year of enrolment.

During 19X5, four new members were enrolled and one other member (who had joined in 19X1) died.

What is the balance on the life membership fund at 31 December 19X5?

A   £3,591
B   £3,841
C   £3,916
D   £4,047

7   In a statement of source and application of funds it is usual to find an 'adjustment for items not involving the movement of funds'. Which one of the following items might appear under such a caption?

A   The profit on disposal of fixed assets
B   The accumulated depreciation on fixed assets
C   The profit and loss account charge for taxation
D   The provision for doubtful debts

8   What is the purpose of charging depreciation in accounts?

A   To allocate the cost less residual value of a fixed asset over the accounting periods expected to benefit from its use
B   To ensure that funds are available for the eventual replacement of the asset
C   To reduce the cost of the asset in the balance sheet to its estimated market value
D   To comply with the prudence concept

9   Which one of the following formulae should be used to calculate the rate of stock turnover in a retail business?

A   Sales divided by average stock
B   Sales divided by year-end stock
C   Purchases divided by year-end stock
D   Cost of sales divided by average stock

10   Splodge plc's accounts contain two errors. A £10,000 bad debt written off has been deducted from sales and a £20,000 credit note received has been added to sales. Before correction, turnover was £1m and cost of sales was £800,000. What is the gross profit margin after correction of these errors?

A   17.8%
B   18.8%
C   21.2%
D   22.2%   **Total Marks = 20**

76   MULTIPLE CHOICE QUESTIONS: SELECTION 2 (specimen paper)   *54 mins*

1   Gross profit for 19X3 can be calculated from

   A   purchases for 19X3, plus stock at 31 December 19X3, less stock at 1 January 19X3

   B   purchases for 19X3, less stock at 31 December 19X3, plus stock at 1 January 19X3

   C   cost of goods sold during 19X3, plus sales during 19X3

   D   net profit for 19X3, plus expenses for 19X3

2   You are given the following information:

   Debtors at 1 January 19X3   £10,000
   Debtors at 31 December 19X3   £9,000
   Total receipts during 19X3 (including cash sales of £5,000)   £85,000

   Sales on credit during 19X3 amount to

   A   £81,000
   B   £86,000
   C   £79,000
   D   £84,000

3   Rent paid on 1 October 19X2 for the year to 30 September 19X3 was £1,200, and rent paid on 1 October 19X3 for the year to 30 September 19X4 was £1,600.

   Rent payable, as shown in the profit and loss account for the year ended 31 December 19X3, would be

   A   £1,200
   B   £1,600
   C   £1,300
   D   £1,500

4   Your cash book at 31 December 19X3 shows a bank balance of £565 overdrawn. On comparing this with your bank statement at the same date, you discover that:

   (a)   a cheque for £57 drawn by you on 29 December 19X3 has not yet been presented for payment;

   (b)   a cheque for £92 from a customer, which was paid into the bank on 24 December 19X3, has been dishonoured on 31 Decemcn 19X3.

   The correct bank balance to be shown in the balance sheet at 31 December 19X3 is

   A   £714 overdrawn
   B   £657 overdrawn
   C   £473 overdrawn
   D   £53 overdrawn

5   Your firm bought a machine for £5,000 on 1 January 19X1, which had an expected useful life of four years and an expected residual value of £1,000; the asset was to be depreciated on the straight-line basis. On 31 December 19X3, the machine was sold for £1,600.

   The amount to be entered in the 19X3 profit and loss account for profit or loss on disposal, is

   A   profit of £600
   B   loss of £600
   C   profit of £350
   D   loss of £400

6   A company's working capital was £43,200. Subsequently, the following transactions occurred.

   (a)   Creditors were paid £3,000 by cheque.
   (b)   A bad debt of £250 was written off.
   (c)   Stock valued at £100 was sold for £230 on credit.

Working capital is now

A   £43,080
B   £46,080
C   £40,080
D   £42,850

7   A company has an authorised share capital of 1,000,000 ordinary shares of £1 each, of which 800,000 have been issued at a premium of 50p each, thereby raising capital of £1,200,000. The directors are considering allocating £120,000 for dividend payments this year.

This amounts to a dividend of

A   12p per share
B   10p per share
C   15p per share
D   12%

8   After calculating your company's profit for 19X3, you discover that:

(a)   a fixed asset costing £50,000 has been included in the purchases account;

(b)   stationery costing £10,000 has been included as closing stock of raw materials, instead of stock of stationery.

These two errors have had the effect of

A   understating gross profit by £40,000 and understating net profit by £50,000
B   understating both gross profit and net profit by £40,000
C   understating gross profit by £60,000 and understating net profit by £50,000
D   overstating both gross profit and net profit by £60,000

9   Your company sells goods on 29 December 19X3, on sale or return; the final date for return or payment in full is 10 January 19X4. The costs of manufacturing the product are all incurred and paid for in 19X3 except for an outstanding bill for carriage outwards which is still unpaid.

The associated revenues and expenses of the transaction should be dealt with in the profit and loss account by

A   including all revenues and all expenses in 19X3

B   including all revenues and all expenses in 19X4

C   including expenses in 19X3 and revenues in 19X4

D   including the revenue and the carriage outwards in 19X4, and the other expenses in 19X3

10   In times of rising prices, the FIFO method of stock valuation, when compared to the average cost method of stock valuation, will usually produce

A   a higher profit and a lower closing stock value
B   a higher profit and a higher closing stock value
C   a lower profit and a lower closing stock value
D   a lower profit and a higher closing stock value

11   The formula for calculating the rate of stock turnover is

A   average stock at cost divided by cost of goods sold
B   sales divided by average stock at cost
C   sales divided by average stock at selling price
D   cost of goods sold divided by average stock at cost

12   Which one of the following would you expect to find in the appropriation account of a limited company, for the current year?

A   Preference dividend proposed during the previous year, but paid in the current year

B   Preference dividend proposed during the current year, but paid in the following year

C   Directors' fees

D   Auditors' fees

13 The suspense account shows a debit balance of £100. This could be due to

A   entering £50 received from A Turner on the debit side of A Turner's account
B   entering £50 received from A Turner on the credit side of A Turner's account
C   undercasting the sales day book by £100
D   undercasting the purchases day book by £100

14 The capital of a sole trader would change as a result of

A   a creditor being paid his account by cheque
B   raw materials being purchased on credit
C   fixed assets being purchased on credit
D   wages being paid in cash

15 A decrease in the provision for doubtful debts would result in

A   an increase in liabilities
B   a decrease in working capital
C   a decrease in net profit
D   an increase in net profit

Total Marks = 30

77 **MULTIPLE CHOICE QUESTIONS: SELECTION 3 (5/95)**   *54 mins*

1   If, at the end of the financial year, a company makes a charge against the profits for stationery consumed but not yet invoiced, this adjustment is in accordance with the concept of

A   Materiality
B   Accruals
C   Consistency
D   Objectivity

2   You are the accountant of ABC Ltd and have extracted a trial balance at 31 October 19X4. The sum of the debit column of the trial balance exceeds the sum of the credit column by £829. A suspense account has been opened to record the difference. After preliminary investigations failed to locate any errors, you have decided to prepare draft final accounts in accordance with the prudence concept.

The suspense account balance would be treated as

A   An expense in the profit and loss account
B   Additional income in the profit and loss account
C   An asset in the balance sheet
D   A liability in the balance sheet

3   A credit balance of £917 brought down on Y Ltd's account in the books of X Ltd means that

A   X Ltd owes Y Ltd £917
B   Y Ltd owes X Ltd £917
C   X Ltd has paid Y Ltd £917
D   X Ltd is owed £917 by Y Ltd

4   Where a transaction is credited to the correct ledger account, but debited incorrectly to the repairs and renewals account instead of to the plant and machinery account, the error is known as an error of

A   Omission
B   Commission
C   Principle
D   Original entry

5   If a purchase return of £48 has been wrongly posted to the debit of the sales returns account, but has been correctly entered in the supplier's account, the total of the trial balance would show

A   The credit side to be £48 more than the debit side
B   The debit side to be £48 more than the credit side
C   The credit side to be £96 more than the debit side
D   The debit side to be £96 more than the credit side

6   The following information relates to a company at its year end.

		£
Stock at beginning of year		
Raw materials		10,000
Work-in-progress		2,000
Finished goods		34,000
Stock at end of year		
Raw materials		11,000
Work-in-progress		4,000
Finished goods		30,000
Purchases of raw materials		50,000
Direct wages		40,000
Royalties on goods sold		3,000
Production overheads		60,000
Distribution costs		55,000
Administration expenses		70,000
Sales		300,000

The cost of goods manufactured during the year is

A   £147,000
B   £151,000
C   £153,000
D   £154,000

7   A company received an invoice from ABC Ltd, for 40 units at £10 each, less 25% trade discount, these being items purchased on credit and for resale. It paid this invoice minus a cash discount of 2%. Which of the following journal entries correctly records the effect of the whole transaction in the company's books?

		Debit £	Credit £
A	ABC Ltd	300	
	Purchases		300
	Cash	292	
	Discount allowed	8	
	ABC Ltd		300
B	Purchases	300	
	ABC Ltd		300
	ABC Ltd	300	
	Discount allowed		8
	Cash		292
C	Purchases	300	
	ABC Ltd		300
	ABC Ltd	300	
	Discount received		6
	Cash		294
D	ABC Ltd	400	
	Purchases		400
	Cash	294	
	Discount received	106	
	ABC Ltd		400

8   For which one of the following accounting uses is a spreadsheet least suitable?

A   Preparing budgets and forecasts
B   Recording the dual aspect of accounting transactions
C   Preparation of final accounts from a trial balance
D   Entering sales invoices in a sales day-book

9   The following is an extract from the trial balance of ABC Ltd at 31 December 19X4.

	Debit £	Credit £
Sales		73,716
Returns	5,863	3,492
Discounts	871	1,267

The figure to be shown in the trading account for net sales is

A   £66,586
B   £66,982
C   £67,853
D   £70,224

10   Following the preparation of the profit and loss account, it is discovered that accrued expenses of £1,000 have been ignored and that closing stock has been overvalued by £1,300. This will have resulted in

A   An overstatement of net profit of £300
B   An understatement of net profit of £300
C   An overstatement of net profit of £2,300
D   An understatement of net profit of £2,300

11   In a not-for-profit organisation, the accumulated fund is

A   Long-term liabilities plus current liabilities plus current assets
B   Fixed assets less current liabilities less long-term liabilities
C   The balance on the general reserves account
D   Fixed assets plus net current assets less long-term liabilities

12   Given a selling price of £350 and a gross profit mark-up of 40%, the cost price would be

A   £100
B   £140
C   £210
D   £250

13   Which of the following transactions would result in an increase in capital employed?

A   Selling stocks at a profit
B   Writing off a bad debt
C   Paying a creditor in cash
D   Increasing the bank overdraft to purchase a fixed asset

14   Stock is valued using FIFO. Opening stock was 10 units at £2 each. Purchases were 30 units at £3 each, then issues of 12 units were made, followed by issues of 8 units.

Closing stock is valued at

A   £50
B   £58
C   £60
D   £70

15   Sales are £110,000. Purchases are £80,000. Opening stock is £12,000. Closing stock is £10,000.

The rate of stock turnover is

A   7.27 times
B   7.45 times
C   8 times
D   10 times

Total Marks = 30

78   MULTIPLE CHOICE QUESTIONS: SELECTION 4 (11/95)   *54 mins*

1   A 'true and fair view' is one which

    A   presents the accounts in such a way as to exclude errors which would affect the actions of those reading them

    B   occurs when the accounts have been audited

    C   shows the accounts of an organisation in an understandable format

    D   shows the assets on the balance sheet at their current market price

2   The cash book shows a bank balance of £5,675 overdrawn at 31 August 19X5. it is subsequently discovered that a standing order for £125 has been entered twice, and that a dishonoured cheque for £450 has been debited in the cash book instead of credited.

The correct bank balance should be

    A   £5,100 overdrawn
    B   £6,000 overdrawn
    C   £6,250 overdrawn
    D   £6,450 overdrawn

3   The historical cost convention

    A   fails to take account of changing price levels over time

    B   records only past transactions

    C   values all assets at their cost to the business, without any adjustment for depreciation

    D   has been replaced in accounting records by a system of current cost accounting

4   A business commenced with a bank balance of £3,250; it subsequently purchased goods on credit for £10,000; gross profit mark-up was 120%; half the goods were sold for cash, less cash discount of 5%; all takings were banked.

The resulting net profit was

    A   £700
    B   £3,700
    C   £5,450
    D   £5,700

5   An income and expenditure account is

    A   a summary of the cash and bank transactions for a period

    B   another name for a receipts and payments account

    C   similar to a profit and loss account in reflecting revenue earned and expenses incurred during a period

    D   a balance sheet as prepared for a non-profit making organisation

6   A fixed asset register showed a net book value of £67,460. A fixed asset costing £15,000 had been sold for £4,000, making a loss on disposal of £1,250. No entries had been made in the fixed asset register for this disposal.

The balance on the fixed asset register is

    A   £42,710
    B   £51,210
    C   £53,710
    D   £62,210

7   Revenue reserves are

    A   accumulated and undistributed profits of a company
    B   amounts which cannot be distributed as dividends
    C   amounts set aside out of profits to replace revenue items
    D   amounts set aside out of profits for a specific purpose

8   A company has £100,000 of ordinary shares at a par value of 10 pence each and 100,000 5% preference shares at a par value of 50 pence each. The directors decide to declare a dividend of 5p per ordinary share.

The total amount (ignoring tax to be paid out in dividends amounts to

A   £5,000
B   £7,500
C   £52,500
D   £55,000

9   A supplier sends you a statement showing a balance outstanding of £14,350. Your own records show a balance outstanding of £14,500.

The reason for this difference could be that

A   the supplier sent an invoice for £150 which you have not yet received
B   the supplier has allowed you £150 cash discount which you had omitted to enter in your ledgers
C   you have paid the supplier £150 which he has not yet accounted for
D   you have returned goods worth £150 which the supplier has not yet accounted for

10 From the following information, calculate the value of purchases.

	£
Opening creditors	142,600
Cash paid	542,300
Discounts received	13,200
Goods returned	27,500
Closing creditors	137,800

A   £302,600
B   £506,400
C   £523,200
D   £578,200

11 The correct ledger entries needed to record the issue of 200,000 £1 shares at a premium of 30p, and paid for by cheque, in full, would be

A	DEBIT	share capital account	£200,000
	CREDIT	share premium account	£60,000
	CREDIT	bank account	£140,000
B	DEBIT	bank account	£260,000
	CREDIT	share capital account	£200,000
	CREDIT	share premium account	£60,000
C	DEBIT	share capital account	£200,000
	CREDIT	share premium account	£60,000
	CREDIT	bank account	£260,000
D	DEBIT	bank account	£200,000
	DEBIT	share premium account	£60,000
	CREDIT	share capital account	£260,000

12 If work-in-progress decreases during the period, then

A   prime cost will decrease
B   prime cost will increase
C   the factory cost of goods completed will decrease
D   the factory cost of goods completed will increase

13 Net profit was calculated as being £10,200. It was later discovered that capital expenditure of £3,000 had been treated as revenue expenditure, and revenue receipts of £1,400 had been treated as capital receipts.

The correct net profit should have been

A   £5,800
B   £8,600
C   £11,800
D   £14,600

14   The rate of stock turnover is 6 times where

    A   sales are £120,000 and average stock at selling price is £20,000
    B   purchases are £240,000 and average stock at cost is £40,000
    C   cost of goods sold is £180,000 and average stock at cost is £30,000
    D   net purchases are £90,000 and closing stock at cost is £15,000

15   A suspense account shows a credit balance of £130. This could be due to

    A   omitting a sale of £130 from the sales ledger

    B   recording a purchase of £130 twice in the purchases account

    C   failing to write off a bad debt of £130

    D   recording an electricity bill paid of £65 by debiting the bank account and crediting the electricity account.

Total Marks = 30

79   MULTIPLE CHOICE QUESTIONS: SELECTION 5 (5/96)   *54 mins*

1   The *main* aim of accounting is to

    A   maintain ledger accounts for every asset and liability
    B   provide financial information to users of such information
    C   produce a trial balance
    D   record every financial transaction individually

2   In the time of rising prices, the historical cost convention has the effect of

    A   valuing all assets at their cost to the business

    B   recording goods sold at their cost price, even if they are worth less than that cost

    C   understanding profits and overstating balance sheet asset values

    D   overstating profits and understating balance sheet asset values

3   The accounting equation can be rewritten as

    A   assets plus profit less drawings less liabilities equals closing capital
    B   assets less liabilities less drawings equals opening capital plus profit
    C   assets less liabilities less opening capital plus drawings equals profit
    D   opening capital plus profit less drawings less liabilities equals assets

4   At the end of the month, an organisation needs to accrue for one week's wages. The gross wages amount to £500, tax amounts to £100, employer's national insurance is £50, employees' national insurance is £40, and employees' contributions to pension scheme amount to £30. The ledger entries to record this accrual would be

A	Debit wages expense	£500	Credit national insurance creditor		£90
			Credit income tax creditor		£100
			Credit pension scheme creditor		£30
			Credit wages accrued		£280
B	Debit wages expense	£550	Credit national insurance creditor		£90
			Credit income tax creditor		£100
			Credit pension scheme creditor		£30
			Credit wages accrued		£330
C	Debit wages expense	£280	Credit wages accrued		£500
	Debit national insurance expense	£90			
	Debit income tax expense	£100			
	Debit pension scheme expense	£30			
D	Debit wages expense	£330	Credit wages accrued		£550
	Debit national insurance expense	£90			
	Debit income tax expense	£100			
	Debit pension scheme expense	£30			

5   An organisation's fixed asset register shows a net book value of £125,600. The fixed asset account in the nominal ledger shows a net book value of £135,600. The difference could be due to a disposed asset not having been deducted from the fixed asset register.

   A   with disposal proceeds of £15,000 and a profit on disposal of £5,000
   B   with disposal proceeds of £15,000 and a net book value of £5,000
   C   with disposal proceeds of £15,000 and a loss on disposal of £5,000
   D   with disposal proceeds of £5,000 and a net book value of £5,000

6   An organisation's cash book has an opening balance in the bank column of £485 credit. The following transactions then took place.

   (i)   cash sales £1,450 including VAT of £150
   (ii)   receipts from customers of debts of £2,400
   (iii) payments to creditors of debts of £1,800 less 5% cash discount
   (iv) dishonoured cheques from customers amounting to £250

The resulting balance in the bank column of the cash book should be

   A   £1,255 debit
   B   £1,405 debit
   C   £1,905 credit
   D   £2,375 credit

7   An organisation restores its petty cash balance to £500 at the end of each month. During January, the total column in the petty cash book was recorded as being £420, and hence the imprest was restored by this amount. The analysis columns, which had been posted to the nominal ledger, totalled only £400. This error would result in

   A   no imbalance in the trial balance
   B   the trial balance being £20 higher on the debit side
   C   the trial balance being £20 higher on the credit side
   D   the petty cash balance being £20 lower than it should be

8   The sales ledger control account at 1 May had balances of £32,750 debit and £1,275 credit. During May, sales of £125,000 were made on credit. Receipts from debtors amounted to £122,500 and cash discounts of £550 were allowed. Refunds of £1,300 were made to customers. The closing balances at 31 May could be

   A   £35,175 debit and £3,000 credit
   B   £35,675 debit and £2,500 credit
   C   £36,725 debit and £2,000 credit
   D   £36,725 debit and £1,000 credit

9   The debit side of a trial balance totals £50 more than the credit side. This could be due to

   A   a purchase of goods for £50 being omitted from the creditor's account
   B   a sale of goods for £50 being omitted from the debtor's account
   C   an invoice of £25 for electricity being credited to the electricity account
   D   a receipt for £50 from a debtor being omitted from the cash book

10 The sales account is

   A   credited with the total of sales made, including VAT
   B   credited with the total of sales made, excluding VAT
   C   debited with the total of sales made, including VAT
   D   debited with the total of sales made, excluding VAT

11 An invoice from a supplier of office equipment has been debited to the stationery account. This error is known as

   A   an error of commission
   B   an error of original entry
   C   a compensating error
   D   an error of principle

12   A club received subscriptions during 19X5 totalling £12,500. Of these, £800 related to 19X4 and £400 related to 19X6. There were subscriptions in arrears at the end of 19X4 of £250. The subscriptions to be included in the income and expenditure account for 19X5 amount to

A   £11,050
B   £11,550
C   £11,850
D   £12,350

13   Stationery paid for during 19X5 amounted to £1,350. At the beginning of 19X5 there was a stock of stationery on hand of £165 and an outstanding invoice for £80. At the end of 19X5, there was a stock of stationery on hand of £140 and an outstanding invoice for £70. The stationery figure to be shown in the profit and loss account for 19X5 is

A   £1,195
B   £1,335
C   £1,365
D   £1,505

14   An increase in stock of £250, a decrease in the bank balance of £400 and an increase in creditors of £1,200 result in

A   a decrease in working capital of £1,350
B   an increase in working capital of £1,350
C   a decrease in working capital of £1,050
D   an increase in working capital of £1,050

15   The purchase of a business for more than the aggregate of the fair value of its separable identifiable assets results in the creation of a

A   share premium account
B   reserve account
C   suspense account
D   goodwill account

Total Marks = 30

80   **MULTIPLE CHOICE QUESTIONS: SELECTION 6 (11/96)**   *54 mins*

1   A credit balance on a ledger account indicates

A   an asset or an expense
B   a liability or an expense
C   an amount owing to the organisation
D   a liability or a revenue

2   An error of principle would occur if

A   plant and machinery purchased was credited to a fixed assets account

B   plant and machinery purchased was debited to the purchases account

C   plant and machinery purchased was debited to the equipment account

D   plant and machinery purchased was debited to the correct account but with the wrong amount

3   If sales (including VAT) amounted to £27,612.50, and purchases (excluding VAT) amounted to £18,000, the balance on the VAT account, assuming all items are subject to VAT at 17.5%, would be

A   £962.50 debit
B   £962.50 credit
C   £1,682.10 debit
D   £1,682.10 credit

4   The accounting concept or convention which, in times of rising prices, tends to understate asset values and overstate profits, is the

    A   going concern concept
    B   prudence concept
    C   realisation concept
    D   historical cost convention

5   An organisation's year end is 30 September. On 1 January 19X6 the organisation took out a loan of £100,000 with annual interest of 12%. The interest is payable in equal instalments on the first day of April, July, October and January in arrears.

How much should be charged to the profit and loss account for the year ended 30 September 19X6, and how much should be accrued on the balance sheet?

	Profit and loss account	*Balance sheet*
A	£12,000	£3,000
B	£9,000	£3,000
C	£9,000	nil
D	£6,000	£3,000

6   Recording the purchase of computer stationery by debiting the computer equipment at cost account would result in

    A   an overstatement of profit and an overstatement of fixed assets
    B   an understatement of profit and an overstatement of fixed assets
    C   an overstatement of profit and an understatement of fixed assets
    D   an understatement of profit and an understatement of fixed assets

7   Depreciation is best described as

    A   a means of spreading the payment for fixed assets over a period of years

    B   a decline in the market value of the assets

    C   a means of spreading the net cost of fixed assets over their estimated useful life

    D   a means of estimating the amount of money needed to replace the assets

8   An organisation's stock at 1 July is 15 units @ £3.00 each. The following movements occur:

    •   3 July 19X6   5 units sold at £3.30 each
    •   8 July 19X6   10 units bought at £3.50 each
    •   12 July 19X6   8 units sold at £4.00 each

Closing stock at 31 July, using the FIFO method of stock valuation would be

    A £31.50   B £36.00   C £39.00   D £41.00

9   Which ONE of the following is a book of prime entry AND part of the double-entry system?

    A   The journal
    B   The petty cash book
    C   The sales day book
    D   The purchase ledger

10   A manufacturer has the following figures for the year ended 30 September 19X6:

Direct materials	£8,000
Factory overheads	£12,000
Direct labour	£10,000
Increase in work-in-progress	£4,000

Prime cost is

    A £18,000   B £26,000   C £30,000   D £34,000

11   A sales ledger control account had a closing balance of £8,500. It contained a contra to the purchase ledger of £400, but this had been entered on the wrong side of the control account.

The correct balance on the control account should be

    A £7,700 debit   B £8,100 debit   C £8,400 debit   D £8,900 debit

12   Working capital will reduce by £500 if

A   goods costing £3,000 are sold for £3,500 on credit
B   goods costing £3,000 are sold for £3,500 cash
C   fixed assets costing £500 are purchased on credit
D   fixed assets with a net book value of £750 are sold for £250 cash

13   From the following information regarding the year to 31 August 19X6, what is the creditors' payment period?

	£
Sales	43,000
Cost of sales	32,500
Opening stock	6,000
Closing stock	3,800
Creditors at 31 August 19X6	4,750

A   40 days   B   50 days   C   53 days   D   57 days

14   A trader who is not registered for VAT purposes buys goods on credit. These goods have a list price of £2,000 and the trader is given a trade discount of 20%. The goods carry VAT at 17.5%.

The correct ledger entries to record this purchase are to debit the purchases account and to credit the supplier's account with

A   £1,600
B   £1,880
C   £2,000
D   £2,350

15   A suspense account was opened when a trial balance failed to agree. The following errors were later discovered.

- A gas bill of £420 had been recorded in the gas account as £240

- A discount of £50 given to a customer had been credited to discounts received

- Interest received of £70 had been entered in the bank account only

The original balance on the suspense account was

A   debit £210   B   credit £210   C   debit £160   D   credit £160

Total Marks = 30

81   **MULTIPLE CHOICE QUESTIONS: SELECTION 7 (5/97)**   *54 mins*

1   If the owner of a business takes goods from stock for his own personal use, the accounting concept to be considered is the

A   prudence concept
B   capitalisation concept
C   money measurement concept
D   separate entity concept

2   A book of prime entry is one in which

A   the rules of double-entry bookkeeping do not apply
B   ledger accounts are maintained
C   transactions are entered prior to being recorded in the ledger account
D   subsidiary accounts are kept

3   A business has opening stock of £12,000 and closing stock of £18,000. Purchase returns were £5,000. The cost of goods sold was £111,000.

Purchases were

A   £100,000   B   £110,000   C   £116,000   D   £122,000

4   An increase in the figure for work-in-progress will

   A   increase the prime cost
   B   decrease the prime cost
   C   increase the cost of goods sold
   D   decrease the factory cost of goods completed

5   A business had a balance at the bank of £2,500 at the start of the month. During the following month, it paid for materials invoiced at £1,000 less trade discount of 20% and cash discount of 10%. It received a cheque from a debtor in respect of an invoice for £200, subject to cash discount of 5%.

   The balance at the bank at the end of the month was

   A £1,970   B £1,980   C £1,990   D £2,000

6   An error of commission is one where

   A   a transaction has not been recorded

   B   one side of a transaction has been recorded in the wrong account, and that account is of a different class to the correct account

   C   one side of a transaction has been recorded in the wrong account, and that account is of the same class as the correct account

   D   a transaction has been recorded using the wrong amount

7   Goodwill is most appropriately classed as

   A   a fixed asset
   B   an intangible asset
   C   a fictitious liability
   D   a semi-fixed asset

8   The double-entry system of bookkeeping normally results in which of the following balances on the ledger accounts?

   Debit balances   *Credit balances*

   A   Assets and revenues   Liabilities, capital and expenses
   B   Revenues, capital and liabilities   Assets and expenses
   C   Assets and expenses   Liabilities, capital and revenues
   D   Assets, expenses and capital   Liabilities and revenues

9   A business commenced with capital in cash of £1,000. Stock costing £800 is purchased on credit, and half is sold for £1,000 plus VAT, the customer paying in cash at once.

   The accounting equation after these transactions would show:

   A   Assets £1,775 less Liabilities £175 equals Capital £1,600
   B   Assets £2,175 less Liabilities £975 equals Capital £1,200
   C   Assets £2,575 less Liabilities £800 equals Capital £1,775
   D   Assets £2,575 less Liabilities £975 equals Capital £1,600

10   A sole trader had opening capital of £10,000 and closing capital of £4,500. During the period, the owner introduced capital of £4,000 and withdrew £8,000 for her own use.

   Her profit or loss during the period was

   A   £9,500 loss
   B   £1,500 loss
   C   £7,500 profit
   D   £17,500 profit

11 Life membership fees payable to a club are usually dealt with by

A   crediting the total received to a life membership fees account and transferring a proportion each year to the income and expenditure account

B   crediting the total received to the income and expenditure account in the year in which these fees are received

C   debiting the total received to a life membership fees account and transferring a proportion each year to the income and expenditure account

D   debiting the total received to the income and expenditure account in the year in which these fees are received

12 A business has made a profit of £8,000 but its bank balance has fallen by £5,000. This could be due to

A   depreciation of £3,000 and an increase in stocks of £10,000
B   depreciation of £6,000 and the repayment of a loan of £7,000
C   depreciation of £12,000 and the purchase of new fixed assets for £25,000
D   the disposal of a fixed asset for £13,000 less than its book value

13 A business operates on a gross profit margin of $33^1/_3$%. Gross profit on a sale was £800, and expenses were £680.

The net profit percentage is

A 3.75%   B 5%   C 11.25%   D 22.67%

14 A company has authorised capital of 50,000 5% preference shares of £2 each and 500,000 ordinary shares with a par value of 20p each. All of the preference shares have been issued, and 400,000 ordinary shares have been issued at a premium of 30p each. Interim dividends of 5p per ordinary share plus half the preference dividend have been paid during the current year. A final dividend of 15p per ordinary share is declared.

The total of dividends payable for the year is

A £82,500   B £85,000   C £102,500   D £105,000

15 A fixed asset costing £12,500 was sold at a book loss of £4,500. Depreciation had been provided using the reducing balance, at 20% per annum since its purchase.

Which of the following correctly describes the sale proceeds and length of time for which the asset had been owned?

	Sale proceeds	*Length of ownership*
A	Cannot be calculated	Cannot be calculated
B	Cannot be calculated	2 years
C	£8,000	Cannot be calculated
D	£8,000	2 years

Total Marks = 30

Suggested Solutions

1   TUTORIAL QUESTION: USERS OF ACCOUNTING STATEMENTS

(a) (i) *Loan creditors*

Lenders are concerned that an enterprise is able to pay back any borrowings. Cash and borrowing positions are therefore quite useful information for them in the short term. In the long term they are interested in the overall health and operational viability of the enterprise.

(ii) *The employee group*

Employees are interested in financial statements for a number of reasons. Job security is one concern, as the long-term financial viability of a company is indicated in the accounts. Also, the profit information might be a basis for judging pay claims. Employees would also be interested in social accounting.

(iii) *Analysts and advisors*

Analysts and advisors are interested in the operating performance of an enterprise as they aim to identify investment opportunities. Their information requirements are quite complex, with an emphasis on profit performance and estimates of future operations.

(iv) *Business contacts (eg suppliers and customers)*

Suppliers are interested in the long term health of a company, to assess whether orders will be continued. They are also interested in an enterprise's liquidity position, to assess whether they will get paid. Customers need to know whether products will still be available. Competitors also are interested, to compare performance.

(v) *The government*

Government departments have an interest in published financial statements. The most obvious examples are the Inland Revenue and the Customs and Excise, for the collection of taxes and duties. Published financial information is used by central and local government in other ways: economic statistics, information for regional policy making, and so forth.

(vi) *The public*

The general public has an interest in financial statements on three counts. Firstly, the activities of any enterprise have social consequences. For example, proponents of 'social accounting' have supported the introduction of statistics of industrial injuries into published financial statements: apart from humanitarian considerations, the cost of treating industrial injuries in the National Health Service is a cost to the tax payer caused by poor safety procedures or dangerous work. Issues related to the environment are also of interest. This expands the scope of purely financial statements to include social issues and social costs. Secondly, in many cases members of the public are potential investors. Thirdly, the public has an interest, as customers, in the activities of an enterprise.

(b) Section (a) demonstrates that different users can have valid uses of the same information, with differences of emphasis. Owners and investors and the analysts who advise them will concentrate in more detail on the financial performance of an enterprise than on information related to more public concerns (eg the environment).

2   ACCOUNTING STATEMENTS

> *Tutorial note.* Try to avoid repetition in answering this question.

(a) *Relevant*

Published financial statements are directed to a number of different user groups: employees; the government; shareholders or owners of an enterprise; bankers; suppliers and customers; investment analysts. All of these user groups have different information needs, all of which must be satisfied in part by the information presented in published financial statements. Relevance in this context means that the information contained serves the needs of users.

There is great debate as to how relevant published financial statements in fact are, especially to investors. The use of historical costs is sometimes felt to obscure the real operating performance of an enterprise. Many users also want more information from financial statements than is currently provided.

Understandable

Many users are not accounting professionals. This is an especially important issue when shareholders are private individuals rather than large investment institutions with teams of analysts. Given that the purpose of financial statements is to convey information to shareholders, if that information is impossible to understand, then it is of little use. Graphs, diagrams, and summary information can be used to make the often technical content of published accounts easier to understand.

Reliable

Reliability means that the information presented in a set of financial statements can be relied on to be an accurate description of the transactions of the enterprise as recorded in the accounting records and show a true and fair view. This means that users should have confidence that the information is correct, and that there are no material errors in the accounts.

Complete

A set of published financial statements is in essence a report on the activities of the enterprise over a particular period, and a description of its assets, liabilities at the end of it. Therefore, completeness is important. All material transactions or circumstances should be recorded so that the user gets a full picture of an enterprise's position and performance. There has been much debate as to whether the exclusion of 'special purpose transactions' or 'off balance sheet finance', by which enterprises hide major transactions or liabilities from published accounts, should be permitted.

Objective

As far as is reasonably possible, the information presented in published financial statements should not be distorted by the wishes of those preparing it. There is always a temptation to overstate profits and performance. It is the task of the auditors to ensure that these statements are objective.

Timely

Financial statements should be produced in such a timescale that the information it contains is still relevant to users. Those who make investment decisions value timeliness, as it allows them to make decisions on recent information. Another feature of the timing of financial reports is the regularity with which they are produced. Producing financial statements every year, covering the same twelve months, enables the time periods to be compared.

Comparable

Comparability has two aspects. Firstly, it means that accounts produced by an enterprise for one accounting period should be readily compared with the accounts for the previous accounting period. This requirement affects accounting policies. If the basis for measuring, say, profit, is different, then comparing two successive profit figures does not give a meaningful appreciation of an improvement or decline in operating performance. Inflation produces problems of comparability, as the value of money, the unit of measurement is declining in successive accounting periods. Secondly, the financial statements of different enterprises in the same industry should be comparable: one might be operating more efficiently than another.

(b) These matters can come into conflict in a number of ways.

The effort required to make a set of accounts absolutely complete may result in extra time being spent to prepare them, thus reducing their timeliness.

Objectivity might conflict with understandability: the transactions of a business enterprise are often complex, especially, for example, with the reporting of taxation. Objectively speaking, the enterprise is complex, and therefore its financial statements may also be complex. Making matters easy to understand may introduce subjectivity or oversimplification.

Objectivity might also be in conflict with comparability. no enterprise is exactly the same, and comparisons drawn may be unjust, especially if different accounting policies are used.

3   PURPOSE OF ACCOUNTS

> *Tutorial note.* A large number of points could be made in answer to this question, and you would not be expected to cover all of them. It is better to *develop* points rather than simply list as many as possible.

In assessing the value of the information in audited accounts we should think not only in terms of degrees of usefulness, but also of the purpose for which they are intended.

Audited financial statements are intended to report on the past accounting period and on the state of the company's affairs at the end of the period. A limited company is required by law to file accounts with the Registrar of Companies. While a bank manager considering an overdraft facility will certainly be interested in such reports, he will be far more concerned about the short and medium term future. He would therefore require the following types of information.

(a) *Forecasts of profit and cash flow.* Published accounts have historically placed much more emphasis on profit than on cash flow, although recent regulatory requirements have endeavoured to remedy this. Profits are important to a bank manager because he will need to know if the firm is likely to stay in business. Cash flow, however, is of paramount importance; the bank will wish to be able to get its money back if need be, and high profits are no guarantee of liquidity. With regard to both those aspects, audited accounts are of limited use because they provide information about the past, rather than the future.

(b) *Current value of assets.* This will be particularly important in the case of secured lending and if the company becomes insolvent and the assets have to be sold. Financial statements are generally prepared under the historical cost convention and may thus give out-of-date values for assets.

(c) *Future developments in the market.* The bank will wish to know if the company will stay in business and remain reasonably profitable. Factors such as the economic climate, competitors' activities and so on will come into play. Audited accounts provide next to no information on these issues.

It is clear, therefore, that the accounts on their own will not provide the bank manager with all the information he requires. This does not mean that they are not worth preparing, only that they are of limited value to this kind of short-term lender.

4   SHAREHOLDER AND SUPPLIER

> *Tutorial note.* Candidates must stop and think before answering this question. It does not matter what opinions they hold on these rather subjective issues as long as the opinions are backed up by rational arguments.

(a) A shareholder in a company needs to know:

(i)   whether the value of his shareholding is secure;
(ii)   whether it is likely to continue to be secure and preferably to grow in value.

A creditor of the company will need to know whether the company is in a position to pay for its purchases within a reasonable time. He therefore needs to know what cash the company has available at present and what other calls there may be on that cash from other creditors (employees, other suppliers, the government, providers of loan capital and so on).

However, it would be misleading to suggest that this distinction was absolute. A creditor will be interested in the future health of the business. He will certainly be concerned mainly with the question of whether the company is a going concern. Moreover, if the company is growing and is profitable, he will be more likely to supply goods on credit in future years.

Similarly, the shareholder will be interested in the current position as well as in future prospects. If the company is in a poor state now, it does not augur well for the future.

(b) Historical cost accounts give a good indication of the current security of a shareholding, but they do not give a good indication of whether the value of shares is likely to be maintained or grow in the future.

Some companies prepare accounts on a 'current cost' basis. The intention is to indicate how far the company has maintained its capital when price increases are taken into account. The adjustments required are complex and are not widely understood.

A compromise is to prepare modified historical cost accounts. This generally means that up-to-date valuations are included in the historical cost balance sheet for some or all of a company's fixed assets Even full current cost accounts, however, do not indicate likely future developments.

5   TUTORIAL QUESTION: ACCOUNTING CONCEPTS

(a) Going concern
(b) Accruals
(c) Prudence
(d) Consistency

6   TUTORIAL QUESTION: TERMINOLOGY

(a) A *balance sheet* is a statement of the assets, liabilities and capital of a business as at a stated date. It is laid out to show either total assets as equivalent to total liabilities and capital or net assets as equivalent to capital. Other formats are also possible but the top half (or left hand) total will always equal the bottom half (or right hand) total. Some balance sheets are laid out vertically and others horizontally.

(b) An *asset* is owned by a business and is expected to be of some future benefit. Its value is determined as the historical cost of producing or obtaining it (unless an attempt is being made to reflect rising prices in the accounts, in which case a replacement cost might be used). Examples of assets are:

   (i)   plant, machinery, land and other long-term or *fixed* assets;

   (ii) *current* assets such as stocks, cash and debts owed to the business with reasonable assurance of recovery: these are assets which are not intended to be held on a continuing basis in the business.

(c) A *liability* is an amount owed by a business, other than the amount owed to its proprietors (ie capital). Examples of liabilities are:

   (i)   amounts owed to the government (VAT or other taxes);
   (ii)   amounts owed to suppliers;
   (iii) bank overdraft;
   (iv)   long-term loans from banks or investors.

It is usual to differentiate between 'current' and 'long-term' liabilities. The former fall due within a year of the balance sheet date.

(d) *Share capital* is the permanent investment in a business by its owners. In the case of a limited company, this takes the form of *shares* for which investors subscribe on formation of the company. Each share has a *nominal* (or face) *value* (eg £1). In the balance sheet, total issued share capital is shown at its nominal value.

(e) If a company issues shares for more than their nominal value (at a *premium*) then by law this premium must be recorded separately from the nominal value in a 'share premium account'. This is an example of a *reserve*. It belongs to the shareholders but cannot be distributed to them, because it is a *capital* reserve. Other capital reserves include the revaluation reserve, which shows the surpluses arising on revaluation of assets which are still owned by the company.

Share capital and capital reserves are not distributable except on the winding up of the company, as a guarantee to the company's creditors that the company has enough assets to meet its debts. This is necessary because shareholders in limited companies have 'limited liability'; once they have paid the company for their shares they have no further liability to it if it becomes insolvent. The proprietors of other businesses are, by contrast, personally liable for business debts.

Revenue reserves constitute accumulated profits (less losses) made by the company and can be distributed to shareholders as *dividends*. They too belong to the shareholders, and so are a claim on the resources of the company.

(f) Balance sheets do not always balance on the first attempt, as all accountants know! However, once errors are corrected, all balance sheets balance. This is because in double entry bookkeeping every transaction recorded has a dual effect. Assets are always equal to liabilities plus capital and so capital is always equal to assets less liabilities. This makes sense as the owners of the business are entitled to the net assets of the business as representing their capital plus accumulated surpluses (or less accumulated deficit).

(g) The balance sheet is not intended as a statement of a business's worth at a given point in time. This is because, except where some attempt is made to adjust for the effects of rising prices, assets and liabilities are recorded at historical cost and on a prudent basis. For example, if there is any doubt about the recoverability of a debt, then the value in the accounts must be reduced to the likely recoverable amount. In addition, where fixed assets have a finite useful life, their cost is gradually written off to reflect the use being made of them.

Sometimes fixed assets are *revalued* to their market value but this revaluation then goes out of date as few assets are revalued every year.

The balance sheet figure for capital and reserves therefore bears no relationship to the market value of shares. Market values are the product of a large number of factors, including general economic conditions, alternative investment returns (eg interest rates), likely future profits and dividends and, not least, market sentiment.

7 TUTORIAL QUESTION: SSAP 2

(a) Fundamental accounting concepts are the broad basic assumptions underlying all financial statements. They are as follows.

(i) *Going concern*. The entity preparing statements is assumed to be continuing in existence for the foreseeable future.

(ii) *Accruals/matching*. Revenue and expenses which are related to each other are matched, so as to be dealt with in the same accounting period, without regard to when the cash is actually received or paid.

(iii) *Prudence*. Revenues and profits are recognised only when realised, losses and liabilities are recognised as soon as they are foreseen. (The prudence concept overrides the accruals concept if the two are in conflict.)

(iv) *Consistency*. Accounting treatments should not be altered from one period to another without good cause. Similar items should be treated alike within each accounting period.

(b) Accounting bases are methods which have been developed for applying fundamental accounting concepts to financial transactions. They include the following.

(i) *Depreciation*. A variety of depreciation methods is possible, including the straight line, reducing balance and sum-of-the-digits method. Each has the same aim of expensing the cost of a fixed asset over its useful life.

(ii) *Stock valuation*. Methods such as FIFO, historical cost and average cost all aim at determining the cost of stock items in the accounts.

(c) Accounting policies are the accounting bases adopted by a business entity as the most appropriate for its circumstances. The entity should disclose material accounting policies in a note to its accounts.

8   EXPLANATIONS AND ILLUSTRATIONS

> *Tutorial note.* The question asks for four explanations, but we have included all five for completeness.
>
> *Examiner's comment.* Many candidates earned reasonable marks on this question.

(a) *Capital maintenance*

The capital of a business is the excess of its assets over its liabilities. It represents the proprietor's interest in the business. One way of measuring profit is to measure how well off a business is at the beginning of a period and compare it with how well off it is at the end of a period. Thus, if the value of a business rises by £500 over the course of a year we can say that the capital of the business has been maintained and that an addition to capital of £500 has been created.

The concept of capital maintenance is particularly important in the context of inflation. When prices are rising, at least some of the profit shown by the historical cost accounts must be ploughed back into the business just to maintain its previous capacity.

(b) *Goodwill*

Goodwill is an intangible fixed asset. It is created by good relationships between a business and its customers, for example through the reputation of the products or staff.

The value of goodwill to a business may be extremely significant. However, it is not usually shown in the accounts because it is subjective and difficult to measure. The exception to this rule is when a business is sold. In this case goodwill will be objectively defined as the difference between the price paid for the business and the fair value of the assets acquired.

(c) *Economic value of assets*

In a conventional balance sheet a fixed asset is normally shown at its net book value, that is historical cost less accumulated depreciation. This is because, in general, accountants prefer to deal with objective 'costs' rather than subjective 'values'.

An alternative way of looking at a fixed asset is in terms of its ability to generate future profits over its remaining life. This is its economic value. It may be calculated by estimating future profits and applying an appropriate discount factor to arrive at a net present value factor.

(d) *Research and development costs*

Large companies often spend significant amounts on research and development activities. The question arises as to whether to write off such expenditure in the period in which it is incurred or to capitalise it and subsequently amortise it.

The treatment required is set out in SSAP 13 *Accounting for research and development* and depends on the nature of the expenditure. Pure and applied research must be prudently written off against profit in the year incurred. Development expenditure (strictly defined) may be capitalised and subsequently amortised over the anticipated product life.

(e) *Prudence*

The *prudence concept* is that where alternative procedures, or alternative valuations, are possible, the one selected should be the one which gives the most cautious presentation of the business's financial position or results. For example, stocks should be stated in the balance sheet at the lower of cost or net realisable value rather than their selling price: to value the stock at selling price would be to anticipate making a profit before the profit had been earned, and would not be 'prudent'.

The other aspect of the prudence concept is that where a loss is foreseen, it should be anticipated and taken into account immediately. If a business purchases stock for £1,200 but because of a sudden slump in the market only £900 is likely to be realised when the stock is sold, the prudence concept dictates that the stock should be valued at £900. It is not enough to wait until the stock is sold, and then recognise the £300 loss. It must be recognised as soon as it is foreseen.

be valued at £900. It is not enough to wait until the stock is sold, and then recognise the £300 loss. It must be recognised as soon as it is foreseen.

9 SUGGESTIONS

> *Tutorial note.* This question puts you in a position that you may very well encounter in real life before long. The MD clearly does not understand certain accounting concepts, so try to keep your report as free from jargon as you can, given the requirements of the question. Try not to be patronising, though, and don't be too officious.

REPORT

To: Managing director
From: Management accountant
Date: 23 November 19X7
Subject: Forecast final accounts for the year ending 31 December 19X7

Further to our recent discussion I set out below my comments on your suggestions regarding the year end accounts.

(a) *Obsolete stock*

Accounting standards require that stock is valued at the lower of cost and net realisable value. This means that each year we must consider all items of stock and adjust downwards the valuation of those that could only be sold for less than their cost. If there are no such items then no provision will be necessary. The provision is adjusted (upwards or downwards) each year to take account of the current position.

In accounting terms this is in accordance with the concept of prudence: if the value of stock is overstated then we would be anticipating profit which will never be earned. To discontinue the policy would also breach the concept of consistency, which requires that in accounting for similar items, the same treatment should be applied from one period to another so that interested parties such as shareholders can make valid comparisons.

A final decision on this matter must await the results of the annual stocktake.

(b) *Depreciation*

Depreciation is a measure of the extent to which a fixed asset has worn out through use or become obsolescent because of changes in technology or the needs of the market. It aims to spread the cost of an asset over the useful life of the asset, in accordance with the matching concept (revenue earned through using assets should be matched with the expenditure incurred on those assets).

If no provision for depreciation is made, therefore, the assumption would have to be made that there has been no reduction in the useful life of our assets over the past year, which is exceedingly unlikely. This policy would also be inconsistent with that adopted in previous years, and imprudent because we would be understating costs and hence overstating profits.

(c) *Research expenditure*

Accounting standards require that all expenditure on research should be written off in the year in which it is incurred. The advantages derived from general research activities are too remote to justify the company carrying the expenditure forward: this would be to anticipate future revenues that cannot, in fact, be anticipated with any certainty at all. To capitalise such costs would once more be in breach of the concepts of prudence, matching and consistency. Even if there were a case for treating any of the R&D Department's costs as development expenditure (which may be capitalised if it fulfils certain stringent conditions) it would still be necessary to provide depreciation (amortisation) in the profit and loss account as soon as the development project went into commercial production.

(d) *Doubtful debts*

Once again the concepts of prudence, matching and consistency require that the company should not change its previous policy and anticipate income that it is not reasonably certain to receive. Doubtful debts are a case in point of income that seems *unlikely* to be received. All unpaid debts should be reviewed to determine the likelihood of payment. If it is believed that all debts will be paid, then no provision will be necessary and provisions made in previous years may indeed be written back.

Each of the above matters (with the exception, perhaps, of (c)) will require further consideration after the year end, once the full year's results and events are known. Each will be investigated carefully by our auditors, who will require adjustments to be made to our final accounts if they do not agree that we are showing a 'true and fair view' of our financial position.

I shall of course be prepared to elaborate upon any of the above matters or consider further suggestions as necessary.

10 TUTORIAL QUESTION: THE ACCOUNTING AND BUSINESS EQUATIONS

(a) Profit £1,051 = Drawings + £733 – £100
£1,051 - £733 + £100 = Drawings = £418

(b) Profit = Drawings + increase in net assets – capital introduced
£205 = £77 + £173   – £45

(c) Capital + liabilities = Assets
Capital + £153 = £174
∴ Capital = £21.

(d) Capital = Assets - Liabilities

£50 + £100 + profit for the year = £90 – £70
£150 + profit for the year = £20
∴ the profit for the year is in fact a *loss* of £130.

11 TUTORIAL QUESTION: THE EFFECT OF TRANSACTIONS

Transaction	*Current assets*	*Current liabilities*	*Profit*
(a)	Increase £2,000 Decrease £2,000	Stay the same	Stay the same
(b)	Stay the same	Stay the same	Stay the same
(c)	Decrease £6,250	Stay the same	Stay the same
(d)	Decrease £2,750	Stay the same	Stay the same
(e)	Decrease £1,400	Stay the same	Decrease £1,400
(f)	Increase £10,000	Stay the same	Stay the same
(g)	Stay the same	Stay the same	Decrease £500
(h)	Increase £775	Stay the same	Increase £125
(i)	Increase £8,000	Increase £8,000	Stay the same
(j)	Decrease £4,000 Increase £5,000	Stay the same	Increase £1,000
(k)	Decrease £820	Stay the same	Decrease £820

12 TUTORIAL QUESTION: CREDIT, CASH AND DISCOUNT

(a) SALES BOOK

19X9		£
1.5	P Dixon	160
4.5	M Maguire	80
5.5	M Donald	304
		544

(b) PURCHASES BOOK

19X9		£
2.5	A Clarke (W)	323
4.5	D Daley	400
6.5	G Perkins	100
		823

(c) CASH BOOK

19X9		Bank £	Cash £	Discount £	19X9		Bank £	Cash £	Discount £
1.5	Balance b/d		224		1.5	Balance b/d	336		
1.5	Cash withdrawal		50		1.5	Cash withdrawal	50		
3.5	Cash sales		45		2.5	R Hill (W)	108		12
5.5	H Larkin	180		20	4.5	Telephone bill	210		
6.5	D Randle	482			5.5	Honour Ltd	135		
6.5	Balance c/d	177			6.5	Balance c/d		319	
		839	319	20			839	319	12
7.5	Balance b/d		319		7.5	Balance b/d	177		

Working

$$£380 \times \frac{85}{100} = £323 \qquad £120 \times \frac{100-10}{100} = £108$$

13   XY'S DAYBOOK

> *Tutorial note.* Part (b) of this question may have caused you problems. The term 'the realisation concept' is not in general usage and a more carefully worded question would no doubt have prompted more candidates to think of prudence and accruals. For part (c) the examiner commented that 'candidates continued to demonstrate their inability to post transactions using double entry principles. It was common for candidates to reverse the debit and credit entries.
>
> You are told not to balance off the accounts, but you might have found it helpful to do so in rough to check that you have made no mistakes. Alternatively, quickly add up all the debits and credits in your debtors ledger accounts (net total £10,575 as given), see that total debits in the nominal ledger equal total credits, and that the balance on the sales ledger control account equals the total debtors ledger balances.

(a) The entry on 17 February suggests that the customer MG Limited returned £600 worth of goods on that day, perhaps because that part of the goods sold on 14 February were faulty or the wrong quantity was delivered.

(b) 'Realisation' is a crucial part of the accounting concept of accruals and prudence: income should only be recognised when it can be said to have occurred with reasonable certainty, that is when it is realised in the form of cash or in a form that is reasonably certain to become cash eventually.

Put more simply, items are recorded in the daybook only when an invoice has been issued, not, for example on receipt of an order.

(c) *Debtors ledger*

ANG LIMITED

		£		£
February				
7	Sales day book	5,405		
25	Sales day book	1,410		

JOHN'S STORES

		£			£
February					
10	Sales day book	3,290			

ML LIMITED

		£			£
February			February		
14	Sales day book	1,175	17	Sales day book	705

Nominal ledger

SALES

		£			£
			February		
			28	Sales ledger control	9,600

VAT

		£			£
February			February		
28	Sales ledger control	105	28	Sales ledger control	1,680

RETURNS INWARDS

		£			£
February					
28	Sales ledger control	600			

SALES LEDGER CONTROL

		£			£
February			February		
28	Sales	9,600	28	Returns inwards	600
28	VAT	1,680	28	VAT	105

(d) A provision for doubtful debts is made to allow for the fact that customers to whom goods are sold may be unable to pay for them. As noted above, prudence requires that income should only be recognised when it can be said to have occurred with reasonable certainty. If there is any possibility that income already recognised will not in fact be realised then a provision for doubtful debts is required. The size of the provision depends partly upon the care taken by the business over credit control (seeing to it that goods are only sold if the customer is able to pay) and partly upon previous experience, but in current economic conditions even customers with impeccable payment histories may find themselves in difficulties and, prudently, some allowance should be made for the economic climate.

14   TRANSACTIONS

> *Tutorial note.* Part (a) tested knowledge of books of prime entry and of the double entry principles, while part (b) required a discussion of stewardship.
>
> *Examiner's comment.* Answers to part (a) ranged from very good to very poor with transaction 5 causing the most problems. Marks were not awarded where candidates did not make it clear that the three credit entries for this transaction indicated *liabilities*, not cash payments. Part (b) produced only 'scant' answers.

(a)

Transaction number	Book of prime entry	Debit entries a/c name	Amount £	Credit entries a/c name	Amount £
1	Purchase day book	Purchases (£3,000 × 75%) VAT a/c	2,250 393.75	J Smith	2,643.75
2	Cash book	L Taylor	2,400	Bank a/c Discounts received	2,280 120
3	Journal	K Green (purchase ledger)	300	K Green	300
4	Journal	Fixed asset cost - motor vehicles	2,000	S Long (sales ledger)	2,000
5	Journal	Wages expense NI cxpcnse	3,000 130	Wages payable PAYE and NI payable	2,430 700

(b) Stewardship when applied to an organisation refers to the primary function of the managers who are responsible for the running of the business on a day to day basis.

As proprietors became further and further removed from the day to day management of the business they owned, the stewardship role encompassed the safeguarding and accounting for the business's assets.

The development of external auditing was based on the 'stewardship' concept of company management. The function of the auditor was to assure the proprietors that the stewardship of the organisation was effectively carried out.

However, the stewardship concept is wider than the requirement to ensure that the assets of an organisation are properly recorded, valued and insured. It should also include the control of costs, the improvement of efficiency and the optimisation of profits Additionally whilst management's stewardship responsibilities extend primarily to the owners of the business it also includes all other users of the accounts.

15   XY LEDGER ACCOUNTS

Tutorial note. Questions asking you to prepare four ledger accounts are relatively uncommon. This question tests both in theory (parts (b) and (c)) and in practice, whether you fully understand accruals and provisions.

(a)   (i)   RENT PAYABLE ACCOUNT

		£			£
1.10.X5	Bal b/fwd	1,500	30.9.X6	Charge to P&L a/c	6,000
30.11.X5	Bank	1,500	30.9.X6	Rent prepaid c/fwd	1,500
29.2.X6	Bank	1,500			
31.5.X6	Bank	1,500			
31.8.X6	Bank	1,500			
		7,500			7,500
1.10.X6	Rent prepaid b/fwd	1,500			

(ii)   ELECTRICITY ACCOUNT

		£			£
5.11.X5	Bank	1,000	1.10.X5	Bal b/fwd	800
10.2.X6	Bank	1,300	30.9.X6	Charge to P&L a/c	5,000
8.5.X6	Bank	1,500			
7.8.X6	Bank	1,100			
30.9.X6	Accrual c/fwd	900			
		5,800			5,800
			1.10.X6	Balance b/fwd	900

(iii)   INTEREST RECEIVABLE ACCOUNT

		£			£
1.10.X5	Bal b/fwd	300	2.10.X5	Bank	250
30.9.X6	Transfer to P&L a/c	850	3.4.X6	Bank	600
			30.9.X6	Accrual c/fwd	300
		1,150			1,150
1.10.X6	Balance b/fwd	300			

(iv)   PROVISION FOR DOUBTFUL DEBTS

		£			£
30.9.X6	Bal c/fwd		1.10.X5	Bal b/fwd	4,800
	(125,000 × 5%)	6,250	30.9.X6	Charge to P&L a/c	1,450
		6,250			6,250
			1.10.X6	Balance b/fwd	6,250

(b) The accruals concept states that revenue must be matched against expenditure incurred in earning it. Hence only income and expenditure relating to the year should be included in the profit and loss account. Rent not relating to the year, ie which is prepaid at 30 September 19X6 is carried forward to be included as an expense of the following year. Electricity costs relating to the year which have not been paid for at 30 September 19X6 are accrued for and included as an expense at the year end. Similarly interest earned during the year but not received by the year end is provided for at 30 September 19X6 and so included in income for the year ending on that date.

The prudence concept states that where a loss is foreseen it must be provided for. From prior experience XY know that not all debtors balances are likely to be collected in full. Hence at 30 September 19X7 a provision is made against those amounts not expected to be collected.

(c) *Rent payable account.* The balance brought down is a prepayment and relates to rent paid in advance for the following financial year, ie to 30 September 19X7. It will be included in debtors in the balance sheet.

Electricity account. The balance brought down is an accrual and relates to the amount of electricity charged to the profit and loss account for the year ended 30 September 19X6 which has not been paid for at that date. It will be included in the balance sheet as a current liability.

Interest receivable account. This balance brought down is accrued income. It comprises an estimate of the amount of interest earned in the period 1 April to 30 September 19X6 which was not received at the year end. It will be included in debtors in the balance sheet.

Provision for doubtful debt account. The balance carried down is a provision against trade debtor balances outstanding at 30 September 19X6 which are not expected to be collected in full. The provision will be shown in the balance sheet as a deduction from trade debtors.

16   BH

(a) The imprest system of maintaining petty cash involves keeping the petty cash balance at an agreed sum or float. Expenses (and income) are recorded on vouchers as they are paid out of or into the float. The vouchers should be signed by the payee and the petty cashier. Invoices or receipts are usually required to evidence the payment.

Hence under this system at any one time the total of petty cash held and expense vouchers paid and income vouchers received will equal the agreed petty cash float, eg £100.

At regular intervals (weekly or monthly) the petty cash float will be topped up to the agreed sum by means of a withdrawal from the bank account and the expense and income vouchers it replaces will be recorded in the petty cash book.

The purpose of using this system is that the petty cash can be easily controlled as the amount of the float is known and can be checked at any time. It allows employees to be reimbursed quickly and makes efficient use of administration time.

(b) An organisation in the course of its day to day business creates and receives source documents, eg invoices, credit notes and cheques. In order to function efficiently the business needs to record these documents so that they can be controlled and dealt with properly.

One method of recording these items is in day books which include the sales day book, purchase day book, sales returns day book, purchase returns day book, cash book and petty cash book. Another name for these books is books of prime entry.

The day books are used for recording source documents as they are raised or received. In addition they are used as a means of analysis, eg the purchase day book will analyse suppliers' invoices into type of expense.

However, their function is not limited to just recording the source documents; they are also used as a means of posting to the nominal ledger accounts. The transactions recorded in the day books are totalled on a periodic basis, eg weekly or monthly. These totals are then posted to the relevant nominal ledger accounts, ie income and expenditure accounts, asset and liability accounts including control accounts for both the sales and purchase ledgers.

Use of the day books in this way contributes to the efficiency and control of the double entry bookkeeping system in that it helps to ensure that both sides of the entry, ie both debit and credit, are posted to the nominal ledger simultaneously. For example, from the sales day book a debit to the sales ledger control account will be matched by credit entries to the sales income and VAT payable accounts in the nominal ledger. Individual transactions, such as an invoice received, will also be recorded in memorandum accounts - in this case the purchase ledger - which do not form part of the double-entry system but which allow balances with individual suppliers to be monitored.

(c)

SALES LEDGER CONTROL ACCOUNT

	£		£
Balance at 1.2.X7	103,670	Balance at 1.2.X7	1,400
Feb sales (175,860 + 10,350)	186,210	Returns	9,500
Refunds	800	Cheques received	126,750
Dishonoured cheques	1,580	Discounts	1,150
Dividend receivable	300	Contra P/L	750
		Bad debts written off	2,300
At 28.2.X7 Balance owing to customers	840	At 28.2.X7 Balance due from customers	151,550
	293,400		293,400
Balance at 1.3.X7	151,550	Balance at 1.3.X7	840

17   TUTORIAL QUESTION: STOCKS

(a) Cost is that expenditure which has been incurred in the normal course of business in bringing the product or service to its present location and condition. This expenditure should include:

   (i)   cost of purchase (including import duties, transport and handling costs and any other directly attributable costs, less trade discounts, rebates and subsidies);

   (ii)   any costs of conversion appropriate to that location and condition (including direct labour and expenses, and attributable production overheads).

(b) Net realisable value is the actual or estimated selling price (net of trade but before settlement discounts) less:

   (i)   all further costs to completion; and
   (ii)   all costs to be incurred in marketing, selling and distributing.

18   SMITH

> *Tutorial note.* This question tests your understanding of a distinction that often causes students difficulties in practice. There are a number of different ways of defining reserves, each of which will gain marks in an examination.

(a)

		£	£
DEBIT	Advisory services (P&L)	2,000	
CREDIT	Creditors (Smith)		2,000
DEBIT	Advisory services (P&L)	700	
CREDIT	Provision (Smith)		700
DEBIT	Profit and loss account	10,000	
CREDIT	Stock replacement reserve		10,000

(b)   The terms may be explained as follows.

   (i)   A *provision* is an amount charged against revenue as an expense and relates either to a diminution in the value of an asset (for example, a provision for doubtful debts) or a known liability, the amount of which cannot be established with any accuracy.

   (ii)   A *creditor* is a person to whom the business owes money. This is a legal obligation as well as an accounting entry.

   (iii) A *reserve* is an appropriation of distributable profits for a specific purpose, for example to replace fixed assets.

The difference, then, is that a provision is an *estimate* of an amount owed, a creditor (and an accrual) is an *actual* amount owed, and a reserve is not an amount owed at all.

(c)   (i)   Invoice for advisory services - creditor
       (ii)   Reminder - provision
      (iii) Transfer - reserve

19   XW

> *Tutorial note.* In part (c) you could have argued that the concept of consistency should be applied to stock, ie the method of valuation chosen should be applied year on year. Whichever concepts you choose, you must argue your case - just a list of three words will earn you no marks.
>
> *Examiner's comment.* Some candidates discussed *users* rather than *uses* of accounts in part (a). In part (b), many candidates obtained full marks. Part (c) was about stock and accounting concepts, and not, as some candidates thought, about methods of stock valuation.

(a)   The purpose of financial accounting records is as follows.

   (i)   To assist in the efficient running of a business. Accounting records are part of the management information system.

   (ii)   To assist in keeping the business' assets secure.

   (iii) To allow information to be produced to interested parties, eg owners, tax authorities etc.

It is also important to note that, by law, a company must keep certain minimum accounting periods. These will be important when the accounts are audited as they must provide an adequate audit trail.

Accounting records are used to prepare historical financial statements such as the balance sheet or profit and loss account. However, they can also be used for forecasts, for example, cash flow forecasts.

(b) Five characteristics of a good coding system are as follows.

(i)	Uniqueness	Each code should be unique to a particular type of stock
(ii)	Flexibility	The system should be capable of allowing for growth of the number of items held. It should also allow for sub-division into different categories of items.
(iii)	Simplicity	It should be as simple as possible to reduce the incidence of errors by users.
(iv)	Check-digit	It should contain a check-digit for use in computer processing to validate data.
(v)	Understandability	It should use a mixture of alpha/numeric digits to allow the category of item to be identified from the alpha part of the code.

(c) Three accounting concepts which govern the valuation of stock are as follows.

(i)	Prudence	Stock should be valued at the lower of cost and net realisable value, ie profits should not be anticipated but losses should be provided for.
(ii)	Going concern	Assumes stock will be sold in the normal trading conditions of a going concern and not on a break-up basis.
(iii)	Matching	The cost of stock is carried forward to be matched against the revenues which its sale is expected to generate, rather than being expensed as incurred.

20 TUTORIAL QUESTION: DEPRECIATION

(a) Where fixed assets are disposed of for an amount which is greater or less than their book value, the surplus or deficiency should be reflected in the results of the year and disclosed separately if material.

(b) A change from one method of providing depreciation to another is permissible only on the grounds that the new method will give a fairer presentation of the results and of the financial position. In these circumstances the unamortised cost of the asset should be written off over the remaining useful life on the new basis commencing with the period in which the change is made. The effect should be disclosed in the year of change, if material.

21 TUTORIAL QUESTION: ASSET DISPOSALS

(a) (i) Straight line depreciation will give the same charge each year for the four years of economic life, as follows.

$$\text{Annual depreciation} = \frac{\text{Cost minus residual value}}{\text{Estimated economic life}}$$

$$\text{Annual depreciation} = \frac{£1,800 - £0}{4 \text{ years}}$$

$$\text{Annual depreciation} = \underline{£450}$$

Annual depreciation charges are therefore 19X1 £450, 19X2 £450, 19X3 £450, 19X4 £450.

(ii) The diminishing balance method at 60% per annum involves the following calculations.

	£
Cost at 1.1.19X1	1,800
Depreciation 19X1	1,080 60% × £1,800
Book value 1.1.19X2	720
Depreciation 19X2	432 60% × £720
Book value 1.1.19X3	288
Depreciation 19X3	173 60% × £288
Book value 1.1.19X4	115
Depreciation 19X4	115(balance remaining)
Residual value at end of estimated economic life	–

Annual depreciation charges are therefore 19X1 £1,080, 19X2 £432, 19X3 £173, 19X4 £115.

(b) (i)

LASER PRINTER ACCOUNT

		£			£
1.1.19X4	Bal b/f	1,800	1.7.19X4	Assets disposals a/c	1,800

(ii)

PROVISION FOR DEPRECIATION - LASER PRINTER ACCOUNT

		£			£
			1.1.19X4	Bal b/f ie £1,080 + £432 + £173	1,685
1.7.19X4	Assets disposals a/c	1,743	1.7.19X4	Depreciation a/c ie 6 mths @ £115 pa	58
		1,743			1,743

(iii)

ASSETS DISPOSALS ACCOUNT

		£			£
1.7.19X4	Laser printer account	1,800	1.7.19X4	Bank a/c	200
31.12.19X4	Profit and loss (profit on disposal)	143	1.7.19X4	Provision for depreciation - (laser printer a/c)	1,743
		1,943			1,943

	£
Proof of profit on disposal:	
Received from sale of laser printer	200
Net book value at date of disposal =	
Cost less accumulated depreciation = £1,800 − £1,743	57
Profit on disposal	143

22   DEPRECIATION

> *Tutorial note.* Part (a) is quite difficult and many candidates did not attempt it, or produced poor answers. Few candidates made the point that depreciation is *not* a fund of money set aside for replacement, which was crucial to a good answer. Common errors in part (b) included preparing separate ledger accounts for each vehicle; including ledger accounts for purchases and sales of motor vehicles; reversing the debit and credit entries, especially in the provision for depreciation account; recording depreciation in the cost account; using the sale proceeds to record the disposal in the 'asset at cost' account; calculating the depreciation charge wrongly; not preparing ledger accounts, but giving journal entries and profit and loss and balance sheet extracts, in spite of very clear requirements in the question.

(a)   REPORT

To: Departmental manager
From: Management accountant
Date: 24 May 19X3
Subject: Depreciation

Measurement of income

Depreciation is a means of spreading the cost of a fixed asset over its useful life, and so matching the cost against the full period during which it earns income for the business. It is in a sense a compromise between two extremes.

(i)   Writing off the cost of the asset to the profit and loss account in full in the period in which it is purchased.

(ii)   Carrying the asset at full cost in the balance sheet throughout its life until it is disposed of.

Both (i) and (ii) are contrary to the concept of accruals which requires that revenue and costs should be matched with one another so far as their relationship can be established. Since the asset earns income over several accounting periods, its cost should also be spread over those accounting periods.

Capital maintenance

The capital of a business is what is owed to the owners and represents the excess of its assets over its liabilities. The concept of capital maintenance suggests that this excess should be at least maintained, and preferably increased. However, most assets wear out over time and decrease in value and this needs to be taken into account in measuring the excess of assets over liabilities. The depreciation charge is an estimate of the amount by which an asset diminishes in value each period.

Furthermore, using the concept of capital maintenance, 'profit is the sum which may be distributed or withdrawn from the business while maintaining intact the capital which existed at the beginning of the period' (Lewis, Pendrill and Simon, *Advanced Financial Accounting*). If no charge were made for depreciation the profits available for distribution would be higher and capital would not be properly maintained if those profits were indeed distributed.

This is not to say that the depreciation provision is a replacement fund: it is merely a means of spreading the *loss* against purchase cost that will occur when the asset is sold (because of its fall in value) over the life of the asset.

Changing price levels

Changing price levels mean that the cost of an asset purchased to replace one that has worn out will be different to the price of the original asset. As noted above, depreciation does not provide a replacement fund. If an organisation wishes to earmark income earned for the replacement of assets it needs to do so by transferring additional funds to a reserve account. Assuming that asset prices are rising due to inflation this means that the amount transferred for asset replacement should be greater than the original asset's fall in value over the period (the depreciation charge) if capital is to be truly maintained.

Sometimes changing price levels can mean that an asset is *more* valuable after it has been owned for some time (land and buildings and vintage cars are examples). Best accounting practice allows this increase in value to be reflected in accounts by creating a revaluation reserve. From the point of view of capital maintenance (and in law), such reserves are not distributable until the asset is actually disposed of and the estimated increase in value is realised in cash.

(b)

MOTOR VEHICLES AT COST

		£			£
01.10.X0	Balance b/f	10,000	24.04.X1	Disposals (MV05)	4,000
31.01.X1	Motor van (MV11)	9,000	30.09.X1	Balance c/f	15,000
		19,000			19,000
01.10.X1	Balance b/f	15,000	31.08.X2	Disposals (MV11)	9,000
20.02.X2	Motor van (MV12)	12,000	30.09.X2	Balance c/f	32,000
31.08.X2	Motor van (MV13)	14,000			
		41,000			41,000
01.10.X2	Balance b/f	32,000			

PROVISION FOR DEPRECIATION OF MOTOR VEHICLES

		£			£
24.04.X1	Disposals (W1)	2,313	01.10.X0	b/f	4,000
30.09.X1	c/f	5,015	30.01.X1	Provision (W2)	3,328
		7,328			7,328
31.08.X2	Disposals (W3)	2,250	01.10.X1	b/f	5,015
30.09.X2	c/f	10,074	30.09.X2	Provision (W4)	7,309
		12,324			12,324

DISPOSALS

		£			£
24.04.X1	MV05	4,000	24.04.X1	Depreciation (MV05)	2,313
			24.04.X1	Cash	500
			30.09.X1	P&L account	1,187
		4,000			4,000
31.08.X2	MV11	9,000	31.08.X2	Depreciation (MV11)	2,250
31.09.X2	P&L account	650		Trade-in allowance	7,400
		9,650			9,650

Workings

1 *Depreciation on motor van MV05*

	Net book value	Depreciation
	£	£
Cost (January 19W8)	4,000	
Depreciation - September 19W8 (25%)	(1,000)	1,000
	3,000	
Depreciation - September 19W9 (25%)	(750)	750
	2,250	
Depreciation - September 19X0 (25%)	(563)	563
	1,687	2,313

2 *Depreciation provision 19X1*

	£
Cost at year end	15,000
Depreciation provision (4,000 – 2,313)	(1,687)
	13,313
Depreciation charge at 25%	3,328

3 *Depreciation on motor van MV11*

	Net book value	
	£	£
Cost - January 19X1	9,000	
Depreciation - September 19X1 (25%)	(2,250)	2,250
	6,750	2,250

4   *Depreciation provision 19X2*

	£
Cost at year end	32,000
Accumulated depreciation (5,015 – 2,250)	(2,765)
	29,235
Depreciation charge at 25%	7,309

23   SBJ

(a)

MOTOR VEHICLES - COST

	£		£
Bal per question	48,000	Bal at 31.12.X4 before annual charge	48,000
	48,000		48,000

MOTOR VEHICLES - ACCUMULATED DEPRECIATION

	£		£
Bal at 31.12.X4 before annual charge	12,000	Bal per question	12,000
	12,000		12,000

PLANT AND MACHINERY - COST

	£		£
Bal per question	120,000	Disposal	30,000
		Adjusted balance at 31.12.X4	90,000
	120,000		120,000

PLANT AND MACHINERY - ACCUMULATED DEPRECIATION

	£		£
Disposal (30,000 – 23,500 – 800)	5,700	Bal per question	30,000
Adjusted balance at 31.12.X4 before annual charge	24,300		
	30,000		30,000

OFFICE EQUIPMENT - COST

	£		£
Bal per question	27,500	Adjusted balance at 31.12.X4	75,960
Addition (W)	48,460		
	75,960		75,960

OFFICE EQUIPMENT - ACCUMULATED DEPRECIATION

	£		£
Bal at 31.12.X4 before annual charge	7,500	Bal per question	7,500
	7,500		7,500

Working

	£
Motor vehicle addition	
List price	24,000
Less 20% trade discount	(4,800)
	19,200
VAT @ 17.5%	3,360
	22,560
Cost of painting name	100
Addition to fixed asset register	22,660

Other equipment addition

Nominal ledger balances

	Cost £	Acc depn £	NBV £
Motor vehicles	48,000	12,000	36,000
Plant and machinery	90,000	24,300	65,700
Office equipment	27,500	7,500	20,000
	165,500	43,800	121,700

Fixed assets register		
Original balance	147,500	
Addition	22,660	
		170,160
Addition to office equipment		48,460

(b) *Depreciation charge for 19X4*

	£	£
Motor vehicles		
£48,000 × 25%	12,000	
£22,660 × 25% × ¼	1,416	
		13,416
Plant and equipment		
£90,000 × 10%		9,000
Office equipment		
£(75,960 – 7,500) × 10%		6,846
		29,262

(c) An organisation charges depreciation on fixed assets in order that the asset is written down to its residual value at the end of its useful life, and that the accounting periods which have benefited from the use of that asset bear the cost.

Depreciation is an example of the accruals concept in that it enables the cost of the asset to be spread over its useful life, so matching it against the whole period during which it earns profits for the business.

The principles which govern the charging of depreciation are laid down by SSAP 12 *Accounting for depreciation* which states:

'Provision for depreciation of fixed assets having a finite useful economic life should be made by allocating the cost (or revalued amount) less estimated residual value of the assets as fairly as possible to the periods expected to benefit from their use. The depreciation methods used should be the ones which are most appropriate having regard to the types of asset and their use in the business.'

24   OBJ PLC

> *Tutorial note.* Remember that it is the *accounts* which are supposed to give a true and fair view of an entity's profit or loss for a period and of its state of affairs at the end of that period, not the *auditors*. The latter merely report on whether, in their opinion, the accounts do in fact give a true and fair view. Note that the examiner was prepared to accept a less detailed format of the answer to part (c) (i) (4) on fixed assets. The format we have given here makes the amount of the profit clear.

(a) Capital expenditure can be defined as expenditure on fixed assets, the net cost of which is to be 'capitalised' and depreciated over the anticipated useful working life of the assets. Substantial improvements to fixed assets can also be treated as capital expenditure.

Revenue expenditure can be defined as expenditure incurred for the purpose of the trade of the business (heat, light, wages etc) or to *maintain* the existing earning capacity of fixed assets.

(b) The concept of a true and fair view (of an entity's profit or loss for a period and of its balance sheet on a particular date) is not defined in either the Companies Act or financial reporting standards. However, accounts will generally be considered by auditors to give a true and fair view if the information contained in them is sufficient in quantity and quality to satisfy the reasonable expectations of users of the accounts. The expectations will have been set by experience of what is the normal practice of accountants in the preparation of accounts. Compliance with the Companies Act and accounting principles and standards is *prime facie* evidence that the accounts show a true and fair view.

Items that are significant in the context of a set of financial statements to the users of those accounts are said to be *material*. An item (a transaction or balance) would be considered material if its inclusion or omission would affect the users' view of the financial statements as a whole.

Whether a set of financial statements can be considered to show a true and fair view must be judged by the treatment of material items. Conversely, the treatment of immaterial items should not affect the true and fair view (the Companies Act and accounting standards are not applicable to immaterial items) unless, in aggregate, they are significant enough to affect the users' perception of the accounts.

(c) (i)

		Debit £	Credit £
(1)	Cost of plant (18,800 – 2,800)	16,000	
	VAT recoverable	2,800	
	Cash		18,800
(2)	Cost of motor vehicles (16,355 – 140)	16,215	
	Vehicle expense	140	
	Cash		16,355
(3)	Vehicle repairs	1,300	
	Cash		1,300
(4)	Accumulated depreciation	20,000	
	Cash	12,000	
	Cost of asset		30,000
	Profit on sale		2,000

(ii) *Net profit*

	£
Unadjusted	475,350
Vehicle expense (1,300 + 140)	(1,440)
Profit on sale of fixed asset	2,000
Adjusted profit	475,910

Fixed assets (net of depreciation)

	£
Unadjusted	272,330
New plant	16,000
New motor vehicle	16,215
NBV asset disposed (£30,000 – £20,000)	(10,000)
Adjusted fixed assets	294,545

25   GOODWILL

> *Tutorial note.* In discussing the three methods of accounting for goodwill you need not confine your answer to SSAP 22. Remember to state the arguments in favour of each of these three methods. (Note that FRS 10 replaced SSAP 22 in December 1997. In theory this could be examined in November 1998 but as the detailed changes go beyond your syllabus we do not cover FRS 10 here).

(a) Purchased goodwill may be treated in one of the following ways.

   (i)   It may be eliminated from the accounts immediately against reserves.

   (ii)   It may be eliminated gradually by amortisation through the profit and loss account.

   (iii) It is possible to leave it at cost in the balance sheet unless its value is permanently impaired.

   Method (i), writing goodwill off to reserves, brings the treatment of purchased goodwill into line with that of non-purchased goodwill. It is felt that goodwill is a unique asset, volatile, difficult to identify and without a structured relationship with the costs incurred in building it up. Accordingly, it should not be capitalised but written off immediately, and this is the treatment preferred by SSAP 22.

   Method (ii), capitalisation and amortisation brings goodwill into line with other fixed assets. Goodwill may be volatile in value and not readily identifiable, but these are not sufficient reasons to disqualify it from recognition in the balance sheet. To show goodwill at a cost-based amount will provide information on the resources that have been deployed in acquisition on the shareholders' behalf and can therefore help provide a basis for assessing management's performance. Furthermore the cost of the asset is being matched with the benefits which it generates over its economic life, as is the case with other fixed assets.

   Method (iii), leaving goodwill at cost in the balance sheet, recognises that, unlike a piece of machinery, goodwill has no predictable finite life. Rather than diminishing in value, it may in fact be increasing, and may well last as long as the business itself.

(b) Goodwill may be distinguished from other intangible fixed assets by reference to the following characteristics.

   (i)   It is incapable of realisation separately from the business as a whole.

   (ii)   Its value has no reliable or predictable relationship to any costs which may have been incurred.

   (iii) Its value arises from various intangible factors such as skilled employees, effective advertising or a strategic location. These indirect factors cannot be valued.

   (iv)   The value of goodwill may fluctuate widely according to internal and external circumstances over relatively short periods of time.

   (v)   The assessment of the value of goodwill is highly subjective.

   It could be argued that, because goodwill is so different from other intangible fixed assets it does not make sense to account for it in the same way. Thus the capitalisation and amortisation treatment would not be acceptable. Furthermore, because goodwill is so difficult to value, any valuation may be misleading, and it is best eliminated from the balance sheets altogether. However, there are strong arguments, as discussed in part (a), for treating it like any other intangible fixed asset. This issue remains controversial.

26 GOODWILL, FIXED ASSETS AND RESEARCH

> *Tutorial note.* Assuming that you know your SSAPs, FRSs and accounting concepts the main problem with this question is avoiding the temptation to write too much. If you remember that you are drafting a report for a non-accountant this may help you to keep to the most important points. The most common errors were failing to use report format and using a name which the marking team believed to be the candidate's own - in direct contravention of the instructions on the examination paper. The examiner also commented that there is no need to quote directly from SSAPs. You must take your own view on this. You will have to learn them at some stage in your studies. (See the Tutorial Note to question 25 on goodwill regarding FRS 10.)

REPORT

To: Managing director
From: Accountant
Date: 18 November 19X6
Subject: The valuation of fixed assets and intangibles

Published accounts are used by many different people and their format and the accounting treatment of individual items within them are therefore governed by laws and by accounting standards, to try to ensure that the view of the company given is a true and fair one.

The rules for the accounting treatment of the items you mentioned are explained below.

(a) *Goodwill*

Goodwill is governed by Statement of Standard Accounting Practice 22 (SSAP 22). This distinguishes between internally generated goodwill, which is *never* shown in the accounts, and purchased goodwill, which sometimes is.

Internally generated goodwill is omitted from the accounts of a business for the following reasons.

(i)   The goodwill is inherent in the business but it has not been paid for, and it does not have an 'objective' value. We can guess at what such goodwill is worth, but such guesswork would be a matter of individual opinion, and not based on hard facts.

(ii) Goodwill changes from day to day. One act of bad customer relations might damage goodwill and one act of good relations might improve it. Staff with a favourable personality might retire or leave to find another job, and be replaced by staff who need time to find their feet in the job. Since goodwill is continually changing in value, it cannot realistically be recorded in the accounts of the business.

The omission of internally generated goodwill from accounts is in accordance with the accounting concept of prudence: its ultimate cash realisation cannot be assessed with any certainty.

However, purchased goodwill can be shown in the balance sheet because it has been paid for. It has no tangible substance, and so it is an intangible fixed asset. Purchased goodwill has been defined as 'the excess of the price paid for a business over the fair market value of the individual assets and liabilities acquired'. Purchased goodwill must be depreciated (amortised).

(b) *Fixed assets*

Most fixed assets depreciate in value as they get older and so they are valued in the accounts at cost less an amount ('depreciation') intended to reflect this diminution in value. Fixed assets are depreciated over their useful lives in accordance with the matching concept. However, because of inflation, or other external factors, it is not uncommon for the value of certain fixed assets to go up, in spite of getting older. Except in the very recent past, this is particularly true of the value of land and buildings.

A business that owns fixed assets which are rising in value is not obliged to revalue those assets on its balance sheet. However, in order to give a true and fair view of the position of the business, it might be decided that some fixed assets should be revalued upwards. The new valuation may be done by a third party or by the company's directors, always remembering that the company's auditors will object if the new values are unrealistic.

Accounting for fixed assets is governed by SSAP 12 (on depreciation) and SSAP 19 (on investment properties) and has been under review for some time, although the position stated above is unlikely to change.

(c) *The costs of research*

Research expenditure is governed by SSAP 13, 'Accounting for research and development'. This requires that research expenditure should always be written off in the period in which it is incurred. This is because although financial advantages may eventually be derived from research they are so remote that it would not be prudent to carry the expenditure forward.

However, *development* expenditure is different. It usually relates to a specific project (for example the development of a new product) which can be profitably exploited in the foreseeable future. Provided the viability of the project has been carefully assessed, there is a strong argument for capitalising the development costs associated with it. This accords with the accruals concept, whereby revenue and costs are matched with one another and dealt with in the profit and loss account of the period to which they relate.

SSAP 13 allows companies to capitalise development expenditure in their accounts if they wish, provided that certain criteria are satisfied. Broadly, it is permissible to carry forward such expenditure in the circumstances described in the previous paragraph.

If a company capitalises development expenditure, it will appear in the balance sheet as an intangible asset. Like capitalised goodwill, it must be depreciated (amortised) when the development project is brought into commercial production.

Please do not hesitate to contact me if I can be of further assistance in this matter.

27   NG NEARING

> *Tutorial note.* Make sure you pick up a few easy marks by presenting your answer correctly in the form of a report as required by the question.

REPORT

To: Research Director
From: Management Accountant   Date: 1.2.X5
Subject: Research and Development

Our company spends significant amounts of money on research and development (R & D) activities. Obviously, any amounts so expended must be credited to cash and debited to an account for research and development expenditure. The accounting problem is how to treat the debit balance on R & D account at the balance sheet date.

There are two possibilities.

(a) The debit balance may be classified as an expense and transferred to the profit and loss account. This is referred to as 'writing off' the expenditure.

(b) The debit balance may be classified as an asset and included in the balance sheet. This is referred to as 'capitalising' or 'carrying forward' or 'deferring' the expenditure.

The argument for writing off R & D expenditure is that it is an expense just like rates or wages and its accounting treatment should be the same.

The argument for carrying forward R & D expenditure is based on the accruals concept. If R & D activity eventually leads to new or improved products which generate revenue, the costs should be carried forward to be matched against that revenue in future accounting periods.

R & D expenditure is the subject of an accounting standard, SSAP 13 *Accounting for research and development*. SSAP 13 (and the Companies Act 1985) requires that *research* expenditure should always be written off in the period in which it is incurred. This is because the advantages derived from general research activities are too remote to justify carrying the expenditure forward.

Development expenditure is different. It usually relates to a specific project (eg the development of a new product) which can be profitably exploited in the foreseeable future. Provided the viability of the project has been carefully assessed, there is a strong argument for capitalising the development costs associated with it.

SSAP 13 allows companies to capitalise development expenditure in their accounts, provided that certain criteria are satisfied. Broadly, it is permissible to carry forward such expenditure in the circumstances described above. Even so, a company is never *obliged* to do so; it is always open to a company to take the most prudent view and write off development expenditure in the same way as research expenditure.

If a company capitalises development expenditure, it will appear in the balance sheet as an intangible asset. It must be depreciated (amortised). The process of amortisation should begin when the development project is brought into commercial production.

Signed: Management Accountant

28   TUTORIAL QUESTION: BANK RECONCILIATIONS

(a)

CASH BOOK

19X8		£	19X8		£
Dec 31	Balance b/d	1,793	Dec 31	Bank charges	18
Dec 31	Dividend	26	Dec 31	Standing order	32
			Dec 31	Direct debit	88
				Balance c/d	1,681
		1,819			1,819

(b)   BANK RECONCILIATION AS AT 31 DECEMBER 19X8

	£	£
Balance per bank statement		1,557
Add unrecorded lodgements:		
V Owen	98	
K Walters	134	
		232
Less unpresented cheques:		
B Oliver (869)	71	
L Philips (872)	37	
		(108)
Balance per cash book (corrected)		1,681

29   SANDILANDS

Tutorial note. The correct procedure is to amend the cash book balance for items omitted and errors by the company, but to correct the bank statement's figure for timing differences and for errors by the bank. Do not make the mistake of re-entering amounts already entered in the cash book.

(a)   (i)   CASH BOOK

31.5.X3	Balance b/d	£ 873	31.5.X3	Bank charges	£ 630
	Error £(936 - 693)	243		Trade journals	52
				Insurance	360
31.5.X3	Balance c/d	2,098		Business rates	2,172
		3,214			3,214
			1.6.X3	Balance b/d	2,098

(ii)   BANK RECONCILIATION

	£	£
Balance per bank statement		(2,954)
Add: outstanding lodgements	6,816	
cheque debited in error	510	
direct debit paid in error	1,000	
		8,326
		5,372
Less unpresented cheques		(7,470)
Balance per cash book		(2,098)

(b)   The regular preparation of bank reconciliations enables errors by both the firm and the bank to be detected. Reconciliations may also highlight poor cash management, for example delays in banking cheques received.

30   MTR LTD

> *Tutorial note.* Part (a) required you to distinguish between financial and management accounts, an essential distinction for aspiring CIMA members! Internal and external audit, tested in part (b) have very different functions and perspectives, although there may be some overlap. Part (c) tested bank reconciliations. This does not usually come up but that does not mean you can leave it behind with your basic bookkeeping studies.

(a)   Management accounts are produced by management for their own use in running the day to day business of a company. They can be produced in any format which suits management needs. Whilst they generally deal with historical results for a designated period (month, quarter, year), they may also contain comparative forecast or budget figures and disclose variances. The figures may deal with the business as a whole, by branch, division or product. The choice is entirely that of management and they will differ from company to company. They are generally not for external use (although they may be supplied to lenders in a summarised form). The common base of all management accounts is cost.

Financial accounts are based on bookkeeping. They are prepared by management for external use and cover a historical period (normally the company's financial year). Limited company accounts are required to be prepared in a prescribed format and, except for very small companies, need to be audited by registered external auditors. They need to be prepared in accordance with company law and with standard accounting practice. This assists external users of the accounts and also allows for comparison of accounts between companies but limits their use for management purposes.

(b)   Internal audit is an element of management's system of internal control. Internal auditors test and report to management on the system of internal controls operating within an organisation and make recommendations where controls are not working. As the auditors are appointed by management they cannot be considered to be wholly independent. Whilst their work predominantly deals with controls in the financial system, it is not limited to this area and may deal with other controls, for example security.

External audit comprises the examination of financial statements by an independent third party who is a registered auditor.

In a limited company external audit of the annual statements is a statutory requirement (except for very small companies). The auditors are appointed by and report to the shareholders by means of their audit report which forms part of the financial statements. They are completely independent of management.

(c)

	£
Per cash book	6,368
Dishonoured cheque	(425)
Bank charges not recorded	(130)
Rates DD not recorded	(844)
	4,969
Credit transfer not recorded	685
Unpresented cheque - VAT	435
	6,089
Uncleared sales ledger receipts	(1,480)
Balance per bank statement	4,609

31 TUTORIAL QUESTION: SALES LEDGER RECONCILIATION

(a)

SALES LEDGER CONTROL

19X8		£	19X8		£
1.12	Balance b/d	50,241		Returns inwards	41,226
	Sales	472,185		Bad debts written off	1,914
	Cheques dishonoured	626		Discounts allowed	2,672
				Cheques received	429,811
			30.11	Balance c/d	47,429
		523,052			523,052

(b)

		£	£
Balance per P Johnson			46,347
Add:	Whitchurch Ltd invoice, previously omitted from ledger	267	
	Rectofen Ltd balance, previously omitted from list	2,435	
	Casting error in list total (£46,747, not £46,347)	400	
			3,102
			49,449
Less:	Error on posting of Bury plc's credit note to ledger	20	
	P Fox & Son (Swindon) Ltd's balance included twice	2,000	
			2,020
Balance per sales ledger control account			47,429

32 HAC

> *Tutorial note.* The CIMA model answer was incorrect in its treatment of the doubtful debt provision and the bad debt recovered, neither of which affect the sales ledger control account. The question has therefore been amended to enable a correct reconciliation to work.

(a)

SALES LEDGER CONTROL ACCOUNT

	£		£
Balance b/fwd	160,387.70	Discount allowed	25,404.36
Discounts received	10,419.76		
Returns outwards	11,376.19	Returns inwards	6,820.24
		Purchase ledger contras	99,032.54
		Decrease in provision for doubtful debts	10,429.61
		SDB mistotalled	2,291.18
		Credit note	270.00
		Balance c/fwd	37,935.72
	182,183.65		182,183.65

Amended control account balance	37,935.72
Total of sales ledger balances	96,484.43
Credit balance recorded as debit	(8,762.44)
Credit note	(270.00)
Purchase ledger contras	(49,516.27)
	37,935.72

(b)   The advantages of using control accounts are as follows.

(i)   They provide a check on the accuracy of entries made in the personal accounts in the sales ledger and purchase ledger. It is very easy to make a mistake in posting entries, because there might be hundreds of entries to make. Figures might get transposed. Some entries might be omitted altogether (possibly deliberately, as part of a fraud), so that an invoice or a payment transaction does not appear in a personal account as it should. Errors are identified as follows.

(1)   The total balance on the debtors control account is compared with the total of individual balances of the personal accounts in the sales ledger.

(2)   The total balance on the creditors account is compared with the total of individual balances on the personal accounts in the purchases ledger.

The control accounts could also assist in the location of errors, where postings to the control account are made daily or weekly, or even monthly. If a clerk fails to record an invoice or a payment in a personal account, or makes a transposition error, it would be a formidable task to locate the errors or errors at the end of a year, say, given the hundreds or thousands of transactions during the year. By using the control account, a comparison with the individual balances in the sales or purchase ledger can be made for every week or day of the month, and the error found much more quickly than if control accounts did not exist.

Where there is a separation of clerical (bookkeeping) duties, the control account provides an internal check. The person posting entries to the control accounts will act as a check on a different person whose job it is to post entries to the sales and purchase ledger accounts.

(ii)   They provide a debtors and creditors balance for producing a trial balance or balance sheet. A single balance on a control account is obviously extracted more simply and quickly than many individual balances in the sales or purchases ledger. This means also that the number of accounts in the double entry bookkeeping system can be kept down to a manageable size, since the personal accounts are memorandum accounts only and the control accounts instead provide the accounts required for a double entry system.

33   BC

> *Tutorial note.* It is a good idea to go through each item in the question before you start and decide whether the control account or the list of balances will be affected.
>
> *Examiner's comment.* Part (a) was well answered. Common errors were failing to include the VAT element of the sales invoice which had been incorrectly recorded and including the provision for doubtful debts in the control account. Parts (b) and (c) were less well answered.

(a)

SALES LEDGER CONTROL A/C

	£		£
Debit balances b/fwd	226,415	Credit balances b/fwd	1,250
Incorrect sales invoice		Reversal of misposted cash	
(6,400 − 4,600) + 17½%	2,115	discounts received	560
Cash sales invoices not		Cash discounts allowed	840
recorded	860	Contra with purchase ledger	750
		Bad debts written off	2,150
		Adjusted balance c/fwd	223,840
	229,390		229,390

(b)   LIST OF INDIVIDUAL BALANCES

	£
Balance b/fwd	225,890
Adjustments	
Credit balances (reversal)	(2,500)
Dishonoured cheque	450
Adjusted balance on sales ledger control account	223,840

(c)   A computerised sales ledger system might offer BC Ltd the following facilities.

(i)   The automatic production of customers' statements and aged debtor listings should assist in both credit control and collection.

(ii)   The system should be both faster and more accurate than a manual system.

(iii) The system will facilitate the production of management information, eg list of largest customers, geographical spread of customers and so on.

(iv) Where it is part of a fully integrated accounts package, it will allow the automatic updating of the nominal ledger. This should ensure that differences between the sales ledger and the control account do not occur.

34   PQR

> *Tutorial note.* This is a fairly straightforward question. Points to watch are as follows.
>
> (a)   Remember that VAT on motor cars is not recoverable and should not, therefore, appear in the VAT account.
>
> (b)   Payments to creditors and receipts from debtors are inclusive of VAT. The VAT has already been accounted for in the sales/purchase day book.

(a)

VAT ACCOUNT

	£		£
Purchases	4,725	Balance b/f	3,250
Administration expenses	420	Sales	14,875
		VAT refund	1,567
Balance c/f	15,072	Purchase returns	525
	20,217		20,217

(b)

BANK ACCOUNT

	£		£
Materials refund	3,525	Balance b/f	6,250
VAT refund	1,567	Motor vehicles	9,400
Debtors	125,000	Administration expenses	2,820
		Creditors	42,000
		Balance c/f	69,622
	130,092		130,092

(c)   Before transferring the relevant balances at the year end to the profit and loss and putting closing balances carried forward into the balance sheet it is crucial to test the accuracy of double entry bookkeeping records by preparing a trial balance. This is done by taking all the balances on every account. Because of the self-balancing nature of the system of double entry the total of the debit balances will be exactly equal to the total of the credit balances.

If they are not equal, there must be an error in recording the transactions in the accounts. A trial balance will disclose the following types of error.

(i)   A *transposition error*, eg entering £359 as £395.

(ii)   An error whereby *only one entry* is posted. For example, advertising expenses are paid and the bank account is credited but the corresponding debit entry to the advertising account is not made.

(iii) Both entries are posted to the same side of the trial balance. For example cash received from a debtor is wrongly recorded as:

DEBIT   Cash
DEBIT   Debtors

(iv) The opening balance on the ledger is brought down on the wrong side of the account, eg a bank overdraft is brought down as a debit.

35 TUTORIAL QUESTION: ERRORS AND JOURNAL ENTRIES

Date		Dr £	Cr £
October 16	D Evans, sales ledger	163	
	P Evans, sales ledger		163

(*Note*. This entry would only be required if a sales ledger control account is not kept.)

Date		Dr £	Cr £
October 17	Office equipment	475	
	Sales ledger control		475
	(*or* J Swanson, sales ledger)		
	Drawings	60	
	Purchases		60
	Bad debts expense	102	
	Sales ledger control		102
	(*or* D Saunders, sales ledger)		
October 18	Motor vehicle servicing costs	124	
	Motor vehicles at cost		124
	Purchase ledger control		
	(*or* A Brigham, purchase ledger)	40	
	Bank		40

(*Note*. You must both correct the misposting and post the entry correctly - so the bank balance is credited by 2 × £20, not just £20.)

Date		Dr £	Cr £
October 19	Sales ledger control		
	(*or* N Quinn, sales ledger)	9	
	Sales (or returns inward)		9
	Purchase ledger control		
	(*or* Boxted Supplies Ltd, purchase ledger)	610	
	Office equipment		610
October 20	Purchases	425	
	Purchase ledger control		
	(*or* EFI Ltd, purchase ledger)		425

36 TUTORIAL QUESTION: SUSPENSE ACCOUNTS

SUSPENSE ACCOUNT

	£		£
		Balance b/d	14,000
Discounts received	14,000	Discounts allowed	6,000
Current a/c - partner's wife	9,600	Creditors control a/c	3,600
	23,600		23,600

37   RST

> *Tutorial note*. The main difficulty here is deciding which items affect the suspense account. The only ones which do are those which affect the balancing of the trial balance. Any items which are normally entered as adjustments on the trial balance *after* the balances have been extracted from the books will not be passed through suspense account. This applies, for example, to the following items.
>
> (a)   Adjustments to provisions, for example for doubtful debts or discounts allowed.
> (b)   Valuation of closing stock.
> (c)   Calculation of closing accruals and prepayments.
>
> For convenience, the suggested solution sets out the journal entries required in respect of those items which do not affect the suspense account.

(a)   STATEMENT OF ADJUSTMENTS TO PROFIT

		£	£
Draft net profit after tax			78,263
Add:	reduction in provision for doubtful		
	debts £1,300 - 2% × £(55,210 − 610)	208	
	equipment incorrectly debited to purchases	9,800	
	closing stock omitted	2,171	
	prepayment omitted	162	
	miscast of wages account	100	
		12,441	
Less:	bad debts	610	
	provision for discounts allowed		
	2% × £(55,210 − 610)	1,092	
	opening rates prepayment omitted	491	
	loss on disposal of vehicle		
	£((8,100 − 5,280) − 1,350)	1,470	
	disposal proceeds wrongly credited to sales	1,350	
	depreciation on equipment originally		
	debited to purchases (20% × £9,800)	1,960	
	accrual omitted	543	
		7,516	
Net increase in profit			4,925
Revised net profit after tax			83,188

(b)   SUSPENSE ACCOUNT

	£		£
Supplier's account		Rates - opening prepayment	
transposition error	90	omitted	491
Wages - miscast	100		
∴ Original balance	301		
	491		491

JOURNAL ENTRIES
(Other than those affecting the suspense account)

Transaction			Debit £	Credit £
(a)	(i)	Bad and doubtful debts (P & L a/c)	610	
		Debtors		610
	(ii)	Provision for doubtful debts	208	
		Bad & doubtful debts (P & L a/c)		208
	(iii)	Discounts allowed (P & L a/c)	1,092	
		Provision for discounts allowed		1,092
(c)		Sales	1,350	
		Accumulated depreciation	5,280	
		Loss on disposal (P & L a/c)	1,470	
		Fixed assets at cost		8,100

Transaction		Debit	Credit
(e)	Equipment at cost	9,800	
	Purchases		9,800
	Depreciation (P & L a/c)	1,960	
	Accumulated depreciation		1,960
(f)	Closing stock (balance sheet)	2,171	
	Closing stock (trading account)		2,171
(g)	Electricity charges (P & L a/c)	543	
	Accrued expenses (balance sheet)		543
	Prepaid expenses (balance sheet)	162	
	Insurance (P & L a/c)		162

38   TD

> *Tutorial note.* In part (b) remember that not all error corrections will affect the suspense account. In adjusting the profit in part (c), do not forget to take account of adjustments already made to gross profit.
>
> *Examiner's comment.* In part (a) candidates displayed a good knowledge of double entry principles, but parts (b) and (c) were less well answered.

(a)

			Dr £	Cr £
(i)	DEBIT	Suspense a/c	1,000	
	CREDIT	Sales		1,000
(ii)	DEBIT	Plant	240	
	CREDIT	Delivery cost		240
(iii)	DEBIT	Cash discount received	150	
	CREDIT	JW a/c		150
(iv)	DEBIT	Stock of stationery	240	
	CREDIT	Stationery expense		240
(v)	DEBIT	Suspense a/c	500	
	CREDIT	Purchases		500
(vi)	DEBIT	Purchase returns	230	
	DEBIT	Sales returns	230★	
	CREDIT	Suspense a/c		460

(b)

SUSPENSE A/C

		£			£
(i)	Sales	1,000		End of year balance	1,040
(v)	Purchases	500	(vi)	Purchase returns/sales returns	460
		1,500			1,500

(c)

	£
Gross profit originally reported	35,750
Sales omitted	1,000
Plant costs wrongly allocated ★	240
Incorrect recording of purchases	500
Sales credit note wrongly allocated	(460)
Adjusted gross profit	37,030

	£
Net profit originally reported	18,500
Adjustments to gross profit (37,030 – 35,750)	1,280
Cash discount incorrectly taken	(150)
Stationery stock	240
Adjusted net profit	19,870

* *Note* It has been assumed that the delivery and installation costs on plant have been included in purchases.

39   TUTORIAL QUESTION: USING COMPUTERS AND SOFTWARE

(a) Accounting packages are ready made programs written to perform the task of maintaining a business accounting system. The growing use of PCs means that even many small businesses are using such packages to process their accounting transactions.

In principle, computerised accounting is exactly the same as manual accounting. Accounting functions retain the same names in a computerised system and the familiar ideas of day books, ledger accounts, double entry and trial balance still apply. The principles of working with computerised sales, purchase and nominal ledgers are exactly what would be expected in the manual methods they replace. The only difference is that these various books of account are invisible. In a computerised system, ledgers are now computer files which are held in a computer-sensible form, ready to be called upon.

An accounting package will consist of several *modules* which may include the following.

(i)   Invoicing
(ii)   Stock
(iii) Sales ledger
(iv)   Purchase ledger, and so on

When a user begins to work with an accounting package he will usually be asked to key in a password. Separate passwords can be used for different parts of the system, for example for different ledgers if required.

The user will be presented with a menu of options such as *entering new data* or *printing accounting reports*. By selecting and keying in the appropriate option number the user will then be guided through the actions needed to enter the data or generate the report.

The computer uses code numbers to identify different ledgers and the accounts within those ledgers. Code numbers also indicate to the computer which accounts to debit and which to credit. A transaction (for example debit a/c 121, credit a/c 140) will be given an identifying number for audit trail purposes.

Each module in the computer may be integrated with the others so that data in one module will be passed automatically or by simple user request through into any other module where the data is of some relevance. For example if the user inputs some data to the invoicing module authorising the despatch of an invoice to a customer, there might be automatic links to other modules such as the sales ledger to update the customer's account and the stock module to update the stock file.

Thus the user does not need to be an accounting specialist because the computer will enter the data correctly according to the code numbers used. In addition the system will not accept incomplete data entries and the user is prompted to provide complete information.

The system will print a variety of output reports, including transaction listings, account balances, sales analyses and so on.

(b) The advantages of accounting packages compared with a manual system are as follows.

(i)   As mentioned in (a), the packages can be used by non-specialists.

(ii)   A large amount of data can be processed very quickly.

(iii)   Computerised systems are more accurate than manual systems.

(iv)   A computer is capable of handling and processing large volumes of data.

(v)   Once the data has been input, computerised systems can analyse data rapidly to present useful control information for managers such as a trial balance or a debtors schedule.

(c)   Databases and spreadsheets are examples of applications software which are often used on PCs.

A spreadsheet appears to the user like a flat piece of paper divided into columns and rows to resemble a sheet of accountant's analysis paper. The intersection of each column and row is referred to as a cell. A cell can contain text, numbers or formulae. Use of a formula means that the cell which contains the formula will display the results of a calculation based on data in other cells. If the numbers in those other cells change, the result displayed in the formula cell will also change accordingly. With this facility, a spreadsheet is used to create financial models.

A database, on the other hand, is a collection of information which can be used in a number of different ways. It is like a filing cabinet, in that it contains items of information which different users can access at will. Information relevant to a particular issue can be selected from the database. The order of items in the database does not depend on the enquiries made of it.

A spreadsheet then is used for the manipulation of data. A database is used for the purposes of data storage and retrieval.

40   INTERLOCKING AND INTEGRATED

> *Tutorial note.* The issues in this question overlap to a certain extent with your cost accounting studies.

(a)   *Financial accounting* is essentially concerned with reporting the results and financial position of a business to *outsiders*, principally shareholders, but also suppliers, customers and the Inland Revenue. This is particularly clear in the context of the published accounts of limited companies. There are detailed regulations prescribed by statute which state what such accounts should contain; this enables shareholders to assess how well the directors have carried out their stewardship function. Accordingly, costs for the period under review are analysed under various prescribed headings, such as administration expenses, distribution costs, cost of sales, and then further as, say, wages and salaries, auditors' remuneration and so on.

Cost accounting, by contrast, is concerned with presenting accounting information in the form most helpful to *management*, essentially for decision making rather than stewardship purposes. Cost accountants generally aim to trace costs to cost units or cost centres, and to separate fixed and variable costs, the latter being important for decision making. They will also be involved in allocating indirect costs in a fair and sensible manner and in comparing budgeted with actual performance.

To sum up, the purposes of financial and cost accounting are quite different and this is reflected in the types of report produced.

(b)   In an *interlocking system*, separate ledger accounts are kept for the cost accounting function and the financial accounting function. The cost ledger contains only costing-type entries, which is better for decision making purposes. It contains a cost ledger control account which is a mirror image of the financial ledger control account in the financial ledger. A disadvantage of such a system is that different profit and loss accounts will be produced by the two ledgers and this will necessitate a reconciliation between the two.

In an *integrated system*, the cost accounting function and the financial accounting function are combined in one system of ledger accounts. The advantage of integrated accounts is the saving in administrative effort. Only one set of accounts needs to be maintained instead of two, and the possible confusion arising from having two sets of accounts with different figures (eg for stock values and profits) does not exist.

The *disadvantage* of integrated accounts is that one set of accounts is expected to fulfil two different purposes, namely external reporting requirements and the provision of internal management information. At times these different purposes may conflict, for example, the valuation of stocks will conform to the requirements of SSAP 9, whereas the cost accountants might have preferred, given their own choice, to value closing stock at, say marginal cost or replacement cost. However a reasonably sophisticated computer system would be able to cost-code expenditures to serve both financial accounting and cost accounting purposes.

41   ASSETS AND STOCKS

> *Tutorial note.* In part (a) many candidates did not use simple computing terminology like 'fields', 'records' and 'files' and many did not answer the question set, instead discussing how to enter data onto the computer or else confusing databases and spreadsheets. In part (b) the examiner found that 'few candidates were able to demonstrate more than rote learning of the definitions of the matching and cost concepts'. You may think that our answer is a simple one, but this was all that was required. The points made will probably seem obvious to you but the *examiner* does not know that they are obvious to you unless you tell her so.

(a) (i)   The following details should be recorded for each asset.

   (1) A description of the asset

   (2) A note of any identifying numbers

   (3) The date of purchase

   (4) The cost

   (5) The name and address of the manufacturer and/or the supplier

   (6) The asset's location and/or the name of its user

   (7) The depreciation method, including the estimated life and residual value

   (8) Accumulated depreciation to date

   (9) The method of paying for the asset, especially if it is leased

   (ii) Any kind of computerised fixed asset record will improve efficiency in accounting for fixed assets because of the ease and speed with which any necessary calculations can be made. Most obvious is the calculation of the depreciation provision which can be an extremely onerous task if it is done monthly and there are frequent acquisitions and disposals and many different depreciation rates in use.

   The particular advantage of using a database for the fixed asset function is its flexibility in generating reports for different purposes. Aside from basic cost and net book value information a database with fields such as those listed in (a) (i) in the record of each asset could compile reports analysing assets according to location say, or by manufacturer. This information could be used to help compare the performance of different divisions, perhaps, or to assess the useful life of assets supplied by different manufacturers. There may be as many more possibilities as there are permutations of the individual pieces of data.

(b) The *cost* concept is applied to stock in that SSAP 9 requires that stocks be valued at the lower of their cost and their net realisable value. For an item of raw material 'cost' usually means the cost of purchasing the item from a supplier. For items of work in progress and finished goods it is necessary to take account of conversion costs (such as direct labour) incurred in working on the raw materials.

The *matching* concept states that, in computing profit, revenue earned must be matched against the expenditure incurred in earning it. Thus the cost of closing stocks is deducted from the cost of opening stock and purchases in a period to determine what cost of sales should be set against revenue. Closing stock is carried forward and matched against revenue earned in the next period.

42   SALES LEDGER PACKAGE

> *Tutorial note.* This is a fairly predictable question on computers in accounting, spanning both financial accounting and cost accounting. It requires a combination of general knowledge and the ability to apply that knowledge to a specific context. If you were properly prepared it should have caused you little difficulty.

(a)   A computerised sales ledger package might benefit a small organisation in the following ways.

   (i)   It would save time, since several tasks that otherwise have to be done separately could be done by means of a single computer entry. For example, compiling day book listings, preparing invoices and making double entries to customer accounts and control accounts could all be done at once. This would free up staff for other duties, or perhaps enable the use of less specialised staff, with no sacrifice in terms of accuracy.

   (ii)   Using an open item system, the computer can identify specific invoices and credit individual payments against them. This allows the identification of the specific invoices that make up the debtors' balances and thus enables aged debtor analyses to be prepared at the touch of a button. This is particularly helpful in compiling lists of potential bad debts.

   (iii)   Monthly statements can easily be prepared. Late payments can be identified in exception reports. Some systems automatically prepare debtors reminder letters to chase late payers once the payment date has been passed.

   (iv)   Credit limits for each customer can be entered and the computer can produce reports of any debtors who have exceeded their limit, so that further sales are not made until payment is received.

   (v)   The system would also be useful for marketing purposes since it would help to identify customers who were interested in specific products.

(b)   A spreadsheet is a general software package used for modelling. It works rather like a blank sheet of paper with a large number of rows and columns, making up many individual cells into which data can be entered. The data can take the form of text, numbers, or formulae which combine cell references, numbers and mathematical symbols. Thus the contents of one cell can operate upon the contents of another cell with the result appearing in yet another cell.

Spreadsheets have a wide variety of applications in accounting. One of the most common uses in cash accounting is for the preparation of budgets.

   (i)   The first part of the spreadsheet would be a group of cells defining certain variables such as forecast sales volumes in month 1, forecast percentage increase each month, materials usage and labour and machine hour requirements and costs per unit, fixed asset values and depreciation rates, fixed costs per period and so forth.

   (ii)   The second part would be a series of columns (one for each period) in each cell of which would be formulae manipulating the data entered in part (i). For example a cell might multiply total sales units required by labour hours and cost per unit to give the expected labour cost for a period. Each column would be totalled by the spreadsheet to show the net result for that period.

   (iii)   Experimentation could then be conducted by altering the variables entered in part (i) ('what if' the expected increase in sales did not occur? 'what if' the labour hour rate was increased? and so on) and observing the changes in the results.

43   SPREADSHEETS

> *Tutorial note.* The suggested solution is longer than you would be required to produce in the examination in order to give comprehensive coverage of the topic.

(a)   *The usefulness of spreadsheets*

Some of the more common accounting applications of spreadsheets are:

(i)   balance sheets;
(ii)   cash flow analysis/forecasting;
(iii)   general ledger;
(iv)   inventory records;
(v)   job cost estimates;
(vi)   market share analyse and planning;
(vii)   profit projections;
(viii) profit statements;
(ix)   project budgeting and control;
(x)   sales projections and records;
(xi)   tax estimation.

What all these have in common is that they all involve data processing with:

(i)   numerical data;
(ii)   repetitive, time-consuming calculations;
(iii)   a logical processing structure.

Spreadsheets provide a basically simple format for modelling, which is why they are provided for PCs rather than more powerful mainframe computers. The great value of spreadsheets, however, derives from their simple format of rows and columns of data, and the ability of the data users to have direct access themselves to their spreadsheet model via their own PC. For example, an accountant can construct a cash flow model with a spreadsheet package on the PC in his or her office(s): he can create the model, input the data, manipulate the data and read or print the output direct. He or she will also have fairly instant access to the model whenever it is needed, in just the time it takes to load the model into his or her PC. Spreadsheets therefore help to bring the computerised data processing more within the everyday reach of data users.

A popular use of spreadsheets is the consideration of 'what if?' problems. One or two key figures are changed and then the computer automatically makes all the consequential changes to all the other figures throughout the spreadsheets.

(b) *Will spreadsheets supersede accounting?*

While it is undoubtedly true that spreadsheets can save a great deal of time on the more tedious and repetitive aspects of accounting, it is by no means the case that accounting is thereby made obsolete. On the contrary, an understanding of the principles of accounting is essential both for the user of a spreadsheet and those involved in its design or modification.

In principle, computerised systems are no different from manual ones. It is unlikely that the former would be understood and used effectively without a thorough understanding of the latter.

44   TUTORIAL QUESTION: ACCOUNTS PREPARATION

MR YOUSEF
PROFIT AND LOSS ACCOUNT FOR THE YEAR ENDED 31 MAY 19X6

	£	£
Sales		138,078
Opening stock	11,927	
Purchases (W1)	84,561	
	96,488	
Less closing stock	13,551	
Cost of goods sold		82,937
Gross profit		55,141
Carriage out (W2)	2,933	
Rent, rates and insurance (W3)	5,952	
Postage and stationery	3,001	
Advertising	1,330	
Salaries and wages	26,420	
Bad debts	877	
Depreciation charge (W4)	8,700	
Increase in provision for bad debts	40	
		49,253
Net profit		5,888

MR YOUSEF
BALANCE SHEET AS AT 31 MAY 19X6

	Cost £	Accumulated depreciation £	NBV £
Fixed assets			
Equipment	<u>58,000</u>	<u>27,700</u>	30,300
Current assets			
Stock		13,551	
Debtors	12,120		
Less provision for bad debts	<u>170</u>		
		11,950	
Prepayment		880	
Cash		177	
Bank		<u>1,002</u>	
		27,560	
Current liabilities			
Creditors		6,471	
Accrual		<u>210</u>	
		6,681	
Net current assets			20,879
			51,179
Capital			
At 1 June 19X2			53,091
Profit for year			<u>5,888</u>
			58,974
Drawings			(7,800)
At 31 May 19X6			51,179

Workings

1   *Purchases*

	£
Per trial balance	82,350
Add carriage inwards	<u>2,211</u>
Per P & L a/c	<u>84,561</u>

2   Carriage out = £5,144 - £2,211 = £2,933.

3   *Rent, rates and insurance*

	£
Per trial balance	6,622
Add rent accrual	210
Less rates prepayment	(880)
Per P & L a/c	<u>5,952</u>

4   Depreciation charge = 15% × £58,000 = £8,700

45   TUTORIAL QUESTION: IDENTIFY FAULTS

The faults in the financial statements are as follows.

(a)   The heading *final accounts* as at 31 May 19X8 is incorrect and should be replaced by the words *trading and profit and loss account* for the year ended 31 May 19X8.

(b)   The item immediately after sales should be returns inwards £2,140 (not return outwards £3,600) and the figure should be deducted from sales not added to it;

(c)   Rents received are incorrectly included in the trading account; they should be included lower down as revenue in the profit and loss account.

(d)   The first item under the heading *cost of goods sold* should be the stock at 31 May 19X7 ie the opening stock of £6,780. This is more correctly dated as 1 June 19X7.

(e)   Returns inwards should be removed and replaced with return outwards £3,600. Also the amount should be deducted from purchases not added to it.

(f)   The figure of discounts received £11,800 should be taken out of the cost of goods sold section and included as revenue in the profit and loss account.

(g)   The last item under the heading *cost of goods sold* should be the closing stock £7,450, ie stock at 31 May 19X8.

(h)   Drawings are incorrectly included as an operating expense in the profit and loss account. Drawings are a distribution of profit and should appear on the balance sheet and reduce the balance of capital remaining in the business at 31 May 19X8.

(i)   The balance sheet title should be amended to read Balance Sheet as at 31 May 19X8.

(j)   Stock at cost is categorised under *Fixed assets* on the balance sheet; this is incorrect: it is a current asset. Also the stock figure should be the closing stock ie stock at 31 May 19X8 - not the opening stock.

(k)   Accumulated depreciation should be moved up two lines and deducted from equipment at cost. A new sub-total of £14,250 should be displayed (in place of the figure of £38,280).

(l)   The section *Current assets* should be amended to read:

	£
Stock at cost	7,450
Trade debtors	11,090
Prepaid expenses	140
Cash on hand	130
	18,810

The items accrued expenses and bank overdraft were wrongly included as they are current liabilities.

(m)   The section *Current liabilities* should read:

	£
Bank overdraft	1,050
Trade creditors	7,530
Accrued expenses	230
	8,810

Prepaid expenses are not included as they are a current asset.

(n)   The current liabilities have been added to the current assets to arrive at working capital; they should have been deducted.

(o)   The net profit is added to the capital as at 1 June 19X7. This is the correct presentation but the figure of £33,930 is incorrect as a result of the many errors made in arriving at the net profit.

(p)   Drawings must be removed from the profit and loss account and deducted immediately after the subtotal of capital as at 1 June 19X7 and net profit is shown.

In order to show the faults in the original financial statements more clearly fully corrected financial statements now follow.

JENNY JAQUES
TRADING AND PROFIT AND LOSS ACCOUNT
FOR THE YEAR ENDED 31 MAY 19X8

	£	£
Sales		127,000
Less returns inwards		2,140
		124,860
Stock at 1 June 19X7	6,780	
Purchases	111,090	
Less returns outwards	3,600	
	114,270	
Stock at 31 May 19X8	7,450	
Cost of goods sold		106,820
Gross profit		18,040
Rents received	2,500	
Discounts received	11,800	
		14,300
		32,340
Selling and distribution expenses	11,800	
Administration expenses	4,670	
		16,470
Net profit		15,870

JENNY JAQUES
BALANCE SHEET AS AT 31 MAY 19X8

	£	£
Fixed assets		
Equipment at cost		28,500
Less accumulated depreciation		14,250
		14,250
Current assets		
Stock at cost	7,450	
Trade debtors	11,090	
Prepaid expenses	140	
Cash on hand	130	
	18,810	
Current liabilities		
Bank overdraft	1,050	
Trade creditors	7,530	
Accrued expenses	230	
	8,810	
		10,000
Net current assets		24,250

	£	£
Capital		
As at 1 June 19X7		18,440
Net profit for the year	15,870	
Less drawings	10,060	
Retained profit for the year		5,810
As at 31 May 19X8		24,250

46   GBA

Tutorial note. This question has a small incomplete records element. Note that in part (c) only *four* transactions are required, but our answer gives five for completeness.

Examiner's comment. Parts (a) and (b) of this question were well answered. In part (c) many candidates were able to think of four transactions which affected the bank balance and not the profit but then failed to explain why the transactions had had these effects.

(a) GBA
     TRADING, PROFIT AND LOSS ACCOUNT
     FOR THE YEAR ENDED 30 JUNE 19X5

	£	£
Sales (625 – 2.3)		622,700
Cost of sales		
Opening stock	98,200	
Purchases (324.5 – 1.7)	322,800	
	421,000	
Less closing stock	75,300	
		345,700
Gross profit		277,000
Other income		
Bank interest (£15,000 × 6% × ½)	450	
Discounts received	2,500	
Decrease in provision for doubtful debts (1,000 – 620)	380	
		3,330
		280,330
Expenses		
Discounts given	1,500	
Packaging materials (12,900 + 200 – 700)	12,400	
Distribution costs	17,000	
Rent, rates & insurance (5,100 – 540)	4,650	
Telephone (3,200 + 500)	3,700	
Car expenses	2,400	
Wages (71,700 – 23,800)	47,900	
Heat & light (1,850 + 400)	2,250	
Sundry expenses (6,700 – 3,500)	3,200	
Loan interest	800	
Bad debts (W1)	600	
Depreciation (W2)	27,000	
		123,400
Net profit		156,930

(b) GBA
     BALANCE SHEET AT 30 JUNE 19X5

	£	£
Fixed assets (W3)		68,500
Current assets		
Stock (75,300 + 700)	76,000	
Debtors (W4)	94,680	
Bank (15,000 + 26,500)	41,500	
	212,180	
Creditors due within one year		
Creditors (W5)	83,100	
Loan (10,000 – 6,400 + 800)	4,400	
	87,500	
Net current assets		124,680
		193,180
Capital		
Opening balance at 1 July 19X4		55,550
Capital introduced		8,000
Profit for year	156,930	
Less drawings (23,800 + 3,500)	(27,300)	
		129,630
		193,180

Workings

1   *Bad and doubtful debts*

Provision for doubtful debts as 30 June 19X5

	£
1% × £20,000	200
2.5% × £12,000	300
5% × £(3,000 – 600)	120
	620

PROVISION FOR DOUBTFUL DEBTS

	£		£
Credit to P & L	380	Balance b/fwd	1,000
Balance to be c/fwd	620		
	1,000		1,000

2   *Depreciation charge*

	£
Delivery vans (20% × 112,500)	22,500
Car (25% × 8,000)	2,000
Equipment 25% × (15,000 – 5,000)	2,500
	27,000

3   *Fixed assets*

	£
NBV at 1 July 19X5:	
Delivery vehicles (112,500 – 35,000)	77,500
Equipment (15,000 – 5,000)	10,000
	87,500
Addition - car	8,000
Depreciation for year (W2)	(27,000)
	68,500

4   *Debtors*

	£
Debtors	95,000
Bad debts written off	(600)
Provision doubtful debts	(620)
Prepayments	450
Accrued income	450
	94,680

5   *Creditors*

	£
Creditors	82,000
Accrued expenses (400 + 500)	900
Unpaid invoice	200
	83,100

(c) (i)   Receipts from debtors and payments to suppliers have no effect on profit. Profits are affected when the sale or purchase is made, not when the goods are paid for or when payment is received.

(ii)   Setting up the deposit account involves moving funds from the current account, ie using one asset to create another. There is no effect on profit until interest is earned.

(iii)   Prepayments - rent, rates and insurance paid for in advance will not be shown as a cost in the 19X5 profit and loss account.

(iv)   Repayment of the loan is made through the bank account but represents a capital transaction and hence has no profit effect.

(v)   Drawings and the payment of the owner's tax bill are not business expenses and therefore have no effect on profit.

47   PLJ

(a)

	Debit £'000	Credit £'000
Stock at 1.5.X6	84	
Capital (228 + 2)		230
Drawings	14	
Plant at cost	83	
Plant depreciation at 1.5.X6		13
Office equipment at cost (31 + 2)	33	
Office equipment depreciation at 1.5.X6		8
Debtors	198	
Creditors		52
Sales		813
Purchases	516	
Returns inwards	47	
Discounts allowed	4	
Provision doubtful debts		23
Administration costs	38	
Salaries	44	
Research costs	26	
Loan	25	
Bank		50
Bad debts written off	77	
	1,189	1,189

(b)   PLJ PROFIT AND LOSS ACCOUNT
      FOR THE YEAR ENDED 30 APRIL 19X7

	£	£
Sales (813 – 47)		766,000
Cost of sales		
Stock at 1.5.X6	84,000	
Purchases	516,000	
	600,000	
Stock at 30.4.X7	74,000	
		526,000
Gross profit		240,000
Expenses		
Depreciation: plant (83 × 10%)	8,300	
office ((33 – 8) × 20%)	5,000	
Discounts allowed	4,000	
Administration (38 – 3)	35,000	
Salaries (44 + 2)	46,000	
Research costs	26,000	
Bad debts	77,000	
		201,300
Net profit		38,700

(c)   PLJ BALANCE SHEET AT 30 APRIL 19X7

	£	£
Fixed assets		
Plant (83 – 13 – 8.3)	61,700	
Office equipment (33 – 8 – 5)	20,000	
		81,700
Current assets		
Debtors (198 – 23 + 25 + 3)	203,000	
Stock	74,000	
	277,000	
Current liabilities		
Creditors (2 + 52)	54,000	
Bank overdraft	50,000	
	104,000	
Net current assets		173,000
		254,700
Capital (230 + 38.7 – 14)		254,700

(d)   PJ believes that her business is growing steadily because she makes a profit every year and her drawings are always less than the amount of her profit. Hence the capital she has tied up in the business is growing from year to year.

However, the amount of profit is dependent on the method used to value the assets and liabilities of the business at the beginning and end of the period. PJ's accounts have been drawn up on an historical cost basis which is accepted convention under normal circumstances, ie assets and liabilities are stated at cost.

But the fundamental problem with preparing accounts on this basis is that there is no adjustment to the profit for the effects of inflation, ie part of the profit will be due to growth in the business volume but part will also be due to the effects of inflation.

Failure to allow for the effects of inflation means that the true success of the business may be overstated (particularly in times of high inflation) and the capital retained in the business may be insufficient to allow it to maintain its output at the same level.

This is the theory of capital maintenance, which states that it is not enough to measure profit (and therefore increase in capital) on an historical cost basis; allowance must be made for the effects of inflation so ensuring that the capital is maintained at a level that allows the trading capacity of the business to continue unimpaired.

48   TUTORIAL QUESTION: INCOME AND EXPENDITURE ACCOUNTS

(a)   HB TENNIS CLUB INCOME AND EXPENDITURE ACCOUNT
FOR THE SIX MONTHS ENDED 30 SEPTEMBER 19X0

	£	£
Income		
Subscriptions (W1)		7,050
Net income from tournaments (465 - 132)		333
Bank interest received		43
Net income from sale of club ties (W2)		103
Life membership fees (W3)		210
		7,739
Expenditure		
Depreciation of equipment (W4)	403	
Groundsman's wages (4,520 + 40)	4,560	
Rent and business rates (636 – 68)	568	
Heating and lighting (674 + 53)	727	
Postage and stationery (41 + 12)	53	
Court maintenance	1,000	
		7,311
Surplus transferred to accumulated fund		428

(b)   HB TENNIS CLUB
BALANCE SHEET AS AT 30 SEPTEMBER 19X0

	£	£	£
Fixed assets			
Equipment at cost			4,080
Depreciation to date			403
			3,677
Current assets			
Stock of ties (W2)		180	
Subscriptions owing (W1)		750	
Prepaid business rates		68	
Bank		6,148	
		7,146	
Current liabilities			
Subscriptions in advance (W1)	6,300		
Accrued expenses	105		
		6,405	
Net current assets			741
			4,418
Financed by			
Accumulated fund			428
Life membership fund £(4,200 - 210)			3,990
			4,418

Workings

1   *Subscriptions income*

	£
Subscriptions received for full year	12,600
∴ subscriptions for six months	6,300
Plus subscriptions outstanding (5 × £150)	750
	7,050

2   *Sale of club ties*

	£	£
Sales income		373
Purchases of ties	450	
less closing stock (40/100 × £450)	180	
		270
Net income from sale of club ties		103

3   *Life membership fees*

	£
Fees received (4 × £1,050)	4,200
One years' instalment (÷ 10)	420
∴ income for six months	210

4   *Depreciation of equipment*

	£
Purchase cost of equipment	4,080
Estimated scrap value	50
	4,030
Annual depreciation (÷ 5 assuming straight line depreciation)	806
Charge for six months	403

49   HAPPY TICKERS

> *Tutorial note.* Sometimes in this kind of question the logic of the double entry adjustments made is not always carried through to the balance sheet. Be sure you understand the concept of deferred income (life subscriptions) being gradually released to the income and expenditure account.

(a) *Cafe operations*

	£	£
Sales		4,660
Stocks at 1.1.Y0	800	
Purchases	1,980	
	2,780	
Stocks at 31.12.Y0	(850)	
		1,930
Gross profit		2,730
Wages		2,000
Net profit		730
Sales of sports equipment		
Sales		900
Opening stock	1,000	
Purchases	500	
	1,500	
Closing stock (balancing figure)	(900)	
Cost of sales (900 × 100/150)		600
Profit		300

	£
(b) Annual subscriptions (W1)	1,300
Life subscriptions (W2)	220
	1,520

Workings

1   *Annual subscriptions*

	£
b/f 31.12.X9 (in advance)	120
Received in year	1,100
Owed for 19Y0 at 31.12.19Y0 (4 × 20)	80
	1,300

2   *Life subscriptions*

	£
Life member subscriptions at 31.12.X9	1,400
New subscriptions in year to 31.12.Y0	200
	1,600
Less 11 × £20 allocated to current year	220
Life subscriptions c/f at 31.12.Y0	1,380

(c) HAPPY TICKERS SPORTS AND SOCIAL CLUB
INCOME AND EXPENDITURE STATEMENT
FOR THE YEAR TO 31 DECEMBER 19Y0

	£	£
Income		
Subscriptions		1,520
Cafe operations		730
Sale of sports equipment		300
		2,550
Expenses		
Rent	1,200	
19X9 subscription written off	20	
Insurance 900 × 12/18	600	
Roller repairs (1/2 × 450)	225	
Write down of used sports equipment*	486	
Depreciation of roller	100	
		2,631
Excess of expenditure over income		81
Accumulated fund brought forward at 1 January 19Y0		2,900
Accumulated fund carried forward at 31 December 19Y0		2,819

Note. The used sports equipment at valuation figure must remain constant, so any additions must be written down. The write-down is calculated as follows:

	£
Total purchases of sports equipment	1,000
∴ Used in club (1/2 × 1,000)	500
Less: used equipment sold	(14)
Additions to be written down	486

HAPPY TICKERS SPORTS AND SOCIAL CLUB
BALANCE SHEET AS AT 31 DECEMBER 19Y0

	£	£	£
Fixed assets			
Half share in motorised roller		500	
New sports equipment unsold (part (a))		900	
Used sports equipment at valuation		700	
			2,100
Current assets			
Rent pre-paid (2 months)	200		
Insurance pre-paid (900 - 150 - 600)	150		
Carefree Conveyancers (half repairs of roller)	225		
Subscriptions in arrears (4 × £20)	80		
Cafe stocks	850		
Cash (1,210 + 6,994 - 7,450)	754		
		2,259	
Current liabilities			
Subscriptions in advance	80		
Life subscriptions (part (b) W2)	1,380		
Cafe supplies	80		
		1,540	
Net current assets			719
Net assets			2,819
Accumulated fund brought forward		2,900	
Less: loss for year		(81)	
Accumulated fund carried forward			2,819

(d) Life subscriptions are treated as a liability because they are monies which have been received from members for services in future periods. They are therefore 'owing' to future periods. Strictly speaking they are not liabilities but *deferred income*.

The principle is similar to that seen at work in the treatment of subscriptions received in advance. These too are shown as credit balances because they are 'owed' to the following year. The life subscriptions are similar but received for many years in advance, not just one.

50   RACKETS

> *Tutorial note.* This is an unusual question which tests your skills in analysing information and interpreting accounting policies even if they strike you as being faulty. You are given the opportunity to express your reservations once you have demonstrated the effect of applying the policy as laid down. Observe the dates of receipt very carefully.

(a)   RACKETS UNLIMITED
TABLE OF SUBSCRIPTIONS INCOME

Member	Income year to 30.6.X0 £	Income year to 30.6.X1 £	Balance c/f at 30.6.X1 Dr £	Balance c/f at 30.6.X1 Cr £
A	10	–	–	–
B	10	10	–	–
C	10	10	–	–
D	10	10	–	17
E	10	9	–	8
F	10	10	–	27
G	10	10	–	80
H	10	10	–	100
I	10	10	–	9
J	–	10	10	–
K	–	10	–	17
1	10	–	–	10
M	10	9	–	–
N	–	10	10	–

(b)   Any two of the following.

(i)   It is not clear what amount is due for a period paid in advance or how this is to be accounted for.

(ii)   Life subscriptions appear to be spread over ten years. It is not clear why this figure has been chosen.

(iii)   Reductions are made for payments in advance. It might be more realistic to treat these reductions as discounts and show the gross amount of the subscription and the discount separately.

51   TUTORIAL QUESTION: INCOMPLETE RECORDS

MISS TEEK
TRADING AND PROFIT AND LOSS ACCOUNT
FOR THE YEAR ENDED 31 MARCH 19X9

	Working	£	£
Sales: cash	1		10,850
credit	2		1,650
			12,500
Opening stock		500	
Purchases	3	7,600	
		8,100	
Closing stock	4	(600)	
Cost of sales			7,500
Gross profit			5,000
Expenses			
Rent		970	
Repairs to canopy		201	
Van running expenses (520 + 80 + 323)		923	
Depreciation		1,000	
Sundry expenses (24 + 31)		55	
Bank interest		47	
Accounting fees		75	
Bad debts		29	
			3,300
			1,700
Profit on disposal of van			1,300
			3,000

MISS TEEK
BALANCE SHEET AS AT 31 MARCH 19X9

Fixed assets	*Working*	£	£	£
Motor van: cost	5			5,000
depreciation	5			1,000
net book value				4,000
Current assets				
Stock	4		600	
Debtors	2		320	
Cash in hand	1		39	
			959	
Current liabilities				
Bank overdraft	1	474		
Bank interest (presumably not paid until 1 April)		27		
Creditors	3	233		
			734	
Net current assets				225
				4,225
Proprietor's capital				
Balance at 31 March 19X8				3,795
Profit for the year			3,000	
Less drawings			2,570	
Retained profit for the year				430
Balance at 31 March 19X9				4,225

Suggested solutions

Workings

1
CASH BOOK

	Cash £	Bank £		Cash £	Bank £
Balance b/d	55	2,800	Drawings (52 × £50)	2,600	
Cash takings banked			Petrol (52 × £10)	520	
(contra entry)		7,521	Sundry expenses	24	
Cheques banked		1,500	Repairs to canopy	201	
Dividend income: drawings a/c		210	Takings banked (contra		
Cash takings (balancing		210	entry)	7,521	
figure)	10,850		Purchase of van		3,200
			Road fund licence		80
			Insurance on van		323
			Creditors		7,777
			Rent		970
			Sundry		31
			Accounting work		75
			Bank interest		20
			Returned cheque: bad debt		29
Balance c/d (overdraft)		474	Balance c/d	39	
	10,905	12,505		10,905	12,505
Balance b/d	39		Balance b/d		474

2
DEBTORS

	£		£
Balance b/d	170	Cash	1,500
Credit sales - balancing figure	1,650	Balance c/d	320
	1,820		1,820

3
CREDITORS

	£		£
Bank	7,777	Balance b/d	230
Balance c/d	233	Purchases (balancing figure)	7,780
	8,010		8,010

Goods taken as drawings

		£
Selling price	(100%)	300
Gross profit	(40%)	120
Cost	(60%)	180

Therefore, purchases taken to the trading account = £7,780 – £180 = £7,600.

4 *Closing stock*

	£
Sales (10,850 + 1,650) (100%)	12,500
Gross profit (40%)	5,000
Cost of goods sold (60%)	7,500
Opening stock	500
Purchases (W3)	7,600
	8,100
Cost of goods sold	7,500
Closing stock (balancing figure)	600

5 *New van*

The bank statement shows that the cash paid for the new van was £3,200. Since there was a part exchange of £1,800 on the old van, the cost of the new van must be £5,000 with first year depreciation (20%) £1,000.

6   *Disposal of van*

	£		£
Van at cost	3,000	Provision for depreciation at	
Profit on disposal	1,300	date of sale	2,500
		Asset account (trade in value for	
		new van)	1,800
	4,300		4,300

7   *Drawings*

	£		£
Cash	2,600	Dividend income	210
Stock	180	Capital account (balance)	2,570
	2,780		2,780

Since there are no investments in the business balance sheet, the dividend income must be separate from the business. However, since it is paid into the business bank account, it should be accounted for, in effect, as a reduction in drawings.

52   SOLE TRADER 'T'

> *Tutorial note.* Candidates for the examination made the mistake of valuing stock at selling price rather than cost. Very few candidates recognised that there has to be a balancing figure in current liabilities which in the absence of a positive bank balance was probably an overdraft.

T - PROFIT AND LOSS ACCOUNT FOR THE YEAR ENDED 30.4.X1

	£	£
Sales		125,000
Cost of sales		
Opening stock (W1)	5,000	
Purchases (balancing figure)	105,000	
	110,000	
Closing stock (W1)	(10,000)	
		100,000
Gross profit (W2)		25,000
Administration expenses		(7,500)
		17,500

T - BALANCE SHEET AS AT 30.4.X1

	£	£
Fixed assets (W5)		3,321
Current assets		
Stock	10,000	
Debtors (W3)	17,124	
	27,124	
Current liabilities		
Creditors (W4)	8,630	
Overdraft (balancing figure)	10,744	
	19,374	
		7,750
Net assets		11,071

Workings

1   *Opening and closing stock*

	£
Sales	125,000
At cost (25% mark up) $125,000 \times \dfrac{100}{125}$	100,000
Closing stock $100,000 \times \dfrac{36.5}{365}$	10,000
$\therefore$ Opening stock $= 10,000 \times 1 = {}^{1}/_{2}$	5,000

2   *Gross profit*

	£
Sales	125,000
Cost of sales (from W1)	100,000
Gross profit	25,000

3   *Debtors*
Debtors payment period: 50 days
Debtors: $50/365 \times 125,000 = 17,124$

4   *Creditors*
Creditors payment period: 30 days
Creditors $30/365 \times 105,000 = 8,630$

5   *Fixed assets*

Current assets	= stock + debtors
	= 27,124
Current liabilities	= $1/1.4 \times 27,124$
	= 19,374
Net current assets	= 27,124 – 19,374
	= 7,750

This represents 70% of capital employed

∴ Fixed assets	= $7,750 \times 30/70$
	= 3,321

53   JAY

Tutorial note. In part (d) you were only asked to comment on one of the accounting policies you mention. Our solution discusses all three for completeness.

Examiner's comment. The following approach to incomplete records questions is recommended.

(a)   Identify those items in the receipts and payments account which are affected by the notes.

(b)   Identify balance sheet items and profit and loss account items.

(c)   Draw up the final accounts and insert the values required using workings (or control accounts) for the more difficult items such as debtors and creditors.

(d)   Use the accounting equation to determine the opening capital from the opening assets and liabilities.

(a)   J: TRADING AND PROFIT AND LOSS ACCOUNT
FOR THE YEAR ENDED 30 SEPTEMBER 19X3

	£	£
Sales (W1)		33,340
Cost of sales		
Opening stock	890	
Purchases (W2)	18,995	
	19,885	
Closing stock	775	
		19,110
Gross profit		14,230
Less expenses		
Bank charges	120	
Rent	2,400	
Postage and stationery	65	
Profit on sale of plant (1,735 – 1,420)	(315)	
Wages (1,750 + 180)	1,930	
Motor expenses (W3)	1,155	
Electricity (270 – 30 + 345)	585	
Business rates (2,800 + 1,300 – 1,400)	2,700	
Depreciation (W4)	2,069	
		10,709
		3,521

(b)   J: CALCULATION OF CAPITAL AT 1 OCTOBER 19X2

	£	£
Assets		
Plant and equipment	6,420	
Motor vehicles	4,200	
Stocks	890	
Debtors	1,260	
Bank	3,520	
Cash	80	
Prepayment	1,300	
		17,670
Liabilities		
Creditors	470	
Accrual	30	
		500
Net assets = capital		17,170

(c)   J: BALANCE SHEET AS AT 30 SEPTEMBER 19X3

	£	£
Fixed assets		
Plant and equipment (5,000 – 750)	4,250	
Motor vehicles (5,275 – 1,319)	3,956	
		8,206
Current assets		
Stocks	775	
Debtors	1,330	
Prepayments (55 + 100 + 1,400)	1,555	
Cash at bank	3,365	
Cash in hand	250	
	7,275	
Current liabilities		
Creditors	265	
Accruals (180 + 345)	525	
	790	
Net current assets		6,485
		14,691
Financed by:		
Opening capital (Part (b))		17,170
Profit		3,521
		20,691
Drawings		(6,000)
		14,691

(d)   Three accounting policies adopted by J are:

(i)   the accruals or matching concept, for example in the treatment of business rates;

(ii)   the valuation of stocks (at cost);

(iii)   the depreciation policy which is to depreciate fixed assets on the reducing balance basis.

The effect of the choice of policy on the final accounts can be analysed as follows.

(i)   If the accounts had been prepared on a cash basis rather than on accruals basis, the motor expenses figure would have been overstated because a full year's tax and warranty would have been charged rather than six months.

(ii)   If closing stock had been valued at selling price rather than cost, profit and net assets would have been overstated.

(iii)   The advantage of the reducing balance method of depreciation as opposed to the straight line method is that it more realistically reflects the fact that some assets lose most value in the early stages of their economic life.

Workings

1   *Sales*

DEBTORS CONTROL ACCOUNT

	£		£
Balance b/f	1,260	Balance c/f	1,330
Credit sales (bal fig)	29,710	Cash received	29,640
	30,970		30,970

Total sales (credit and cash): 29,710 + 3,630 = £33,340

2   *Purchases*

CREDITORS CONTROL ACCOUNT

	£		£
Balance c/f	265	Balance b/f	470
Cash paid	12,740	Purchases (bal fig)	12,535
	13,005		13,005

Total purchases (credit and cash): 12,535 + 6,460 = £18,995

3   *Motor expenses*

	£
Per cash book	980
Road fund licence (6/12 × 110)	55
Petrol	20
Maintenance warranty (6/12 × 200)	100
	1,155

4   *Depreciation*

		£
Plant:	Balance at 1.10.92 (NBV)	6,240
	Disposal (NBV)	(1,420)
	Balance at 30.9.93	5,000

∴ Depn charge 15% × £5,000 = £750

	£'000
Motor vehicles:	
Balance at 1.10.92	4,200
Addition 1,405 - (110 + 20 + 200)	1,075
	5,275

∴ Depn charge 25% × £5,275 = £1,319

Total depreciation charge : 750 + 1,319 = £2,069

54   JB

Tutorial note. Part (a) and (b) required you to prepare accounts from incomplete data. This is a popular topic as it tests whether you have a really sound grasp of double entry. In part (b) you were required to explain the benefits of the system of double entry bookkeeping.

(a) JB
PROFIT AND LOSS ACCOUNT
FOR THE YEAR ENDED 31 DECEMBER 19X5

	£	£
Sales (417,300 (W1) + 10,160 (W2))		427,460
Opening stock	30,500	
Purchases (W3)	178,700	
	209,200	
Less closing stock	(27,850)	
Cost of sales		181,350
Gross profit		246,110
Expenses		
Rent (22,000 + 2,500 – 2,700)	21,800	
Wages (W4)	99,260	
General expenses (12,500 + 2,600/2)	13,800	
Depreciation (W5)	31,850	
Bad debt written off (16,000 × 80%)	12,800	
		179,510
Operating profit		66,600
Interest paid		9,500
Net profit		57,100

(b) JB
BALANCE SHEET AS AT 31 DECEMBER 19X5

	£	£
Fixed assets (128,000 + 45,000 + 5,000 – 31,850)		146,150
Current assets		
Stocks	27,850	
Debtors (22,300 + 2,700 + 1,300 – 12,800)	13,500	
Cash at bank	106,700	
	148,050	
Creditors: amounts due within one year (W6)	27,950	
Net current assets		120,100
		266,250
Creditors: amounts due in more than one year (W7)		74,000
		192,250

Financed by:
JB's capital account (W8)	192,250

(c) Maintaining books and ledgers allows JB to keep control of her business. At any point during the year she can ascertain who owes her money, how much she has in the bank and who she owes money to. Keeping financial records also simplifies the task of preparing the year end accounts.

Double entry bookkeeping is the method of maintaining books of account where each transaction is entered twice, once as a debit entry and once as an equal credit entry.

Use of double entry bookkeeping gives JB a means of confirming that she has carried out her posting of transactions correctly. This is because of the year end or at any time during the year she can extract a trial balance from the nominal ledger and check that the total of debits and credits agree.

Workings

		£
1	*Credit sales*	
	Cash received	427,500
	Closing debtors	22,300
		449,800
	Less opening debtors	(32,500)
	Credit sales	417,300

			£
2	*Cash sales*		
	Opening bank balance		(8,850)
	Add total receipts		449,500
	Less total payments		(342,550)
	Theoretical balance at y/e		98,100
	Per bank statement		106,700
	Difference		8,600
	Add back cash wages (£30 × 52)		1,560
	Cash sales		10,160

3	*Purchases*		
	Paid to suppliers		175,600
	Closing creditors		12,200
			187,800
	Less opening creditors (17,600 – 4,300)		13,300
	Credit purchases		174,500
	Cash purchases		4,200
			178,700

4	*Wages*		
	Payments		90,000
	Accrued at 1/1/X5		(4,300)
	Cash wages		6,750
	JB's daughter (W2)		1,560
	Accrued at 31/12/X5		5,250
			99,260

5	*Depreciation*		
	Plant and machinery 128,000 × 20%		25,600
	Office equipment 45,000 × 10/9 = £50,000 Cost £50,000 × 20%		5,000
	Motor vehicle £50,000 × 25%)		1,250
			31,850

6	*Creditors < 1 year*		
	Current portion loan (20,000 – 9,500)		10,500 ★
	Due to suppliers		12,200
	Wages owing		5,250
			27,950

★ It has been assumed that the loan repayments are fixed from year to year.

7	*Creditors > 1 year*		
	Loan at 1/1/X5		95,000
	Payments 19X5 (20,000 – 9,500)		(10,500)
	Included in creditors < 1 year		(10,500)
			74,000

			£
8	*Capital account*		
	Opening balance		117,050
	Vehicle transferred		5,000
	Capital paid in		22,000
	Profit for year		57,100
			203,150
	Cash withdrawn (22,450 – 6,750 – 4,200 – 2,600)		(8,900)
			192,250

55   TUTORIAL QUESTION: COMPANY ACCOUNTS

TRADING AND PROFIT AND LOSS ACCOUNT
FOR THE YEAR ENDED 31 DECEMBER 19X8

	£	£
Sales (W1)		96,000
Opening stock (per question)	15,000	
Purchases (W2)	57,000	
	72,000	
Closing stock (per question)	18,000	
Cost of sales		54,000
Gross profit		42,000
Operating expenses (W3)	13,000	
Selling expenses (W4)	6,900	
Administration expenses (W5)	10,500	
Profit on sale of fixed assets (W7)	(2,000)	
		28,400
Net profit for the year		13,600
Profit and loss account brought forward		19,000
Profit and loss account carried forward		32,600

BALANCE SHEET AT 31 DECEMBER 19X8

Fixed assets	Cost	Depre-ciation	NBV
	£	£	£
Land and buildings	40,000	-	40,000
Plant and machinery (W6)	40,000	16,000	24,000
			64,000

Current assets		
Stock	18,000	
Prepayments (W5)	500	
Debtors less provision (W9)	17,100	
	35,600	
Current liabilities		
Creditors per question	7,000	
Accrued debenture interest (W5)	3,000	
Bank account (W10)	9,000	
	19,000	
Net current assets		16,600
Debenture loan		30,000
Net assets		50,600
Share capital (10,000 + 5,000) (W9)		15,000
Share premium (W9)		3,000
Profit and loss account		32,600
Owner's equity		50,600

Workings

		£	£
1	Sales	100,000	
	less returns incorrectly recorded	(1,000)	
			99,000
	Returns	2,000	
	add returns incorrectly recorded	1,000	
			(3,000)
	Net sales		96,000
2	Purchases		61,000
	less returns		(4,000)
	Net purchases		57,000

		£
3	Operating expenses	9,000
	Depreciation on plant (W6)	4,000
		13,000

		£
4	Selling expenses	6,000
	Adjust provision wrongly credited	800
	Increase in bad debt provision £900 (W8) – £800	100
		6,900

		£
5	Administration expenses	7,000
	Debenture interest (30,000 × 10%)	3,000
	Rates (£1,000 × 3/6)	500
		10,500

The remaining £500 is a prepayment, to be included in current assets.

6		Cost	Depreciation	NBV
		£	£	£
	Plant and machinery	50,000	22,000	28,000
	Disposal of fully depreciated asset	10,000	10,000	NIL
		40,000	12,000	28,000
	Depreciation for year (40,000 × 10%)		4,000	4,000
		40,000	16,000	24,000

7	*Profit on disposal of fixed asset*	
	Sale proceeds (W9)	2,000
	Original cost (£10,000) less depreciation (£10,000)	NIL
	Profit	2,000

8	*Debtors*	
	Sales ledger control account	20,000
	Less: returns incorrectly debited	1,000
	adjustment to a credit	1,000
		18,000
	Provision (5% × £18,000)	900
	Net debtors	17,100

9	Suspense account balance	10,000
	of which Share capital 5,000 × £1	(5,000)
	Share premium 5,000 × £0.60	(3,000)
	∴ Balance is fixed asset sale proceeds	2,000

10	Bank overdraft per question	8,000
	Rates standing order	1,000
		9,000

56   ABC

Tutorial note. To gain a pass standard in part (a) you should have got the layout right plus at least three of the figures shown in the workings. However, minor arithmetical mistakes, as opposed to errors of principle, will not be penalised too heavily. 10 marks are allocated to part (c), the discussion question. You should therefore devote no less than 18 minutes to this part of your answer.

(a) ABC LIMITED
DRAFT TRADING AND PROFIT AND LOSS ACCOUNT
FOR THE YEAR ENDED 31 OCTOBER 19X4

	£	£
Sales	123,740	
Returns inwards	4,243	
		119,497
Cost of sales		
Opening stock	4,950	
Purchases	76,297	
	81,247	
Closing stock (W1)	4,948	
		76,299
Gross profit		43,198
Less expenses		
Carriage outwards	1,325	
Postage, stationery etc	1,249	
Wages and salaries (28,291 + 624)	28,915	
Bad debts (W4)	962	
Depreciation (W5)	7,535	
Business rates (W2)	8,490	
Lighting and heating (3,624 + 393)	4,017	
		52,493
Net loss		(9,295)

(b) ABC LIMITED
DRAFT BALANCE SHEET AS AT 31 OCTOBER 19X4

	Cost	Dep'n	NBV
	£	£	£
Fixed assets			
Premises	60,000	26,400	33,600
Equipment	23,400	9,350	14,050
Vehicles	12,800	7,925	4,875
	96,200	43,675	52,525
Current assets			
Stock (W1)		4,948	
Debtors	12,095		
Less provision	1,210		
		10,885	
Prepayment		3,750	
Bank		1,236	
		20,819	
Current liabilities			
Trade creditors		8,742	
Accruals (624 + 393)		1,017	
		9,759	
Net current assets			11,060
Net assets			63,585
Financed by			
Share capital			50,000
Profit and loss account (22,880 – 9,295)			13,585
			63,585

(c) (i) The fact that the company has made a loss is not, in itself, a reason for eliminating the provision for bad and doubtful debts. The decision on whether to provide for doubtful debts should not be biased by the need to show a good result.

The setting up of a provision for doubtful debts is governed by the fundamental accounting concept of *prudence*, described in SSAP 2 as follows.

'Revenue and profits are not anticipated, but are recognised by inclusion in the profit and loss account only when realised in the form either of cash or of other assets the ultimate cash realisation of which can be assessed with reasonable certainty; provision is made for all known ... expenses and losses whether the amount of these is known with certainty or is a best estimate in the light of the information available.'

If there is uncertainty as to whether some of the sales will be realised in the form of cash, the prudence concept dictates that the amount in question should not be included in the profit for the year.

While it would not be correct to jettison the provision for doubtful debts because it is no longer convenient, it might still be appropriate to review the policy. There is no point in being over-prudent.

We are told that 'it is company policy' to provide for doubtful debts on the basis described. This policy should not be applied mechanically. For example, it may be that a large customer always pays late, but always pays up! Furthermore, the percentages seem rather high. It might be better to improve credit control and investigate slow payers instead of adopting a blanket policy.

(ii) As is the case with the provision for doubtful debts, the company cannot stop providing for depreciation simply because to do so would present a more favourable picture of the company's results.

The Companies Act 1985 requires that all fixed assets having a limited economic life should be depreciated. SSAP 12 gives a useful discussion of the purpose of depreciation and supplements the statutory requirements in important respects.

Depreciation is defined in SSAP 12 as 'the measure of the wearing out, consumption or other reduction in the useful economic life of a fixed asset whether arising from use, effluxion of time or obsolescence through technological or market changes'. This definition covers the amortisation of assets with a pre-determined life, such as a leasehold, and the depletion of wasting assets such as mines.

The need to depreciate fixed assets arises from the accruals concept. If money is expended in purchasing an asset then the amount expended must at some time be charged against profits. If the asset is one which contributes to an enterprise's revenue over a number of accounting periods it would be inappropriate to charge any single period (eg the period in which the asset was acquired) with the whole of the expenditure. Instead, some method must be found of spreading the cost of the asset over its useful economic life.

Workings

1   *Stock*

		£
At cost		6,492
Write down (2,089 – 545)		1,544
		4,948

2   *Business rates*

		£
Per trial balance		12,240
Less prepayment $^5/_6 \times 4,500$		3,750
		8,490

3   *Debtors*

		£
Per trial balance		12,595
Less bad debt w/o		500
		12,095

4   *Doubtful debts*

	£
Provision required	
3% × 6,500	195
10% × 3,440	344
20% × 1,355	271
50% × 800	400
	1,210

Provision b/d: £748

∴ Increase in provision: £1,210 – £748 = £462

Total bad debt expense = £500 + 462 = £962

5   *Depreciation*

	£
Premises: 4% × 60,000	2,400
Equipment: 15% × 23,400	3,510
Vehicles: 25% × (12,800 – 6,300)	1,625
Total depreciation expense	7,535

57   JAYKAY

> *Tutorial note.* Many candidates obtained full marks on (a) and (b). Others had problems with carriage in and carriage out, interest received, tax and dividends. Part (c) was less well answered and future candidates should take note of this in their revision.

(a)   JK LIMITED
TRADING, PROFIT AND LOSS ACCOUNT
FOR THE YEAR ENDED 31 MARCH 19X3

	£	£
Sales		647,400
Less cost of sales		
Opening stock	15,400	
Purchases	321,874	
Carriage in	13,256	
Closing stock	(19,473)	
		(331,057)
Trading profit		316,343
Carriage out	32,460	
Electricity (6,994 + 946)	7,940	
Business rates	8,940	
Wages and salaries (138,292 + 2,464)	140,756	
Postages and stationery	6,984	
Rent (14,600 – 2,800)	11,800	
Depreciation (W1)	7,040	
		215,920
		100,423
Interest receivable		7,200
Profit before tax		107,623
Corporation tax		30,000
		77,623
Dividend		2,500
Retained profit for the year		75,123
Retained profit brought forward		76,597
Retained profit carried forward		151,720

(b)   JK LIMITED
BALANCE SHEET AS AT 31 MARCH 19X3

	Cost £	Dep'n £	Net book value £
Fixed assets			
Motor vehicles (W1)	49,400	28,280	21,120
Current assets			
Stock		19,473	
Trade debtors		82,851	
Prepayments		2,800	
Cash at bank (90,000 + 77,240 + 7,200)		174,440	
		279,564	
Current liabilities			
Trade creditors	41,936		
VAT	16,382		
PAYE	4,736		
Accruals and provisions (W2)	35,910		
		98,964	
Net current assets			180,600
Total assets less current liabilities			201,720
Capital			
Ordinary shares of £1 each			50,000
Retained profit			151,720
			201,720

(c)   *Debtors payment period*

$$\frac{\text{Trade debtors}}{\text{Sales}} \times 365 = \frac{82,851}{647,400} \times 365 = 46.7 \text{ days}$$

Creditors payment period

$$\frac{\text{Trade creditors}}{\text{Cost of sales}} \times 365 = \frac{41,936}{331,057} \times 365 = 46.2 \text{ days}$$

Stockholding period

$$\frac{\text{Cost of sales}}{\text{Average stock}} = \frac{331,057}{0.5 \times (15,400 + 19,473)} = 18.9 \text{ days}$$

The debtors and creditors payments periods are approximately equal but debtors are twice as large as creditors and therefore effectively the company is lending around £40,000 to debtors for 47 days, interest free. There is no comparative information available, nor do we know what kind of business is being operated, so it is not possible to comment on whether this represents good or bad performance. We are not told what JK Ltd's terms of trade are, so we cannot even judge by its own standards.

The stockholding period of around 19 days shows that stock is relatively fast moving. Stock has increased by 26% during the year, which may indicate a slight loss of control or may simply be in line with the growth of the business generally. Again comparative data is needed to make meaningful comments.

Workings

1   *Depreciation on motor vehicles*

	£
Cost	49,400
Depreciation b/f	21,240
	28,160

	£
Depreciation at 25%	7,040
Depreciation b/f	21,240
Depreciation c/f	28,280
Cost	49,400
Net book value c/f	21,120

2   *Accruals and provisions*

	£
Electricity	946
Wages and salaries	2,464
Corporation tax	30,000
Dividend	2,500
	35,910

58   DWS

Tutorial note. It is essential that you are familiar with the method of preparation of a trading and profit and loss account and balance sheet since this will certainly be required in the examination.

Examiner's comment. In part (a) many candidates did not show the accepted sub-totals such as net sales and purchases. This aspect was better dealt with in part (b). Part (c) was reasonably well answered.

(a)   DWS LIMITED
TRADING, PROFIT AND LOSS ACCOUNT
FOR THE YEAR ENDED 30 SEPTEMBER 19X4

	£	£
Sales (188 – 8)		180,000
Cost of sales		
Opening stock	31,000	
Purchases (W1)	110,200	
	141,200	
Closing stock	(53,000)	
		88,200
Gross profit		91,800
Expenses		
Selling expenses	12,000	
Heat and light	8,000	
Wages and salaries (14 + 1.5)	15,500	
Directors fees (5 + 3.6 (W2))	8,600	
Printing and stationery	6,000	
Telephone and fax (6 – 1)	5,000	
Rent, rates and insurance (4 – 1)	3,000	
Provision for doubtful debts (W3)	600	
Bank charges	4,000	
Auditors' fees	3,500	
Depreciation (W4)	22,100	
		88,300
Net profit before tax		3,500
Corporation tax		1,000
Profit after tax		2,500
Dividends: interim paid	2,000	
final proposed (W5)	3,000	
		5,000
Retained loss for the year		(2,500)
Transfer to general reserve		(10,000)
Profit and loss account brought forward		34,000
Profit and loss account carried forward		21,500

(b)   DWS LIMITED
      BALANCE SHEET AS AT 30 SEPTEMBER 19X4

	£	£
Fixed assets		
Plant and machinery (W6)	84,500	
Office equipment (W7)	19,200	
		103,700
Current assets		
Stock	53,000	
Debtors (W8)	35,400	
Cash in hand	1,000	
	89,400	
Creditors: amounts due within one year (W10)	(46,600)	
Net current assets		42,800
		146,500
Capital and reserves		
Issued share capital		100,000
Share premium account		8,000
General reserve (7 + 10)		17,000
Profit and loss account		21,500
		146,500

(c)   Current ratio $= \dfrac{\text{current assets}}{\text{current liabilities}}$

$= \dfrac{89,400}{46,600}$

$= 2$

Quick ratio $= \dfrac{\text{current assets less stocks}}{\text{current liabilities}}$

$= \dfrac{89,400 - 53,000}{46,600}$

$= 0.78$

(d)   The current ratio measures how many times current liabilities are covered by current assets, ie to what extent will liquidation of a company's current assets meet its current liabilities. The quick ratio recognises that for many companies stock is not a very liquid asset and so excludes it and measures current liabilities against debtors and cash.

Both ratios are a measure of liquidity which in general terms would be expected to exceed 1, so indicating that the company can meet its current liabilities when they fall due. However it is difficult to state what is an acceptable liquidity ratio as it is very much dependent on the nature of the company's business. For example, a supermarket group would tend to have a lower ratio than say a manufacturing group. What is important is to compare the trend of these ratios over time for a particular company and for the relevant industry sector.

Workings

1   *Purchases*

	£
Per question	115,000
Returns	(6,000)
Mis-posting to office equipment	1,200
	110,200

2   *Directors' fees*

Net sales (£180,000) at 2% = £3,600

3   *Provision for doubtful debts*

PROVISION FOR DOUBTFUL DEBTS

	£		£
Credit to P & L (bal fig)	2,400	Bal b/fwd	4,000
Bal to be carried forward			
($£35,000 - £3,000$) × 5%	1,600		
	4,000		4,000

Bad debt expense = $£(3,000 - 2,400) = £600$.

4   *Depreciation charge*

	£
Plant and Machinery	
10% × £125,000	12,500
Office equipment	
$33\frac{1}{3}\% \times £(45,000 - 1,200 - 15,000)$	9,600
	22,100

5   *Final dividend*

£100,000 of 50p ordinary shares

= 200,000 shares

1.5p final dividend

$= 200,000 \times \dfrac{1.5}{100}$

$= £3,000$

6   *Plant and machinery NBV*

	£	£
Cost		125,000
Depreciation		
- accumulated	28,000	
- charge for year	12,500	
		40,500
		84,500

7   *Office equipment*

	£	£
Cost		45,000
Adjustment for mis-posting		(1,200)
		43,800
Depreciation		
- accumulated	15,000	
- charge for year	9,600	
		24,600
		19,200

8   *Debtors*

	£
Trade	35,000
Bad debts written off	(3,000)
Prepayments	2,000
Suspense account (W11)	3,000
Provision for doubtful debts	(1,600)
	35,400

9   *Bank overdraft*

	£
Balance per cash book	3,000
Bank charges	(4,000)
Correction of misposting	(2,600)
	(3,600)

10   *Creditors: amounts due in less than one year*

		£
Trade creditors		33,000
Mis-posting of payment		(2,600)
Bank overdraft (W9)		3,600
Final dividend		3,000
Corporation tax		1,000
Accruals (1,500 + 3,600 + 3,500)		8,600
		46,600

11   *Suspense account*

SUSPENSE ACCOUNT

	£		£
Balance b/d	3,000	Creditors	2,600
Bank	2,600	Prepayments (bal fig)	3,000
	5,600		5,600

59   TUTORIAL QUESTION: MANUFACTURING ACCOUNTS

MANUFACTURING ACCOUNT FOR THE YEAR ENDED 31 DECEMBER 19X5

	£	£
Raw materials		
Stock on hand 1 January 19X5		25,000
Purchases		80,000
		105,000
Less stock on hand at 31 December 19X5		24,000
		81,000
Direct wages accrued (33,300 + 700)		34,000
Prime cost		115,000
Work in progress		
Balance at 1 January 19X5 at prime cost	5,800	
Less balance at 31 December 19X5 at prime cost	5,000	
	800	
Indirect factory expenses		
Manufacturing expenses	61,900	
Depreciation 7/10 × (39,000 + 30,000 − 60,000) (note 1)	6,300	
		68,200
Factory cost of finished goods produced		184,000
(transferred to trading account)		

TRADING AND PROFIT AND LOSS ACCOUNT
FOR THE YEAR ENDED 31 DECEMBER 19X5

	£	£
Sales		243,000
Less cost of sales		
Finished goods stock at 1 January 19X5	51,000	
Factory cost of finished goods produced	184,000	
	235,000	
Less finished goods stock at 31 December 19X5	52,000	
		183,000
Gross profit		60,000
Less selling and distribution expenses		
Sundry (16,800 − 1,200 prepayments)	15,600	
Depreciation (1/10 × £9,000) - see note 1	900	
Discount allowed	5,400	
Bad debts	1,100	
	23,000	
Administration expenses		
Sundry (16,200 + 600 prepayments b/f + 1,100 accrued c/f)	17,900	
Depreciation (2/10 × £9,000) - see note 1	1,800	
	19,700	
	42,700	
Less discount received	1,700	
		41,000
Net profit for the year		19,000
Retained profit at the beginning of the year		1,000
Retained profit at the end of the year		20,000

Note 1

	Fixed assets at cost £	Net book value £	Accumulated depreciation £
At 31 December 19X4	60,000	39,000	21,000
At 31 December 19X5	90,000	60,000	30,000
Depreciation charge for the year			9,000
Manufacturing share 70%			6,300

60   FACTORY

> *Tutorial note.* The CIMA model answer contains an error in the calculation of the figure for factory power in (a) and hence produces an incorrect final answer for all three parts. There are a lot of simple calculations to do in this question and a careful layout will help you to avoid making errors. Also, the instructions clearly ask for accounts for *each product* as well as in total for parts (a) and (b) (but not for (c)) so take care to follow this requirement.

(a) ABC LIMITED
     MANUFACTURING ACCOUNT
     FOR THE YEAR ENDED 31 OCTOBER 19X3

	Alpha £	Beta £	Total £
Raw materials			
Opening stock			12,987
Purchases			133,759
Carriage inwards			982
Closing stock			(3,728)
Apportionment (1:3)	36,000	108,000	144,000
Direct labour (68,471 + 2,350) (2:1)	47,214	23,607	70,821
Royalties paid	14,500	-	14,500
	97,714	131,607	229,321
Production overheads			
Rent and business rates	4,320	4,320	8,640
Factory power	12,948	12,948	25,896
Salaries	10,360	5,180	15,540
Factory indirect wages	17,862	8,931	26,793
Depreciation - buildings	1,200	1,200	2,400
- equipment	5,593	5,593	11,186
- vehicles	1,524	1,524	3,048
Heat and light	2,735	2,735	5,470
	154,256	174,038	328,294
Work in progress			
Opening stock	7,530	7,938	15,468
Closing stock	(5,820)	(6,187)	(12,007)
Production cost of finished goods	155,966	175,789	331,755

(b) ABC LIMITED
     TRADING ACCOUNT
     FOR THE YEAR ENDED 31 OCTOBER 19X3

	Alpha £	Beta £	Total £
Sales (1:1)	229,935	229,935	459,870
Opening stock	(6,362)	(6,541)	(12,903)
Production cost (per (a))	(155,966)	(175,789)	(331,755)
Closing stock	5,239	4,792	10,031
Gross profit	72,846	52,397	125,243

(c) ABC LIMITED
PROFIT AND LOSS ACCOUNT
FOR THE YEAR ENDED 31 OCTOBER 19X3

	£	£
Gross profit (per (b))		125,243
Rent and business rates (W1)	2,160	
Salaries (W1)	23,310	
Depreciation - buildings (W1)	1,600	
- equipment (W1)	4,794	
- vehicles (W1)	4,572	
Heat and light (W1)	5,470	
Postage and stationery	3,560	
Carriage outwards	1,103	
		(46,569)
		78,674
Discount allowed (W2)	(1,458)	
Discount received (W2)	2,131	
Net discount received		673
		79,347
Debenture interest (£100,000 × 8%)		(8,000)
		71,347
Corporation tax		(24,000)
		47,347
Dividends £(2,500 + 12,500)		(15,000)
Retained profit for the year		32,347

Workings

1

	Alpha £	Factory Beta £	%	Total £	%	Admin Total £	Overall total £
Rent and business rates (1:1)							
(15,800 − 5/6 × 6,000)	4,320	4,320	80	8,640	20	2,160	10,800
Factory power (1:1)							
(22,436 + 3,460)	12,948	12,948	100	25,986	0		25,896
Salaries (2:1)	10,360	5,180	40	15,540	60	23,310	38,850
Factory indirect wages (2:1)	17,862	8,931	100	26,793	0		
Depreciation (1:1)							
Buildings	12,00	1,200	60	2,400	40	1,600	4,000
Equipment	5,593	5,593	70	11,186	30	4,794	15,980
Motor vehicles	1,524	1,524	40	3,048	60	4,572	7,620
Heat and light (1:1)	2,735	2,735	50	5,470	50	5,470	10,940
	56,542	42,431		98,973		41,906	114,086

2 We are not told what type of discounts we are dealing with. The assumption made is that they are *not* trade discounts. They have been grouped together for ease of reallocation if information to the contrary is obtained.

61 MANUFACTURING

Tutorial note. When calculating the increase in provision for doubtful debts in part (b), do not forget that, since the debt is more than six months old and has been written off the company will be entitled to bad debt relief on the VAT. The VAT element of the debt does not, therefore, need to be written off.

(a)   ABC LIMITED
MANUFACTURING ACCOUNT FOR THE YEAR ENDED 31 OCTOBER 19X3

	£'000	£'000	£'000
Opening stock of raw materials		27	
Purchases of raw materials	826		
Less returns outwards	(18)		
		808	
		835	
Less closing stock of raw materials		(24)	
Cost of direct materials used			811
Direct wages (575 + 15)			590
Prime cost			1,401
Factory overheads			
Heat, light and power (50% × 242)		121	
Salaries (20% × (122 + 8))		26	
Rent, rates, insurance 1/3 × (114 – 21)		31	
Depreciation: plant 10% × 350		35	
premises 25% × 2% × 600		3	
			216
Factory cost of goods produced			1,617
Change in work in progress (18 – 19)			(1)
Factory cost transferred to trading and profit and loss account			1,616

(b)   ABC LIMITED
TRADING AND PROFIT AND LOSS ACCOUNT
FOR THE YEAR ENDED 31 OCTOBER 19X3

	£'000	£'000
Sales		2,350
Less returns inwards		(38)
		2,312
Less cost of goods sold		
Opening stock of finished goods	255	
Factory cost of goods transferred	1,616	
	1,871	
Closing stock of finished goods	(147)	
		1,724
Gross profit		588
Less expenses		
Heat, light and power (50% × 242)	121	
Salaries 80% × (122 + 8)	104	
Printing, post and stationery	32	
Rent, rates and insurance 2/3 × (114 – 21)	62	
Depreciation: premises 75% × 2% × 600	9	
equipment 20% × (125 – 35)	18	
Loan interest 250 × 20%	50	
Decrease in doubtful debt provision (W)	(5)	
Bad debt written off	40	
Stock written off (8 – 3)	5	
		436
Net profit before tax		152
Corporation tax		35
		117
Dividends: interim	10	
final 500,000 × 10p	50	
		60
Retained profit for the year		57
Retained profits b/f		442
Retained profits c/f		499

(c)   ABC LIMITED
BALANCE SHEET AS AT 31 OCTOBER 19X3

	Cost £'000	Acc'd depn £'000	NBV £'000
Fixed assets			
Premises	600	207	393
Plant	350	175	175
Office equipment	125	53	72
	1,075	435	640
Current assets			
Stocks			
Raw materials	24		
Work in progress	19		
Finished goods (147 – 5)	142		
		185	
Debtors (287 – 47)	240		
Less provision	(6)		
		234	
Prepayments (17 + 4)		21	
Bank		509	
		949	
Current liabilities			
Creditors	75		
Accruals (W2)	61		
VAT (W3)	19		
Corporation tax	35		
Proposed dividend	50		
Loan repayable in one year	100		
		340	
Net current assets			609
Total assets less current liabilities			1,249
Loan repayable after one year (250 – 100)			150
			1,099
Capital and reserves			
Share capital			500
Share premium account			100
Profit and loss account			499
			1,099

Workings

1   *Decrease in doubtful debt provision*

	£'000
Debtors per trial balance	287
Less bad debt w/o (excl VAT) 47 ÷ 1.175	40
	247
$2^{1}/2$ % × 247	6
Provision b/d	11
∴ Decrease	5

2   *Accruals*

	£'000
Direct wages	15
Salaries	8
Loan interest (50 – 12)	38
	61

3   *VAT creditor*

	£'000
Per trial balance	26
Less bad debt relief	7
	19

62   FPC

Tutorial note. In parts (a) and (b) you were presented with a trial balance and certain adjustments and required to prepare a manufacturing, trading and profit and loss appropriation account for a limited company. Part (c) tested your knowledge of the fundamental accounting concepts when applied to stocks of raw materials, goods on sale or return and provisions for doubtful debts.

Examiner's comment. Some candidates were unable to distinguish properly between items to be entered in the manufacturing account and those to be entered in the trading, profit and loss account. Some candidates included expenses in both accounts 'to be on the safe side'. This is clearly incorrect.

(a)   MANUFACTURING ACCOUNT
FOR THE YEAR ENDED 31 MARCH 19X6

	£	£
Raw materials		
Opening stock	60,000	
Purchases (1,500 – 22 + 15)	1,493,000	
	1,553,000	
Less closing stock	(80,000)	
		1,473,000
Factory wages (600 + 17.5)		617,500
Prime cost		2,090,500
Production overhead		
Rent & rates (120 – 10) × 20%	22,000	
Insurance (100 – 20) × 20%	16,000	
Depreciation: premises (2% × 900) × 25%	4,500	
plant (10% × 150) × 75%	11,250	
Factory supervisors' salaries	150,000	
		203,750
Production cost		2,294,250
Work in progress		
Opening stock	30,000	
Closing stocks	(42,500)	
Increase in WIP stocks		(12,500)
Production cost of finished goods produced		2,281,750

(b) TRADING AND PROFIT AND LOSS APPROPRIATION ACCOUNT
FOR THE YEAR ENDED 31 MARCH 19X6

	£	£
Sales (2,960 – 14 – 35)		2,911,000
Opening stock finished goods	70,000	
Cost of finished goods produced	2,281,750	
	2,351,750	
Less closing stock (100 + 27)	(127,000)	
Cost of goods sold		2,224,750
Gross profit		686,250
Discounts received		2,500
		688,750
Expenses		
Carriage outwards	10,000	
Discounts allowed	4,000	
Rent & rates (120 – 10) × 80%	88,000	
Insurance (100 – 20) × 80%	64,000	
Office wages and salaries	175,000	
Sales officers' commission (2,911 × 5%)	145,550	
Administration expense $(45 - (9.4 \times \frac{17.5}{117.5}))$	43,600	
Depreciation: premises (900 × 2%) × 75%	13,500	
plant (150 × 10%) × 25%	3,750	
Bad debts written off	6,500	
Provision doubtful debts (220 – 35) × 5% – 7	2,250	
Debenture interest (200 × 10%) × 6/12	10,000	
		566,150
Net profit before taxation		122,600
Corporation tax		22,000
Net profit after taxation		100,600
Appropriations		
Dividend - ordinary final (750 × 3p)		22,500
Retained profit for the year		78,100
Retained profit brought forward		98,000
Retained profit carried forward		176,100

Notes and assumptions

1   Goods on sale or return have been taken out of the trading account for the year ended 31 March 19X6. This is because acceptance of the goods and hence the sale will not take place until 15 April 19X6. Therefore sales and debtors will be reduced by £35,000 (this will also affect the provision for doubtful debts) and closing stock in the profit and loss account will be increased by £27,000.

2   Discounts have been assumed to be settlement discounts.

(c) (i)   The consistency concept requires that:

(1)   similar items within a set of financial statements should be given similar accounting treatment;

(2)   the same treatment should be applied from one period to another in accounting for similar items.

This means that for stocks of raw materials all items should be valued on a similar basis (eg FIFO) and in addition the method of valuing raw materials should be consistent from one accounting period to another.

(ii)   The matching concept requires that expense must be matched to the revenue to which it relates. The realisation concept states that profits should only be recognised when they have been realised.

Hence in the case of goods on sale or return, the sale of these goods (and the profit arising) should only be recognised when the goods have been accepted (ie on 15 April 19X6). Similarly the cost of these goods sold would be recognised at the same time. Hence at the year end the sale is not recognised and these goods are included in stock.

(iii) The prudence concept states that where a loss is foreseen it should be provided for immediately. Thus, where the collection of some debtors' balance is considered to be doubtful, a provision should be made for any amount not expected to be received.

63 TUTORIAL QUESTION: RATIOS AND CASH FLOWS

(a)

			19X0	*19X1*
(i)	ROOE		$\frac{15}{75} = 20\%$	$\frac{5}{80} = 0.25\%$
(ii)	ROCE		$\frac{15}{75} = 20\%$	$\frac{5}{80+60} = 3.5\%$
(iii)	Current ratio		$\frac{85}{90} = 0.94{:}1$	$\frac{100}{80} = 1.25{:}1$
(iv)	Gearing ratio	$\frac{\text{Debt}}{\text{Equity}}$	N/A	$\frac{60}{80} = 0.75{:}1$
	or	$\frac{\text{Debt}}{\text{Capital employed}}$	N/A	$\frac{60}{140} = 42.8{:}1$
(v)	Debtors turnover		$\frac{50 \times 365}{500}$ $= 36.5$ days	$\frac{60 \times 365}{700}$ $= 31.2$ days

(vi) Stock turnover

Firstly we must calculate the cost of sales. We are told that gross profit on sales is 30%.

ie
Sales		100
less gross profit		30
Cost of sales		70

∴ Cost of sales

	19X0	*19X1*
	$500 \times 0.7 = 350$	$700 \times 0.7 = 490$
∴ Stock turnover	$\frac{30 \times 365}{350}$	$\frac{30 \times 365}{490}$
	31.2 days	22.3 days

Comment

Clearly something has gone disastrously wrong with Dozy's business, or there is something very unusual about the figures he has provided. The decline in ROCE from 20% to 6.25% might be the result of a devastating increase in inefficiency: on the other hand, Dozy might have been using very old fixed assets, whose reported value might not have been adjusted to reflect inflation, thus artificially inflating ROCE.

In other aspects, Dozy's business appears to be doing quite well. Sales are up by 40%, and the gross profit margin has been retained at 30%. Moreover Dozy appears to be managing his *current assets* efficiently. He is more liquid: current assets in 19X1 exceed current liabilities, his credit control has improved (reducing the debtors collection period by four days). Alternatively, Dozy might have been carrying a bad debt, with no provision, which he has now written off. It is indisputable that he is keeping good control over stock - unless he was carrying obsolete stock which he has now written off.

Some explanation must be available to account for the decline in net profit from £15,000 to £5,000. Dozy is paying from £6,000 a year in interest which might account for a lot of the decrease. Also there is an increased depreciation charge by £10,000 a year.

Clearly, Dozy is going through a difficult patch. However, if his sales continue increasing, he hopefully will be able to generate enough cash to pay back the loan with interest and improve his overall profitability.

(b)   (i)   The aim of a cash flow statement should be to assist users:

(1)   to assess the enterprise's ability to generate positive net cash flows in the future;

(2)   to assess its ability to meet its obligations to service loans, pay dividends etc;

(3)   to assess the reasons for difference between reported profit and related cash flows;

(4)   to assess the effect on its finances of major transactions in the year.

The statement therefore shows changes in cash and cash equivalents rather than working capital, cash equivalents being highly liquid short-term investments. The opening and closing figures given for cash will be those shown in the balance sheet. Receipts and payments should not be netted off. A reconciliation of net income to cash flow from operating activities must be given.

(ii)   The statement should classify cash receipts and payments as resulting from investing, financing or operating activities. Examples of each are:

(1)   investing in or making loans, acquiring or disposing of fixed assets;

(2)   financing by borrowing or repaying money, making an issue of shares, paying dividends;

(3)   operating receipts from customers, payments to employees and suppliers, any other cash flows from transactions not classified as investing or financing.

The format laid down by FRS 1 (revised) in *simplified form* is as follows.

CASH FLOW STATEMENT

	£
Net cash inflow (or outflow) from operating activities	X
Net cash inflow (or outflow) from returns on investments and servicing of finance	X
(eg interest received or paid)	X
Tax paid	X
Capital expenditure (eg fixed assets, sold or purchased)	X
Equity dividends paid	X
Management of liquid resources (eg purchase or sale of treasury bills)	X
Financing (eg shares issued)	X
Increase (or decrease) in cash	X

64   VICTOR

> *Tutorial note.* It is not a requirement of the CIMA *Financial accounting fundamentals* exam that you follow the FRS 1 (revised) format entirely, but observing the logical divisions of the format will help structure your answer.

VICTOR PLC
CASH FLOW STATEMENT FOR THE YEAR ENDED 31 DECEMBER 19X7

	£'000	£'000
Operating activities		
Cash received from customers (670 + 60 – 64)	666	
Cash paid to suppliers (323 + (100 – 76) + 99 – 79)	(367)	
Wages paid (112 + 5 – 6)	(111)	
Expenses paid (27 + 9 – 6 + 5)	(18)	
Corporation tax paid	(60)	
Cash flow from operating activities		110
Interest paid		(35)
		75
Capital expenditure		
Land bought (230 – 140)	(90)	
Buildings bought (258 – 168)	(90)	
Motor vehicles bought	(69)	
Motor vehicles sold (42 – 27 + 7)	22	
		(227)
Equity dividends paid		(30)
		(257)
Financing		
Shares issued (60 +48)	108	
Debentures issued	40	
Cash flow from financing activities		148
Net decrease in cash		(34)
Cash as at 1 January 19X7		10
Overdraft as at 31 December 19X7		(24)

65   GH

> *Tutorial note.* You should start off with the reconciliation of operating profit to net cash inflow from operating activities. This appears as the first part of the cash flow statement under the revised FRS 1. (You do not have to know FRS 1, but its logical structure makes it an easy format to remember.)
>
> *Examiner's comment.* This was the less popular of the two optional questions on the paper, but was well answered. Answers to part (b) were rather brief. Note that there are six marks for this part of the question, so a list is not sufficient.

(a)   GH
CASH FLOW STATEMENT FOR THE YEAR ENDED 30 APRIL 19X5

Reconciliation of net profit to net cash inflow from operating activities

	£'000
Net profit	92
Depreciation (W1)	13
Loss on sale of fixed assets	6
Increase in stocks	(4)
Increase in debtors	(1.5)
Decrease in creditors	(7)
Net cash inflow from operating activities	98.5

CASH FLOW STATEMENT

	£'000	£'000
Net cash inflow from operating activities		98.5
Investing activities		
Payments to acquire tangible fixed assets	(120)	
Receipts from sales of tangible fixed assets	30	
Net cash outflow from investing activities		(90.0)
Net cash inflow before financing		8.5
Financing		
Capital introduced	20	
Drawings	(30)	
Long-term liabilities repaid	(40)	
Net cash outflow from financing		(50.0)
Decrease in cash		(41.5)

Assumptions

(i)   There is no tax paid
(ii) There is no interest received/paid

Working: deprecation charge

	£'000
NBV fixed assets at 1.5.X4	206
Disposals (48 – 12)	(36)
Purchases	120
	290
Closing balance	(277)
Charge for depreciation	13

(b)   The accounting information requirements of different user groups are as follows. (Note that only *four* are required by the question.)

(i)   *Managers of the organisation*, appointed by the owners to supervise the day-to-day activities. They need information about the organisation's current financial situation and what it is expected to be in the future. This enables them to manage the business efficiently and to take effective control of planning decisions.

(ii)   *Owners of the organisation* who will want to assess how effectively management is performing its stewardship function. They will want to know how profitably management is running the organisation's operations and how much profit they can afford to withdraw from the business for their own use.

(iii)   *Providers of finance* to the organisation, for example a bank granting an overdraft facility or a loan. They will want to ensure that the organisation is able to keep up with interest payments and eventually to repay the amounts advanced.

(iv)   The *Inland Revenue* who will want to know about business profits in order to assess the tax payable by the company.

(v)   *Investment analysts* will be interested in profitability and growth, and also the level of dividends.

(vi)   *Creditors* of a business will be very interested in liquidity since they will want to be paid. This is of more immediate concern to them than whether the firm is profitable.

66   SH LTD

> *Tutorial note*. You do not need to know the FRS 1 format for Paper 1, but if you follow the logical structure it will help. FRS 1 was revised in October 19X6. The new format is examinable from November 1997, and examples can be found in the body of the Kit for those taking the exam then.

(a)   SH LIMITED
CASH FLOW STATEMENT FOR THE YEAR ENDED 30 JUNE 19X6

Reconciliation of operating profit to net cash outflow from operating activities.

	£'000
Operating profit	250
Add back: depreciation	255
loss on disposals (W)	30
	535
Increase in stocks	(350)
Decrease in debtors	135
Decrease in creditors	(650)
Net cash outflow from operating activities	(330)

CASH FLOW STATEMENT

	£	£
Net cash outflow from operating activities		(330)
Capital expenditure		
Payments to acquire fixed assets (W)	(730)	
Proceeds from sale of fixed assets	145	
Net outflow from investing activities		(585)
		(915)
Dividends paid		(75)
Financing		
Issue of ordinary share capital		800
Decrease in cash		(190)

Working

Fixed assets

	£'000
Cost	
At 1.7.X5	3,000
Disposals during year	(230)
	2,770
Additions (balancing figure)	730
At 30.6.X6	3,500

	£
Accumulated depreciation	
At 1.7.X5	2,100
Charge for year	255
	2,355
Less balance at 30.6.X6	2,300
Relating to disposals	55

	£
Profit/loss on disposals	
Cost	230
Accounting depreciation	(55)
Net book value	175
Proceeds	145
Loss on disposal	30

(b)   The cash flow statement for the year ended 30 June 19X6 shows a decrease in cash over the year of £190,000. This may indicate a problem with liquidity. However, the cash flow statement may be misleading as it shows cash inflows and outflows on long-term and capital items as well as current items. Hence a more useful measure of liquidity is the current ratio which measures current assets against current liabilities.

Whilst there is no fixed acceptable level, a ratio of at least one is considered desirable.

The current ratios for 19X5 and 19X6 are 1.65 and 1.90 respectively. Both are greater than one and there is a significant improvement in 19X6.

Another liquidity ratio which is often considered a better measure (because it excludes stocks which are not so readily converted into cash) is the quick ratio. Again SH Ltd has a quick ratio for both years greater than one and 19X6 shows a ratio of 1.63 as compared to 1.49 for 19X5. Both the current and quick ratios therefore indicate that SH Ltd should not have any liquidity problems; in other words it will be able to meet its liabilities as and when they arise.

Calculations

			19X5	19X6
Current ratio	$\dfrac{\text{Current assets}}{\text{Current liabilities}}$	=	$\dfrac{8,375}{5,075}$	$\dfrac{8,400}{4,430}$
			= 1.65	= 1.90
Quick ratio	$\dfrac{\text{Current assets} - \text{stock}}{\text{Current liabilities}}$	=	$\dfrac{8,375 - 825}{5,075}$	$\dfrac{8,400 - 1,175}{4,430}$
			= 1.49	= 1.63

67   CONTROLS

> *Tutorial note.* A general overview of types of control is all that is expected at this level. In particular, the examiner has stated that details of audit procedures are not required to be known.

(a)   The following controls should prevent errors or fraud in the operation of the purchase ledger.

   (i)   Cheques should only be signed by an appropriate authorised official.

   (ii)   There should be adequate segregation of duties. For example authorisation of payments should not be carried out by the person responsible for recording the payment.

   (iii)   Invoices from suppliers should be checked against goods received notes before paying them.

   (iv)   Invoices should be matched up with order forms to ensure the order is valid.

   (v)   Creditors reconciliations should be carried out where statements are received from creditors.

   (vi)   A possible fraud might involve collusion with a third party, ie a 'creditor' sends a fictitious invoice or overcharges on a genuine one. Management must watch out for unusual transactions or excessive zeal on the part of an employee to deal with one particular company. Periodic 'surprise' visits by the internal auditors should be an effective deterrent.

(b)   The purposes of internal controls were outlined by the old Auditing Practices Committee (forerunner of the Auditing Practices Board) as being:

   (i)   to carry on the business in an orderly and efficient manner;
   (ii)   to ensure adherence to management policies;
   (iii)   to safeguard the assets; and
   (iv)   to secure, as far as possible the completeness and accuracy of the records.

Eight types of control have been identified:

   (i)   segregation of duties
   (ii)   physical
   (iii)   management
   (iv)   supervision
   (v)   authorisation and approval

(vi)   organisation

(vii) arithmetical and accounting (eg reconciliation)

(viii) personnel.

Of the above, (i), (iii), (v) and (vii) have been discussed in part (a). *Physical* controls involve such matters as custody of assets and security. *Supervision* is self-explanatory: the supervision of day-to-day transactions is required, and of the recording of those transactions. *Organisation* control means that a business should have clear lines of authority and responsibility. *Personnel* control means controls over the selection of staff. This includes questions of honesty (eg references should be taken up) and competence (a company accountant should be suitably qualified).

To summarise, accounting controls are required in order to:

(i)   prevent errors from happening; and

(ii)   detect errors if they do happen.

68 EXTERNAL AND INTERNAL AUDIT

> *Tutorial note.* It is important to address part (a) directly, not just to talk in general terms about the difference between internal and external audit.
>
> *Examiner's comment.* Many of the suggestions raised in part (b) were trivial, for example, showing the external audit staff round the office.

(a)   External audit is a statutory requirement whereby approved auditors independent of the company are appointed by the members of the company to report to them as to whether the annual financial statements have been properly prepared as required by statute and show a true and fair view.

In order to comply with this requirement the external auditors carry out an examination of the accounting systems and records of the company so as to allow them to express an opinion. As a result of their work they may identify matters which need to be brought to the attention of the management but this is not their primary role.

In contrast, internal auditors are employees of the company who report directly to management The scope and extent of their work is determined by management and may cover some or all of the following areas.

(i)   Review of accounting systems and related internal controls.

(ii)   Examination of financial and operating information for management, including detailed testing of transactions and balances.

(iii)   Review of the economy, efficiency and effectiveness of operations and of the functioning of non-financial controls.

(iv)   Review of the implementation of corporate policies, plans and procedures.

(v)   Special investigations.

Because the internal audit function addresses management concerns and investigates and reports to them on these concerns, they will be perceived as being far more useful than external auditors whose work is determined by the need to satisfy statutory requirements.

(b)   Assuming that the external auditor is satisfied with the qualifications and experience of the internal auditor such that he is prepared to place reliance on to the internal auditor's work, their are a number of ways that the internal audit department can assist the external auditor. Examples of these are as follows.

(i)   At an early stage in the financial period discussions can be held between the two parties to decide upon a joint approach which will enable both to restrict their tests to a minimum comparable with their individual responsibilities and to ensure that all important audit areas are covered.

(ii)   Showing of important procedures such as attendance at stock counts, particularly in companies with a number of branches.

(iii) Work performed and information produced by the internal auditor can be used by the external auditor and will prevent duplication of effort and extra time eg debtors circularisation assets verification.

(iv) The internal auditor's intimate knowledge of the company may be of assistance to the external auditor and the latter may be able to rely to a large extent on the internal auditor to monitor the continuous operation of the system of internal control.

69   GTZ

> *Tutorial note.* Part (a) tested your appreciation of accounting controls. Part (b) required you to prepare stock records. Layout is important here.
>
> *Examiner's comment.* Part (a) was not well answered because comments were too general. Part (b) was generally well answered except that some candidates could not deal with the 50% mark up. Part (c) presented no problems.

(a) (i) Reconciliation of suppliers' statements with individual creditors accounts on a regular basis (eg monthly) with investigation and resolution of any differences

Recording of all purchase invoices in a purchase day book immediately on receipt

Assignment of a sequential reference number to purchase invoices

(ii) Issue of monthly debtors statements to allow them to check the balance

Use of a sales day book to record invoices and credit notes issued

Segregation of duties between accounts clerks

Regular reconciliation of the debtors control account

(iii) Regular bank account reconciliations which would highlight a returned cheque

Regular reconciliation of the debtors control account will highlight a difference

(iv) Refunds should be authorised, as should all petty cash payments

Petty cash vouchers should only be authorised if a receipt/invoice is available to substantiate them

Regular bank account reconciliation

Regular reconciliation of the debtors control account

(b) FIFO

Date	Units movement	Total units	Unit cost £	Value movement £	Total value £
1/4	100	100	10	1,000	1,000
8/4 $(360 \times 2/3) \times 1/£10$	(24)	76	10	(240)	760
18/4	38	114	12	456	1,216
20/4	(50)	64	10	(500)	716
23/4	(35)	29	$26 \times £10$ $9 \times £12$	(368)	348
28/4	20	49	13	260	608

49 units with total cost of £608

AVCO

Date	Units movement	Total units	Unit cost £	Value movement £	Total value £
¼	100	100	10	1,000	1,000
8/4	(24)	76	10	(240)	760
18/4	38	114	12	456	1,216
20/4	(50)	64	10.67	(533)	683
23/4	(35)	29	10.67	(373)	310
28/4	20	49	11.63	260	570

49 units with total cost of £570

(c) The following may be reasons for the discrepancy

(i) Error on physical count
(ii) Inaccurate recording of movements on the stock card

70 TUTORIAL QUESTION: RATIOS

Tutorial note. Although the question requires only two ratios to be calculated under each heading, for the benefit of students additional ratios are shown in the suggested solution below.

(a) Ratios which would be of interest to *shareholders* include the following.

		19X6	19X7
Earnings per share			
$\dfrac{\text{Profit after tax}}{\text{Number of shares}}$		$\dfrac{9,520}{39,680}$	$\dfrac{11,660}{39,680}$
	=	24p	29p
ROCE			
$\dfrac{\text{Profit before interest and tax}}{\text{Capital employed}}$	=	$\dfrac{17,238}{60,580}$	$\dfrac{20,670}{69,840}$
	=	28.5%	29.6%
ROSC			
$\dfrac{\text{Profit before tax}}{\text{Shareholders' funds}}$	=	$\dfrac{15,254}{40,740}$	$\dfrac{18,686}{50,000}$
	=	37.4%	37.4%
Dividend cover			
$\dfrac{\text{Profit after tax}}{\text{Dividend payable}}$	=	$\dfrac{9,520}{2,240}$	$\dfrac{11,660}{2,400}$
	=	4.25	4.86

(b) Ratios relevant to *trade creditors* include the following.

		19X6	19X7
Current ratio			
$\dfrac{\text{Current assets}}{\text{Current liabilities}}$	=	$\dfrac{92,447}{36,862}$	$\dfrac{99,615}{42,275}$
	=	2.5	2.4
Acid test ratio			
$\dfrac{\text{Current assets - stock}}{\text{Current liabilities}}$	=	$\dfrac{92,447 - 40,145}{36,862}$	$\dfrac{99,615 - 50,455}{42,475}$
	=	1.42	1.16

(c) Ratios relevant to *internal management* include the following.

Stock turnover (Assuming year end stock equates to average level)

		19X6	*19X7*
$\dfrac{\text{Sales}}{\text{Average stock}}$	=	$\dfrac{486,300}{40,195}$	$\dfrac{583,900}{50,455}$
	=	12 times	11.6 times

Debtors collection period (assuming all sales are credit)

		19X6	*19X7*
$\dfrac{\text{Debtors} \times 365}{\text{Sales}}$	=	$\dfrac{40,210 \times 365}{486,300}$	$\dfrac{43,370 \times 365}{583,900}$
	=	30.2 days	27.1 days

Gearing

$\dfrac{\text{Long - term debt}}{\text{Long - term debt} + \text{equity}}$	=	$\dfrac{19,840}{40,740 + 19,840}$	$\dfrac{19,840}{50,000 + 19,840}$
	=	32.7%	28.4%

71 ARH

Tutorial note. This question required an understanding of the difference between profit and cash flow, as well as the ability to calculate ratios and interpret them.

Examiner's comment. Some candidates confused their answers to parts (a) and (b). Markers were instructed to award marks where candidates had included relevant calculations and comments.

(a)

				19X4	*19X5*
Gross profit %	=	$\dfrac{\text{Gross profit}}{\text{Sales}} \times 100\%$		$\dfrac{2,600}{14,400} = 18\%$	$\dfrac{4,400}{17,000} = 26\%$
Net profit %	=	$\dfrac{\text{Net profit}}{\text{Sales}} \times 100\%$		$\dfrac{1,400}{14,400} = 10\%$	$\dfrac{2,400}{17,000} = 14\%$

Return on capital employed

			19X4	*19X5*
	=	$\dfrac{\text{Profit}}{\text{Capital employed}}$	$\dfrac{1,400}{6,700} = 21\%$	$\dfrac{2,400}{5,720} = 42\%$

(Total assets less current liabilities)

(b) The profitability for 19X5 as demonstrated by the above ratios is much improved on 19X4. Gross profit is up 8% and return on capital employed has doubled. However, net profit has only increased by 4% indicating that administrative costs must be increasing out of proportion to the increase in sales, particularly given the fact that debenture interest costs are no longer included.

However, despite this improved profitability the bank balances have reduced.

Liquidity ratios

		19X4	*19X5*
Current ratio			
$\dfrac{\text{Current assets}}{\text{Current liabilities}}$		$\dfrac{5,700}{1,500} = 3.8$	$\dfrac{4,420}{2,700} = 1.6$
Quick ratio			
$\dfrac{\text{Current assets less stock}}{\text{Current liabilities}}$		$\dfrac{5,700 - 1,300}{1,500} = 2.9$	$\dfrac{4,420 - 2,000}{2,700} = 0.9$

Liquidity ratios demonstrate a marked reduction in liquidity from 19X4 to 19X5. This is highlighted by the quick ratio which has fallen from nearly 3 in 19X4 to less than 1 in 19X5.

The reasons for this decrease may be as follows.

(i)   A fall in the bank balance due to repayment of the 10% debenture

(ii)   An increase in creditors. This may be due to the increases in stock holdings and expenses and the company taking longer to pay because of liquidity problems

(iii) A fall in debtors despite an increase in sales, indicating a more rigorous collection policy, again to maximise liquidity

(iv)   Acquisitions of fixed assets, funded from operating activities

(c)   Reserves are part of the ordinary shareholders' equity in a company. They are distinct from the share capital and comprise:

(i)   amounts that the company is required to set aside by law and which are not available for distribution as dividends. These are termed statutory reserves;

(ii)   amounts arising from profits which have not yet been distributed to shareholders as dividends but which are available to do so.

The revaluation reserve in ARH plc probably arose from the revaluation of the company's fixed assets, particularly property. The excess of valuation over cost is required to be taken to a revaluation reserve. Depreciation of the revalued proportion of the asset may then be charged against this reserve via the profit and loss account.

72   JK

> *Tutorial note*. Do not neglect part (b), the discussion part. It is worth 3/5 of the available marks.

(a) (i)   *Net profit percentage*

$$\frac{\text{Net profit}}{\text{Sales}} = \frac{30,560}{385,200} \times 100\% = 7.93\%$$

(ii)   *Return on capital employed*

$$\frac{\text{Net profit}}{\text{Average capital employed}} = \frac{30,560}{206,152.5} = 14.82\%$$

Note. This is the method the examiner says she wants you to use (CIMA *Guidance Notes*). Average capital employed can be calculated very easily as you are given the opening capital figure. If you are not given this you can calculate it by subtracting the profit for the year from the closing capital.

ROCE may also be calculated as:

$$\frac{\text{Net profit}}{\text{Closing capital employed}} = \frac{30,560}{215,230} = 14.2\%$$

(iii) *Current ratio*

$$\frac{\text{Current assets}}{\text{Current liabilities}} = \frac{130,575}{62,385} = 2.09$$

(iv)   *Quick (acid test) ratio*

$$\frac{\text{Current assets} - \text{stocks}}{\text{Current liabilities}} = \frac{130,575 - 84,630}{62,385} = 0.74$$

(b) (i)   *Depreciation policy*

The use of the reducing balance method of calculating depreciation accords better with the *accruals or matching concept* than the straight line method, particularly for assets such as vehicles or machinery. This is because such items lose more value in earlier years. However, the *change* in depreciation policy conflicts with the *consistency concept* which states that items should be treated in the same way from year to year.

Both ROCE and net profit percentage would reduce as a result of the change, because profit would be reduced as a consequence of the increased depreciation charge.

(ii) *Debtors*

The *prudence* concept requires that provision be made for any loss which is foreseen. Doubtful debts should therefore be provided for.

As a result of the business's failure to follow the prudence concept, profit is overstated by the amount of the bad debts not provided for. It follows that the ratios for net profit and ROCE are also overstated.

Because debtors are overstated, both the current and quick ratios are overstated.

(iii) *Accrued expenses*

The *accruals concept* states that, in computing profit, revenue earned should be matched against the expenditure incurred in earning it. Such expenditure must be taken into account as it is incurred not as it is paid.

The business has not complied with this concept; the expenses for which invoices have not been received should be accrued for in the accounts. Failure to do so means that:

(1) profit (hence net profit ratio and ROCE) is overstated;
(2) liabilities are understated, so the liquidity ratios are overstated.

73 MBC

> *Tutorial note.* In part (b) it is important to show your workings for the ROCE calculation as it is not altogether straightforward. You need to go back to first principles.
>
> *Examiner's comment.* In parts (a) and (b) the formula was usually clearly and accurately stated but the calculations were often incorrect. Part (c) produced some good attempts.

(a) Gearing $= \dfrac{\text{Prior charge capital}}{\text{Total capital}} \times 100\%$

$= \dfrac{10}{48} \times 100\%$

$= 20.8\%$

(b) ROCE $= \dfrac{\text{Profit before interest and tax}}{\text{Average capital employed}} \times 100\%$

$= \dfrac{5.6 \ (\text{W1})}{46.25 \ (\text{W2})} \times 100\%$

$= 12.1\%$

Workings

1 *Profit before interest and tax*

	£m
Profit before interest and tax (bal. fig.)	5.6
Interest (10 × 6%)	0.6
Tax	1.0
Profit after tax	4.0

2 *Average capital employed*

	£m
Capital at end of year	48.0
Returned profit (4 – 0.5)	3.5
Capital at start of year	44.5

$\therefore$ Average capital employed $= \dfrac{48 + 44.5}{2} = £46.25\text{m}$

(c) (i) *Gearing*

If £10m is raised by the issue of shares the effect on the gearing ratio will be to reduce it. This is because the total capital will increase but the amount of prior charge capital will not.

ie $\dfrac{10}{58} \times 100\% = 17.2\%$

However, if the capital is raised by the issue of debentures, the effect on the gearing ratio will be to increase it. This is because whilst the total amount of capital will increase, the amount of prior charge capital will increase proportionately more.

ie $\dfrac{20}{58} \times 100\% = 34.5\%$

(ii) *ROCE*

However the £10m of new capital is raised, the effect on the average capital employed would be the same.

Average capital employed $= \dfrac{48 + 58}{2} = 53$

If debentures were issued additional interest would be payable. However this would have no effect on ROCE as profit is taken before charges for interest and tax. Therefore ROCE would be reduced to the same extent as if equity were raised.

ie $\dfrac{5.6}{53} \times 100\% = 10.6\%$

(d) The different types of research and development are as follows.

(i) *Pure research:* experimental or theoretical work undertaken primarily to acquire new scientific or technical knowledge for its own sake rather than directed towards any specific aim or application.

(ii) *Applied research:* original or critical investigation undertaken in order to gain how scientific or technical knowledge and directed towards a specific practical aim or objective.

(iii) *Development:* use of scientific or technical knowledge in order to produce new or substantially improved materials, devices, products or services, or install new processes or systems prior to the commencement of commercial production or commercial applications, or to improving substantially those already produced or installed.

The accounting standard SSAP 13 *Accounting for research and development* requires that expenditure on pure and applied research should be written off to profit and loss as it is incurred. This involves the operation of the prudence concept.

Development expenditure may be carried forward in line with the matching concept to the extent that its recovery can reasonably be assured.

74   R LTD

(a) *Appropriation accounts*

	19X4	19X5	19X6
	£'000	£'000	£'000
Net profit after tax	32	41	8
Dividends proposed	(5)	(10)	(10)
Transfer to general reserve	—	(18)	—
Profit/(loss) retained for the year	27	13	(2)

(b) *Capital section of balance sheets*

	19X4 £'000	19X5 £'000	19X6 £'000
Share capital	100	100	100
Share premium	60	60	60
General reserve	-	18	18
Profit and loss account	27	40	38
	187	218	216

(c) (i) *Debtors' collection period*

$$\frac{\text{Debtors}}{\text{Credit sales}} \times 365$$

19X4	19X5	19X6
$\frac{40}{360} \times 365$	$\frac{45}{375} \times 365$	$\frac{52}{390} \times 365$
41 days	44 days	49 days

(ii) *Creditors' payment period*

$$\frac{\text{Creditors}}{\text{Credit purchases}} \times 365$$

19X4	19X5	19X6
$\frac{(33-5)}{230} \times 365$	$\frac{(45-5-10)}{250} \times 365$	$\frac{(43-6-10)}{280} \times 365$
44 days	44 days	35 days

(iii) The above results indicate that R Ltd have gradually allowed their customers extended periods of credit. The collection period over the three years has increased from 40 to 49 days.

Creditor payments periods, whilst being maintained at 44 days for 19X4 and 19X5, have fallen to 35 days in 19X6.

This means that the company is paying its suppliers more quickly than it receives payment from its customers. This will increase the level of overdraft required as the company needs to finance payments to creditors for an additional 14 days before monies are received from debtors. Ideally, to minimise overdraft requirements, the two periods should be the same length or preferably the creditors' payment period should be slightly longer than the debtors' collection period.

75 MULTIPLE CHOICE QUESTIONS: SELECTION 1

1 C

	Total £	Ordinary sales £	Private drawings £
Cost of sales	144,000	142,200	1,800
Mark-up:			
12% on cost	216	-	216
20% on sales (= 25% on cost)	35,550	35,550	
Sales	179,766	177,750	2,016

2 B

	Total £	Sales in first three quarters (9/15) £	Sales in final quarter (6/15) £
Sales	210,000	126,000	84,000
Mark-up:			
25% on cost (= 20% on sales)	16,800		16,800
20% on cost (=16$\frac{1}{2}$ % on sales)	21,000	21,000	
	37,800		

3 A We need to calculate credit sales first in order to calculate cash sales.

DEBTORS

	£		£
Bal b/f	2,100	Bank	24,290
∴ Credit sales	23,065	Bal c/f	875
	25,165		25,165

CASH

	£		£
Balance b/f	240	Expenses	1,850
Cash sales		Bank	9,300
(41,250 – 23,065)	18,185	∴ Theft	7,275
	18,425		18,425

4 D

	£	£
Subscriptions received in 19X5		790
Less: amounts relating to 19X4	38	
amounts relating to 19X6	80	
		118
Cash received relating to 19X5		672
Add: subs paid in 19X4 relating to 19X5	72	
19X5 subs still to be paid	48	
		120
		792

Alternatively, in ledger account format:

SUBSCRIPTIONS

	£		£
Balance b/f	38	Balance b/f	72
∴ Income and expenditure a/c	792	Cash	790
Balance c/f	80	Balance c/f	48
	910		910

5 B

	£
Subscriptions received in 19X5	1,024
Less amounts relating to 19X6	58
	966
Add subs paid in 19X4 relating to 19X5	14
	980

Alternatively, in ledger account format:

SUBSCRIPTIONS

	£		£
∴ Income and expenditure a/c	980	Balance b/f	14
Balance c/f	58	Bank	1,024
	1,038		1,038

6 B

	£	£
Balance at 1 January		3,780
New enrolments		480
		4,260
Less release to income:		
1 × £80	80	
63 × £5	315	
4 × £6	24	
		419
		3,841

7 A

8 A

9 D

			£'000
10	C		
		Turnover (£1m + £10,000 – £20,000)	990
		Cost of sales (£800,000 – £20,000)	780
		Gross profit	210

$$\text{Gross profit margin} = \frac{210}{990} \times 100\% = 21.2\%$$

76   MULTIPLE CHOICE QUESTIONS: SELECTION 2

1   D

2   C

3   C

4   B

5   D

6   A   Transaction (a) would have no effect on working capital.

7   C   (£1,200,000 ÷ 800,000)

8   A

9   B

10   B

11   D

12   B

13   D

14   D   In the other three cases only balance sheet accounts are affected and there is an equal and opposite debit and credit.

15   D

77   MULTIPLE CHOICE QUESTIONS: SELECTION 3

> *Tutorial note.* The examiner commented that candidates scored well in this set of multiple choice questions with several scoring full marks. However, some questions caused more difficulty than others, in particular questions 4, 6, 8 and 15.

1   B

2   D

3   A

4   C

5   D   Debits will exceed credits by 2 × £48 = £96

6   A

	£	£
Raw materials		
Opening stock	10,000	
Purchases	50,000	
Closing stock	11,000	
Cost of raw materials		49,000
Direct wages		40,000
Prime cost		89,000
Production overheads		60,000
		149,000
Increase in work in progress		
4,000 – 2,000		(2,000)
Cost of goods manufactured		147,000

7   C   Trade discounts are not included in the cost of purchases.

8   B

9   C   Sales less returns inward. Discounts allowed are a deduction from gross profit.

10   C

11   D   Accumulated fund = net assets

12   D $£350 \times \dfrac{100}{140} = £250$

13   A

14   C   Closing stock = 20 units @ £3 each = £60

15   B   Stock turnover $= \dfrac{\text{Cost of sales}}{\text{Average stock}}$

Cost of sales $= 12 + 80 - 10 = 82$

Average stock $= \dfrac{12 + 10}{2} = 11$

∴ Stock turnover $= \dfrac{82}{11} = 7.45$ times

78   MULTIPLE CHOICE QUESTIONS: SELECTION 4

> *Tutorial note.* The examiner said that there was a wide spread of marks on this question with poorer candidates getting fewer than five questions correct. Very few obtained full marks.

1   A

2   D

Balance b/d	5,675 o/d
Less standing order	(125)
Add dishonoured cheque (450 × 2)	900
	6,450 o/d

3   A

4   C

		£
Sales (10,000 × 220% × 50%)		11,000
Opening stock	-	
Purchases	10,000	
	10,000	
Closing stock	(5,000)	
Cost of goods sold		5,000
Gross profit		6,000
Less discount (5% × 11,000)		550
Net profit		5,450

5   C

6   D

	£
Balance b/d	67,460
Less NBV of fixed asset sold	
15,000 – (15,000 – (4,000 + 1,250))	5,250
	62,210

7   A

8   C

9   B

10	D	CREDITORS CONTROL ACCOUNT				
			£		£
		Bank	542,300	Balance b/d	142,600
		Discounts	13,200	∴ Purchases	578,200
		Returns	27,500		
		Balance c/d	137,800		
			720,800		720,800

11	B
12	D
13	D
14	C
15	B

79   MULTIPLE CHOICE QUESTIONS: SELECTION 5

Tutorial note. Questions 4, 8 and 12 are the trickiest. Remember, difficult MCQs are worth the same number of marks as easy ones.

Examiner's comment. Candidates performed less well on this selection than in previous examinations, although there were no individual questions which were consistently answered wrongly.

1	B

2	D

3   C   Assets less liabilities = opening capital plus profits less drawings

∴ Assets less liabilities less opening capital plus drawings = profit

4   B   The cost to the business consists of gross wages plus employees' NI

5   A   If disposal proceeds were £15,000 and profit on disposal is £5,000, then net book value must be £10,000, the difference between the fixed asset register figure and the fixed asset account in the nominal ledger.

6	B

7	C

8	C

9	A

10	B

11	D

12   B

	£
Subscriptions received	12,500
Add subscriptions in arrears c/f	250
	12,750
Deduct: subscriptions in arrears b/f	800
subscriptions in advance c/f	400
	11,550

13	C		£
		Opening stock	165
		Purchases (1,350 – 80 + 70)	1,340
			1,505
		Closing stock	140
		Stationery in P&L	1,365

14 A

15 D

80 MULTIPLE CHOICE QUESTIONS: SELECTION 6

1 D

2 B

3 B

	£
Output VAT £27,612.50 $\times \dfrac{17.5}{117.5}$ =	4,112.50
Input VAT £18,000 $\times \dfrac{17.5}{100}$ =	3,150.00
$\therefore$ Balance on VAT a/c (credit) =	962.50

4 D

5 B

6 A

7 C

8 D   2 @ £3.00 + 10 @ £3.50 = £41.00

9 B

10 A   Prime cost is direct materials plus direct labour. There are no *direct* expenses.

11 A

12 C

13 D   Purchases = £(32,500 – 6,000 + 3,800)

                  = £30,300

$\therefore$ Creditors' payment period = $\dfrac{}{30,300} \times 365$ = 57 days

14 B   The trader cannot recover the VAT so it is included in purchases.

15 A

SUSPENSE ACCOUNT

	£		£
Balance b/d	210	Gas bill (420 – 240)	180
Interest	70	Discount (2 × 500)	100
	280		280

81   MULTIPLE CHOICE QUESTIONS: SELECTION 7

1   D

2   C

3   D

	£
Opening stock	12,000
Purchases (bal. fig)	122,000
Purchase returns	(5,000)
Closing stock	(18,000)
Cost of goods sold	111,000

4   D

5   A

	£
Opening bank balance	2,500
Payment (£1,000 – £200) × 90%	(720)
Receipt (£200 – £10)	190
Closing bank balance	1,970

6   C

7   B

8   C

9   D

	£
Assets	
Opening cash £(1,000 + 175 VAT)	1,000
Cash received	1,175
Closing cash	2,175
Stock £(800-400)	400
	2,575
Liabilities	
Opening liabilities	-
VAT creditor	175
Purchase stock	800
Closing liabilities	975
Capital	
Opening capital	1,000
Profit on sale of stock £(1,000 – 400)	600
Closing capital	1,600

10   B

	£
Opening capital	10,000
Capital introduced	4,000
Drawings	(8,000)
Loss (bal.fig)	(1,500)
Closing capital	4,500

11   A

12 C

	£
Profit	8,000
Add back: depreciation	12,000
Net cash inflow	20,000
Purchase of fixed assets for cash	(25,000)
Decrease in cash	5,000

13 B

	%	£
Sales	100	2,400
Cost of sales	66 $^{2}/_3$	1,600
Gross profit	33 $^{1}/_3$	800
Expenses	28 $^{1}/_3$	680
Net profit	5	120

14 B

	£
Interim ordinary dividends 5p × 400,000	20,000
Preference dividend (50,000 × £2 × 5%)/2	2,500
Paid to date	22,500
Final ordinary dividend 15p × 400,000	60,000
Preference dividend (must be paid before final ordinary dividend)	2,500
	85,000

15 A

Test your knowledge

Test your knowledge

1   What is the business equation?

2   Define capital expenditure and revenue expenditure.

3   Distinguish between trade discounts received and settlement discounts received. What is the correct accounting treatment for each?

4   What accounting treatment should be adopted where it is found that a fixed asset's useful life has been estimated incorrectly?

5   At what amount should stocks normally be valued?

6   List five possible methods of establishing the cost of a stock item which is continually being purchased and sold.

7   What are the four fundamental accounting concepts identified in SSAP 2?

8   List six different users of accounts.

9   What differences are apparent between the accounts of a non-trading organisation and those of a business?

10   What items of expense would usually be found in the category *selling and distribution expenses* in the profit and loss account?

11   Give the formulae for:

   (a)   return on capital employed;
   (b)   debtors' collection period.

12   How would you define 'useful information'?

13   Distinguish between:

   (a)   an ordinary share; and
   (b)   a preference share.

14   List four differences between debentureholders and shareholders.

15   Distinguish between authorised, issued, called up and paid up share capital.

16   Distinguish between a reserve and a provision.

17   Why is a suspense account opened?

18   Joan's first accounting period begins on 1.1.X6 and ends on 31.3.X7. If she has paid a year's rent of £2,800 in advance on 2.1.X6, and six months rent of £1,500 pa on 3.1.X7, what is the rent expense for her first accounting period?

19   If an accrual is mistakenly treated as a prepayment, what is the effect on profit?

20   If a customer goes bankrupt after his debt has been provided for as doubtful, what is the double entry required?

21   Wol's cashier has disappeared, presumably in company with the cash from the till, which vanished at the same time. The petty cash on 1.1.X0 was £150 and total sales since then are known to be £89,260. Credit customers owed £5,750 on 1.1.X0 and now owe £6,920. The bank statements show that credit customers have paid (by cheques) £72,460 in the period to date. Cash expenses are known to be £1,300 and cash takings banked are £4,480. How much cash has disappeared?

22   A club's bar stocks at 1 January 19X9 cost £7,500. Cash takings banked for 19X9 were £56,680. Bar wages of £100 weekly were paid from the takings before banking. Bar purchases were £42,400. If the gross profit percentage is fixed at 40%, what was the closing bar stock at cost?

23   In the above example, what is the net profit for the year on bar trading to be taken to the income and expenditure account?

24   Which account is the odd one out?

   A   Motor vehicles
   B   Office furniture and equipment
   C   Plant and machinery
   D   Stock and materials

25   If a purchases return of £48 is wrongly posted to the debit of the sales returns account, but correctly entered in the purchase ledger control account the totals of the trial balance would show:

   A   the credit side to be £48 more than the debit side
   B   the debit side to be £48 more than the credit side
   C   the credit side to be £96 more than the debit side
   D   the debit side to be £96 more than the credit side

26   The total of the discounts column on the debit side of the cash book, recording cash discounts deducted by customers when paying their accounts, is posted to

   A   the debit of the discounts received account
   B   the credit of the discounts received account
   C   the debit of the discounts allowed account
   D   the credit of the discounts allowed account

27   You have received a cheque for £285 from a customer, in settlement of his account of £300 from which a cash discount of £15 had been deducted, have banked it and made all the correct entries in your books. The cheque was then returned to you by the bank marked 'refer to drawer'. You would now make the following entries in your books:

   A   debit bank account £285, debit discount received account £15 and credit the debtors account £300

   B   credit bank account £285, credit discount received account £15 and debit the debtors account £285

   C   credit bank account £270, credit discount allowed account £15 and debit the debtors account £285

   D   credit bank account £285, credit discount allowed account £15 and debit the debtors account £300

28   The following information relates to a company's year-end stock of finished goods.

	Direct costs of material and labour £	Production overheads incurred £	Expected selling and distribution overheads £	Expected selling price £
Stock category 1	2,470	2,100	480	5,800
Stock category 2	9,360	2,730	150	12,040
Stock category 3	1,450	850	290	2,560
	13,280	5,680	920	20,400

At what amount should finished goods stock be stated in the company's balance sheet?

   A   £13,280
   B   £18,730
   C   £18,960
   D   £19,650

29   At 31 December 19X5 the provision for doubtful debts in the books of X Ltd included a specific provision for a balance owed by Mr Y. In 19X6 Mr Y was declared bankrupt and X Ltd wishes to write off the balance as a bad debt. The journal entry required is:

   A   DEBIT   Bad and doubtful debts expense account
         CREDIT   Debtors control account

B   DEBIT   Bad and doubtful debts expense account
     CREDIT   Provision for doubtful debts account

C   DEBIT   Provision for doubtful debts account
     CREDIT   Bad and doubtful debts expense account

D   DEBIT   Provision for doubtful debts account
     CREDIT   Debtors control account

30   Which one of the following occurrences might explain the existence of a credit balance on an individual debtor's account?

A   The bookkeeper failed to make a posting from the returns inwards book to the debtors ledger
B   The debtor took advantage of a settlement discount and paid less than the full amount invoiced
C   The bookkeeper failed to post an invoice from the sales day book to the debtors ledger
D   The bookkeeper posted a total from the returns inwards book to the debtors control account twice by mistake

31   A public company's ordinary share capital consists of 10,000,000 50p shares, issued at a premium of 20p each. They are currently being traded on The Stock Exchange at a price of 90p. The company has just announced a 12% final ordinary dividend for 19X6.

The total amount of the net dividend paid out by the company will be:

A   £600,000
B   £840,000
C   £1,080,000
D   £1,200,000

32   Which of the following is not a book of prime entry?

A   Bank statements
B   Petty cash book
C   Journal
D   Sales return day book

33   What transaction is represented by the entries: debit bank, credit M Jones?

A   Sale of goods to Jones for cash
B   Purchase of goods from Jones for cash
C   Receipt of cash from Jones
D   Payment of cash to Jones

34   Which of the following statements are true?

(1)   A utility program is an example of applications software.
(2)   Integrated software means less entry of data for the operator.
(3)   An off-the-shelf package is likely to be more expensive than a tailor made package.
(4)   A real time system is likely to be more expensive than a batch processing system.

A   (1), (2) and (4)
B   (1), (3) and (4)
C   (2) and (4)
D   (1), (2) and (3)

35   At what amount should stocks and work in progress, other than long-term contract work in progress, be stated in periodic financial statements?

36   Suggest four situations in which the net realisable value of stock is likely to be less than cost

37   Under what circumstances should freehold land be depreciated?

1   The business equation is

$$P = I + D - C$$

where   P = profit for period
         I = increase in net assets over the period (after taking account of drawings)
         D = drawings in period
         C = new capital injected during period

2   Capital expenditure is expenditure which results in the acquisition of fixed assets or an improvement in their earning capacity.

Revenue expenditure is expenditure incurred either in the day-to-day running of the business (eg administration expenses or distribution expenses) or to maintain the existing earning capacity of fixed assets.

3   Trade discount received is a reduction in the cost of goods purchased, usually because of large or frequently recurring orders. The accounting treatment is to deduct the discounts from the cost of purchases in the *trading account*.

Settlement discount received is a discount awarded for prompt payment of debts. The accounting treatment is to include the discount as a credit in the *profit and loss account*.

4   The asset's remaining net book value should be depreciated over its remaining useful life, as newly estimated.

5   At the lower of their cost and their net realisable value.

6   Possible methods include FIFO, LIFO, average cost, standard cost, base stock, sales price less estimated profit margin.

7   Going concern; accruals; consistency; prudence.

8   Any six of: shareholders; trade creditors; customers; long-term lenders; government; employees; general public; analysts and journalists.

9   Differences include:
income and expenditure account vs profit and loss account;
surplus/deficit for period vs profit/loss for period;
accumulated fund vs proprietor's capital/share capital;
usually no trading account for non-trading organisations (but sometimes, say, a bar trading account).

10   (a) Salaries of sales director or management
      (b) Salesmen's salaries and commission, and expenses
      (c) Marketing, advertising and sales promotion costs
      (d) Vehicle expenses for delivery vans
      (e) Settlement discounts given
      (f) Bad debt expense

11   (a) Possible formulae include:

$$\frac{\text{Profit after tax}}{\text{Shareholders ' funds}} \times 100\%$$

$$\frac{\text{Earnings}}{\text{Ordinary share capital plus reserves}} \times 100\%$$

$$\frac{\text{Profit before interest and tax}}{\text{Fixed assets plus net current assets}} \times 100\%$$

      (b)
$$\frac{\text{Debtors}}{\text{Sales} / 365}$$

12   Useful information, for users of accounts or indeed for anyone, is that which is relevant, comprehensible, reliable, complete, objective, timely and which aids comparison.

13   (a)   Ordinary shares carry no right to a fixed dividend but are entitled to all profits left after payment of any preference dividend.

      (b)   Preference shares usually carry the right to a fixed dividend, in priority to any dividends on ordinary shares. They usually have priority over ordinary shares for the return of capital in a liquidation. They do not usually carry voting rights.

14   Shareholders are members of a company, while debentureholders are creditors; shareholders receive dividends (an appropriation of profit), while debentureholders receive interest (an expense charged against revenue); debentureholders can enforce payment of interest by legal action, while shareholders cannot enforce payment of dividends; debentures are often secured on company assets, while shares are not.

15   *Authorised share capital:* the maximum amount of share capital that a company is empowered to issue.

      Issued share capital: the amount of share capital that has been issued to shareholders.

      Called up share capital: the amount the company has asked shareholders to pay, for the time being, on shares issued to them.

      Paid up share capital: the amounts actually paid by shareholders on shares issued to them.

16   A reserve is an appropriation of distributable profits for a specific purpose, while a provision is an amount charged against revenue as an expense.

17   Common reasons include:

      (a)   bookkeeper's inability to complete double entry when a transaction first happens (eg on disposal of fixed asset)

      (b)   to make the trial balance balance until errors are detected.

18

	£
19X6 rent	2,800
19X7 rent (£1,500 × 3/6)	750
	3,550

19   Profit is overstated by twice the amount of the accrual because it is deducted instead of being added to the expense account involved.

20   DEBIT   Doubtful debts provision
      CREDIT   Sales ledger control

      The previous entry would have been:

      DEBIT   Bad and doubtful debts expense
      CREDIT   Doubtful debts provision

      Now that there is no doubt that the debt is bad, the accounts can be 'cleared out' by eliminating all reference to the debt. There is no further profit effect.

21

	£
Credit sales	
Cheques	72,460
Less opening debtors	5,750
Add closing debtors	6,920
	73,630
∴ Cash sales = 89,260 - 73,630 =	15,630
Add cash balance b/f	150
	15,780
Less cash expenses	1,300
cash takings banked	4,480
Missing cash	10,000

		£
22		
Cash banked		56,680
Wages (£100 × 52)		5,200
∴ Sales for the year		61,880
Cost of sales @ 60%		37,128
Less opening stock		7,500
Less purchases		42,400
∴ closing stock		12,772

23   Net profit = £61,880 - £37,128 - £5,200 = £19,552

24   E   the only current asset: the rest are fixed assets (except for specialised businesses, such as car dealers, furniture suppliers etc).

25   D   a purchase return should be a credit entry. Since it has been debited to the wrong account, and in addition a debit entry has been made in the purchase ledger control account, debits must exceed credits by 2 × £48 = £96.

26   C   the discounts allowed in the cash book provide the data for the posting to the discounts allowed account. (The double entry is debit discounts allowed, credit debtors.)

27   D   the original entries (debit cash £285, debit discounts allowed £15, credit debtors £300) are reversed, as indicated in D.

28   B   because this valuation (£13,280 + £5,680) includes all costs incurred to bring the stock to its present location and condition.

29   D   because there is no profit and loss effect, as the debt has already been provided for via the bad debt provision. This entry is made purely to tidy up the balance sheet.

30   C   because cash received, crediting the ledger account, would not be matched by a debit recording the invoice. A and B would result in a debit balance and D would not affect the ledger account at all.

31   A   10,000,000 × 50p × 12%.

32   A   bank statements are not records originated by the business.

33   C   this entry indicates an accounting system with no control accounts.

34   A   Statement (3) is incorrect. Packages are generally a lot cheaper than custom-built applications. The time and expense of designing an application from scratch is incurred only once, even though the application is sold to several customers.

35   At the total of the lower of cost and net realisable value of the separate items of stock or of groups of similar items. (SSAP 9 para 26).

36   Possibilities:

(a)   an increase in costs or a fall in selling price;
(b)   physical deterioration of stocks;
(c)   obsolescence of products;
(d)   a decision as part of the company's marketing strategy to manufacture and sell products at a loss;
(e)   errors in production or purchasing. (SSAP 9, appendix 1 para 20).

37   (a)   When it is subject to depletion (for example by mining).
(b)   When there is a reduction in the desirability of its location. (SSAP 12 para 23)

Financial Accounting Fundamentals

FAF

INSTRUCTIONS TO CANDIDATES

You are allowed three hours to answer this question paper.
Answer ONE question from section A (consisting of fifteen sub-questions).   *Answer the TWO questions in section B.*   *Answer ONE question ONLY from section C.*

DO NOT OPEN THIS PAPER UNTIL YOU ARE READY
TO START UNDER EXAMINATION CONDITIONS

SECTION A - 30 MARKS

ANSWER *ALL* FIFTEEN SUB-QUESTIONS

Each of the sub-questions numbered from 1.1 to 1.15 inclusive, given below, has only ONE correct answer.

REQUIREMENT:

On the SPECIAL ANSWER SHEET provided at the end of this question paper, place a circle 'O' around the letter (either *A*, *B*, *C*, or *D*) that gives the correct answer to each sub-question.

If you wish to change your mind about an answer, block out your first attempt and then encircle another letter. If you do not indicate clearly your final choice, or if you encircle more than one letter, no marks will be awarded for the sub-question concerned.

Your special answer sheet MUST be attached to your answer book before it is handed in.

1.1   Your company auditor insists that it is necessary to record items of plant separately and to depreciate them over several years, but that items of office equipment, such as hand-held stapling machines, can be grouped together and written off against profits immediately.

The main reason for this difference in treatment between the two items is because

A   treatment of the two items must be consistent with treatment in previous periods
B   items of plant last for several years, whereas hand-held stapling machines last only for months
C   hand-held stapling machines are not regarded as material items
D   items of plant are revalued from time to time, whereas hand-held stapling machines are recorded at historical cost

1.2   Which of the following *best* explains what is meant by 'capital expenditure'?

Capital expenditure is expenditure

A   on fixed assets, including repairs and maintenance
B   on expensive assets
C   relating to the issue of share capital
D   relating to the acquisition or improvement of fixed assets

1.3   On 1 July 1997, your fixed asset register showed a net book value of £47,500. The ledger accounts showed fixed assets at cost of £60,000 and provision for depreciation of £15,000. It was discovered that the disposal of an asset for £4,000, giving rise to a loss on disposal of £1,500, had not been recorded in the fixed asset register.

After correcting this omission, the fixed asset register would show a balance which was

A   £3,000 lower than the ledger accounts
B   £1,500 lower than the ledger accounts
C   equal to the ledger accounts
D   £1,000 higher than the ledger accounts

1.4   The bank statement on 31 October 1997 showed an overdraft of £800. On reconciling the bank statement, it was discovered that a cheque drawn by your company for £80 had not been presented for payment, and that a cheque for £130 from a customer had been dishonoured on 30 October 1997, but that this had not yet been notified to you by the bank.

The correct bank balance to be shown in the balance sheet at 31 October 1997 is

A   £1,010 overdrawn
B   £880 overdrawn
C   £750 overdrawn
D   £720 overdrawn

1.5   A credit entry of £450 on X's account in the books of Y could have arisen by

A   X buying goods on credit from Y
B   Y paying X £450
C   Y returning goods to X
D   X returning goods to Y

1.6   The *main* purpose of an audit is to

A   detect errors and fraud
B   ensure that the accounts are accurate
C   determine that the accounts show a true and fair view of the financial state of the organisation
D   ensure that all transactions have been recorded in the books of account

1.7   A computerised spreadsheet package is *most* suitable for

A   recording the dual effect of accounting transactions
B   maintaining an audit trail of transactions
C   performing bank reconciliations
D   preparing a cash budget

1.8   Where a transaction is entered into the correct ledger accounts, but the wrong amount is used, the error is known as an error of

A   omission
B   original entry
C   commission
D   principle

1.9   At 1 September, the motor expenses account showed 4-months' insurance prepaid of £80 and petrol accrued of £95. During September, the outstanding petrol bill is paid, plus further bills of £245. At 30 September there is a further outstanding petrol bill of £120.

The amount to be shown in the profit and loss account for motor expenses for September is

A   £385   B   £415   C   £445   D   £460

1.10 Your organisation sold goods to PQ Limited for £800 less trade discount of 20% and cash discount of 5% for payment within 14 days. The invoice was settled by cheque five days later. The entries required to record BOTH of these transactions are:

		Debit £	Credit £
A	PQ Limited	640	
	Sales		640
	Bank	608	
	Discount allowed	32	
	PQ Limited		640

		Debit £	Credit £
B	PQ Limited	640	
	Sales		640
	Bank	600	
	Discount allowed	40	
	PQ Limited		640

		Debit £	Credit £
C	PQ Limited	640	
	Sales		640
	Bank	608	
	Discount received	32	
	PQ Limited		640

		Debit £	Credit £
D	PQ Limited	800	
	Sales		800
	Bank	608	
	Discount allowed	182	
	PQ Limited		800

1.11 A fixed asset was purchased at the beginning of Year 1 for £2,400 and depreciated by 20% per annum by the reducing balance method. At the beginning of Year 4 it was sold for £1,200. The result of this was

A a loss on disposal of £240.00
B a loss on disposal of £28.80
C a profit on disposal of £28.80
D a profit on disposal of £240.00

1.12 You are given the following information for the year ended 31 October 1997:

	£
Purchases of raw materials	112,000
Returns inwards	8,000
Decrease in stocks of raw materials	8,000
Direct wages	42,000
Carriage outwards	4,000
Carriage inwards	3,000
Production overheads	27,000
Increase in work-in-progress	10,000

The value of factory cost of goods completed is

A £174,000   **B** £182,000   **C** £183,000   **D** £202,000

1.13 Your organisation uses the weighted average cost method of valuing stocks. During August 1997, the following stock details were recorded:

Opening balance 30 units valued at £2 each
5 August   purchase of 50 units at £2.40 each
10 August   issue of 40 units
18 August   purchase of 60 units at £2.50 each
23 August   issue of 25 units

The value of the balance at 31 August 1996 was

A £172.50   **B** £176.25   **C** £180.00   **D** £187.50

1.14 During September, your organisation had sales of £148,000, which made a gross profit of £40,000. Purchases amounted to £100,000 and opening stock was £34.000.

The value of closing stock was

A £24,000   **B** £26,000   **C** £42,000   **D** £54,000

1.15 During the year ended 31 October 1997, your organisation made a gross profit of £60,000, which represented a mark-up of 50%. Opening stock was £12,000 and closing stock was £18,000.

The rate of stock turnover was

A 4 times   **B** 6.7 times   **C** 7.3 times   **D** 8 times

Total Marks = 30

SECTION B - 50 MARKS

ANSWER ***BOTH*** QUESTIONS

2.   TYR Limited produced the following trial balance at 31 October 1997.

	Dr £'000	Cr £'000
Share capital		1,000
Reserves		425
12% debentures, repayable 2010		250
Land at valuation	495	
Premises at cost	350	
- depreciation to 1 November 1996		20
Plant and machinery at cost	220	
- depreciation to 1 November 1996		30
Patents and trade marks	200	
Stock at 1 November 1996	210	
Debtors	875	
Cash in hand	12	
Creditors		318
Bank		85
Administration expenses	264	
Selling and distribution expenses	292	
Dividends	20	
Debenture interest	15	
Sales		2,569
Purchases	1,745	
Carriage inwards	15	
Carriage outwards	18	
Returns outwards		34
	4,731	4,731

The following additional information at 31 October 1997 is available.

(a)   A physical stock check reveals stocks at cost of £194,000.

(b)   Prepaid administration expenses amount to £12,000 and prepaid selling and delivery expenses amount to £28,000. Accrued administration expenses amount to £17,000.

(c)   During October 1997 goods were sold on a 'sale or return' basis, with the final date for return being 25 November. The sale has been recorded as normal in the sales day book and debtors' account, and the stock has been excluded from the stock count.

The goods cost £7,000 and had a selling price of £12,000.

(d)   The land is to be revalued at £550,000.

(e)   The Share Capital account comprises 200,000 5% preference shares of £1 each with the balance made up of 50p ordinary shares.

(f)   The Reserves account consists of Share Premium of £100,000, Revaluation Reserve of £135,000 with the balance representing undistributed profits.

(g)   The premises are to be depreciated at 4% per annum straight line.
The plant and machinery is to be depreciated at 10% per annum straight line.

(h)   Corporation tax of £40,000 is to be provided for the year.

(i)   The Dividends account represents a half-year's preference dividend and an interim ordinary dividend. A final dividend of 5p per ordinary share is proposed.

REQUIREMENTS:

(a)   Prepare the trading and profit and loss appropriation account for the year ended 31 October 1997.

10 Marks

(b)   Prepare a balance sheet at 31 October 1997

10 Marks

(c)   Given the following ratios for the previous year, calculate the comparable ratios for the current year and comment on your results. Suggest reasons for any changes in the ratios between the two years.

(i)   Gross profit mark-up   50%
(ii) Net profit percentage   3% (using net profit before tax)
(iii) Current ratio   2.4:1
(iv) Acid test ratio   1.8:1

10 Marks

Total Marks = 30

3.   At the beginning of September 1997, GL had the following balances on the accounts of three of his debtors.

A Barton   £400
C Dodd   £1,200
F Gray   £340

During September, the following sales and returns took place for the above debtors.

Sales

*   on 3 September to A Barton   goods £200 less trade discount of 20%, plus VAT at 17.5%
*   on 8 September to C Dodd   goods £800 plus VAT at 17.5%
*   on 12 September to C Dodd   goods £360 plus VAT at 17.5%

Sales returns

*   on 5 September from A Barton   25% of the goods sold to him on 3 September
*   on 18 September from C Dodd   goods of £120 plus VAT at 17.5%

The balance at the bank was £347 overdrawn on 1 September 1997.

The following bank transactions took place during September 1997.

4 Sept   A Barton paid the amount outstanding at 1 September, less 5% cash discount

8 Sept   C Dodd paid the amount outstanding at 1 September, less 2.5% cash discount

10 Sept   Paid J Swinburn, a creditor, for an invoice of £1,200, less 5% cash discount

15 Sept   Paid VAT of £832 to Customs and Excise, re the quarter ended 31 August 1997

17 Sept   Paid P Taylor, a creditor, £400 less 5% cash discount

20 Sept   Paid by cheque for a motor car costing £9,550, including £150 vehicle licence tax and VAT at 17.5%

22 Sept   C Dodd paid the invoice of 8 September, less the credit note of 18 September. There was no cash discount allowed on this payment

25 Sept   Received a cheque from F Gray for 50% of his debt; the remainder is to be written off as a bad debt

30 Sept   Paid wages to employees, made up as follows.

Gross wages	£2,500
Employees' National Insurance	£200
Employers' National Insurance	£200
Income tax deducted under PAYE	£300

30 Sept   Banked receipts from debtors   £10,500
           Paid cheques to creditors   £11,200

GL has a computerised Sales Ledger system, which produced the following aged debtors' printout at 30 September 1997.

Current month	£12,000
30 to 60 days	£7,500
60 to 90 days	£3,600
over 90 days	£1,100

The balance on the Provision for Doubtful Debts account at 1 September 1997 was £450 credit. No further provisions against debtors have been made since that date. You are given the following additional information.

(a) The 'Current month' total includes £60 for discounts allowed to debtors not recorded in the Sales Ledger.

(b) The '30 to 60 day' total includes a balance of £200 to be taken as a contra entry in the Purchase Ledger.

(c) The 'over 90 days' total includes a debt of £240 to be written off as bad.

(d) The company decides to amend the provision for doubtful debts to the following amounts.

over 90 days	20%
60 to 90 days	10%
30 to 60 days	5%
current month	nil

REQUIREMENTS:

(a) Write up a cash book for September 1997, with columns for Bank and Cash Discount, and balance off at 30 September 1997.

Note. You are NOT required to complete the double-entry EXCEPT where asked to do so in part **(b)** below.

7 Marks

(b) Write up the ledger accounts (in date order) for A Barton, C Dodd and F Gray.　　**6 Marks**

(c) Calculate the change in the provision for doubtful debts.　　**4 Marks**

(d) Explain the principal accounting concept which governs the provision for doubtful debts.

3 Marks

Total Marks = 20

SECTION C - 20 MARKS

ANSWER *ONE* QUESTION ONLY

4. PM is considering buying a small manufacturing business, but she has no experience of accounting. She has obtained the accounts of a well-established business and is trying to negotiate a purchase price for the business.

REQUIREMENTS:

(a) Explain to PM the problems which can affect the values of items appearing in the balance sheet, and the extent to which she can rely on them.   **12 Marks**

(b) Since the accounts were drawn up, the following transactions have occurred:

    (i)   dividends for the year just ended have been paid by cheque;

    (ii) fixed assets have been disposed of on credit, for more than their net book value;

    (iii) a long-term bank loan has been repaid by increasing the overdraft;

    (iv) goods sold on credit have been returned and the original sales value has been credited to the debtors' account.

REQUIRED:

State, for EACH of the above transactions, whether there will be an increase, a decrease, or no change to each of:

- fixed assets
- working capital
- profit   **8 Marks**

Total Marks = 20

5. The Monarch Sports Club has the following summary of its cash book for the year ended 30 June 1997.

	£	£
Opening bank balance		12,500
Receipts		
Subscriptions	18,000	
Life membership fees	3,000	
Competition receipts	7,500	
Entrance fees	2,500	
Equipment sold	1,000	
		32,000
Payments		
Transport to matches	3,700	
Competition prizes	4,300	
Coaching fees	2,100	
Repairs to equipment	800	
Purchase of new equipment	4,000	
Purchase of sports pavilion	35,000	
		49,900
Closing balance (overdrawn)		5,400

The following information is available regarding the position at the beginning and end of the accounting year.

	1 July 1996	30 June 1997
	£	£
Subscriptions in advance	1,100	900
Subscriptions in arrears	200	300
Coaching fees outstanding	150	450

Of the subscriptions outstanding at the beginning of the year, only half were eventually received.

The equipment sold during the year had a net book value of £1,200 at 1 July 1996. Equipment is to be depreciated at 20% per annum straight line. Life membership fees are taken to cover 10 years.

The treasurer insists that no depreciation needs to be charged on the sports pavilion, as buildings do not decrease in value. He says that the last club of which he was treasurer did charge depreciation on its buildings but that when the club came to replace them, there was still insufficient money in the bank to pay for the new building.

REQUIREMENTS:

(a) Explain the difference between a receipts and payments account and an income and expenditure account.   **4 Marks**

(b) Prepare an income and expenditure account for the Monarch Sports Club for the year ended 30 June 1997.   **8 Marks**

(c) Explain what is meant by the 'accumulated fund' in the accounts of a not-for-profit organisation.   **2 Marks**

(d) Discuss whether or not you agree with the treasurer's opinion that no depreciation needs to be charged on the pavilion, AND explain the accounting concepts which govern the charging of depreciation.   **6 Marks**

Total Marks = 20

NOVEMBER 1997 EXAMINATION: FINANCIAL ACCOUNTING FUNDAMENTALS

SPECIAL ANSWER SHEET

*REQUIREMENT: Place a circle 'O' around the letter (either **A**, **B**, **C**, **D**) that gives the correct answer to each sub-question.*

If you wish to change your mind about an answer, block out your first attempt and then encircle another letter. If you do not indicate clearly your final choice, or if you encircle more than one letter, no marks will be awarded for the sub-question concerned.

1.1	A	B	C	D
1.2	A	B	C	D
1.3	A	B	C	D
1.4	A	B	C	D
1.5	A	B	C	D
1.6	A	B	C	D
1.7	A	B	C	D
1.8	A	B	C	D
1.9	A	B	C	D
1.10	A	B	C	D
1.11	A	B	C	D
1.12	A	B	C	D
1.13	A	B	C	D
1.14	A	B	C	D
1.15	A	B	C	D

SUGGESTED SOLUTIONS

DO NOT TURN THIS PAGE UNTIL YOU
HAVE COMPLETED THE TEST PAPER

SECTION A

1.1 C

1.2 D

1.3 A

Ledger accounts

	£
As at 1.1.97	
Cost	60,000
Depreciation	15,000
	45,000

Fixed asset register

At 1.1.97	
Net book value	47,500
Disposal of asset which cost £(4,000 + 1,500)	(5,500)
	42,000

1.4 B

	£
Balance per bank statement	(800)
Unpresented cheque	(80)
Dishonoured cheque (affects cash book only)	-
	(880)

1.5 D

1.6 C

1.7 D

1.8 B

1.9 A

MOTOR EXPENSES

	£			£
1.9 Prepayment b/d	80	1.9	Accrual b/d	95
Cash	95	30.9	Prepayment (80 ×3/4)	60
Cash	245		P&L c/d	385
30.9 Accrual c/d	120			
	540			540

1.10 A

	£	Dr	Cr
Sales price	800		
Less 20% trade discount	120		
Sale	640	PQ Ltd	Sales
Cash discount 5%	32	Discount allowed	
Cash payment	608	Bank	
	640		PQ Ltd

1.11 B

		£
Year 1	Purchase	2,400.00
Year 1	Depreciation	(480.00)
		1,920.00
Year 2	Depreciation	(384.00)
		1,536.00
Year 3	Depreciation	(307.20)
		1,228.80
Year 4	Sale proceeds	1,200.00
	Loss on disposal	(28.80)

1.12 B

	£
Purchase of raw materials	112,000
Decrease in stock of raw materials	8,000
Carriage inwards	3,000
Raw materials used	123,000
Direct wages	42,000
Prime cost	165,000
Production overheads	27,000
Increase in WIP	(10,000)
Factory cost of finished goods	182,000

1.13 C

	Units	Unit cost £	Total £	Average £
Opening stock	30	2	60	
5 August purchase	50	2.40	120	
	80		180	2.25
10 August issue	(40)	2.25	(90)	
	40		90	
18 August purchase	60	2.50	150	
	100		240	2.40
23 August issue	(25)	2.40	(60)	
	75		180	

1.14 B

		£	£
Sales			148,000
COS	Opening stock	34,000	
	Purchases	100,000	
		134,000	
	Closing stock (bal fig)	(26,000)	
			108,000
			40,000

1.15 D

	%	£
Sales	150	180,000
COS	100	(120,000)
Gross profit	50	60,000

$$\therefore \text{Stock turnover} = \frac{120,000}{(12,000 + 18,000)\,/\,2} = 8$$

SECTION B

2

> *Tutorial note.* In part (a) care was needed in calculating the final proposed ordinary dividend, to ensure that the dividend of 5p per share was calculated on the correct number of shares.

(a) TYR LIMITED
TRADING, PROFIT AND LOSS AND APPROPRIATION ACCOUNT
FOR THE YEAR ENDED 31 OCTOBER 1997

	£	£
Sales (W2)		2,557,000
Cost of sales		
Opening stock	210,000	
Purchases (W1)	1,726,000	
	1,936,000	
Less: closing stock (W3)	(201,000)	
Cost of goods sold		(1,735,000)
Gross profit		822,000
Less expenses		
Administration expenses (W5)	269,000	
Selling and delivery expenses (W6)	264,000	
Carriage outwards	18,000	
Debenture interest (£250,000 × 12%)	30,000	
Depreciation (W4)	36,000	
		(617,000)
Profit before tax		205,000
Corporation tax		40,000
Profit after tax		165,000
Dividends		
Interim paid preference dividend	5,000	
Interim paid ordinary dividend	15,000	
Final proposed preference dividend	5,000	
Final proposed ordinary dividend (W7)	80,000	
		(105,000)
Retained profit for the year		60,000
Profit and loss account brought forward (W8)		190,000
Profit and loss account carried forward		250,000

(b) TYR LIMITED
BALANCE SHEET AS AT 31 OCTOBER 1997

	Cost or valuation £	Dep'n £	Net book value £
Tangible fixed assets			
Land	550,000	-	550,000
Premises	350,000	34,000	316,000
Plant and machinery	220,000	52,000	168,000
	1,120,000	86,000	1,034,000
Intangible fixed assets			
Patents and trademarks	200,000	-	200,000
	1,320,000	86,000	1,234,000
Current assets			
Stock		201,000	
Trade debtors (W9)		863,000	
Prepayments (W10)		40,000	
Cash in hand		12,000	
		1,116,000	
Creditors due within one year			
Trade creditors	318,000		
Bank overdraft	85,000		
Accruals and provisions (W11)	72,000		
Final dividends	85,000		
		(560,000)	
Net current assets			556,000
Total assets less current liabilities			1,790,000
Creditors due in more than one year			
Debenture stock			(250,000)
			1,540,000
Capital and reserves			
Share capital			1,000,000
Share premium account			100,000
Revaluation reserve (£135,000 + £55,000)			190,000
Retained profit			250,000
			1,540,000

(c)

		Previous year	Current year
Gross profit mark-up =	$\dfrac{\text{Gross profit}}{\text{Cost of sales}}$	50%	$\dfrac{822}{1,735} = 47\%$
Net profit % =	$\dfrac{\text{Net profit}}{\text{Sales}}$	3%	$\dfrac{205}{2,557} = 8\%$
Current ratio =	$\dfrac{\text{Current assets}}{\text{Current liabilities}}$	2.4:1	116:560 = 1.99:1
Acid test ratio =	$\dfrac{\text{Current assets} - \text{stock}}{\text{Current liabilities}}$	1.8:1	915:560 = 1.63:1

The gross profit ratio fell slightly. This could be due to a rising cost of sales which the company is unable to pass on to customers, increased competition in the market place which has meant the company has had to cut back on its margins or a deliberate policy of reducing its margins in order to increase the volume of sales.

The net profit margin has risen. This indicates that expenses have risen at a lower rate than sales. This could be because the company has become more efficient or because a higher volume of sales means that benefit has been derived from economies of scale.

Both the current ratio and acid test ratio have fallen. This indicates an increase in liquidity perhaps due to more vigorous debt collecting policies or due to the taking of extended periods of credit.

Workings

1   *Purchases*

	£
Purchases per trial balance	1,745,000
Carriage inwards	15,000
Returns outwards	(34,000)
	1,726,000

2   *Sales*

	£
Sales per trial balance	2,569,000
Less: goods sold on sale or return basis	(12,000)
	2,557,000

3   *Closing stock*

	£
Per stock count	194,000
Add back: goods sold on sale or return basis	7,000
	201,000

4   *Depreciation charge*

	£
Premises at 4%	14,000
Plant and machinery at 10%	22,000
	36,000

5   *Administration expenses*

	£
Per trial balance	264,000
Prepaid amount	(12,000)
Accrued expenses	17,000
	269,000

6   *Selling and delivery expenses*

	£
Per trial balance	292,000
Prepaid amount	(28,000)
	264,000

7   *Final proposed ordinary dividend*

	£
Share capital account	1,000,000
Less: 200,000 £1 preference shares	(200,000)
Value of ordinary shares	800,000

Ordinary shares are 50p shares which means that there are 1,600,000 (800,000 × 2) shares and a proposed dividend of 5p per share gives a total proposed final dividend of 1,600,000 × £0.05 = £80,000.

8   *Profit and loss account brought forward*

	£
Reserves account	425,000
Share premium	(100,000)
Revaluation reserve	(135,000)
Profit and loss account b/f	190,000

9   *Trade debtors*

	£
Per trial balance	875,000
Goods sold on sale or return basis	(12,000)
	863,000

10   *Prepayments*

	£
Administration expenses	12,000
Selling and delivery expenses	28,000
	40,000

11   *Accruals and provisions*

	£
Administration expenses	17,000
Corporation tax	40,000
Debenture interest	15,000
	72,000

3

> *Tutorial note.* The bank account was overdrawn at the beginning of September and so you should have an opening *credit* balance in your cash book. *Gross* wages include employees' NIC and income tax but employees' NIC and PAYE deductions are not paid to the tax authorities at the same time as the *net* wages paid to employees. You should therefore have included only £2,000 for *net* wages in your cash book.

(a)

GL CASH BOOK

Date 19X7	Notes	Transaction detail	Cash discount £	Bank £	Date 19X7	Notes	Transaction detail	Cash discount £	Bank £
4/9	(2)	A Barton (debtor)	20	380	1/9	(1)	Balance b/f		347
8/9	(3)	C Dodd (debtor)	30	1,170	10/9	(4)	J Swinburn (creditor)	60	1,140
22/9	(7)	C Dodd (debtor)		799	15/9		VAT a/c		832
25/9	(8)	F Gray (debtor)		170	17/9	(5)	P Taylor (creditor)	20	380
30/9		Debtors a/c		10,500	20/9	(6)	Motor vehicle asset a/c		9,400
30/9		Balance c/f		12,430	20/9		Motor vehicle expenses a/c		150
					30/9	(9)	Wages a/c		2,000
					30/9		Creditors a/c		11,200
			50	25,449				80	25,449
					1/10		Balance b/f		12,430

Notes

1   The bank account was overdrawn at 1 September and so the opening balance is a credit balance.

2   Amount received = £400 × 95% = £380
     Discount = £(400 – 380) = £20

3   Amount received = £1,200 × 97.5% = £1,170
     Discount = £(1,200 – 1,170) = £30

4   Amount paid = £1,200 × 95% = £1,140
     Discount = £(1,200 – 1,140) = £60

5   Amount paid = £400 × 95% = £380
     Discount = £(400 – 380) = £20

6   Motor vehicles asset a/c = £(9,550 – 150) = £9,400

7   Amount received = £(800 – 120) × 117.5% = £799

8   Amount received = £340 × 50% = £170

9   Gross wages include employees' national insurance contributions and income tax, which are not paid at the time of payment of the wages, although the figures are posted to PAYE and employees' NIC control accounts. The wages paid = £(2,500 – 200 – 300) = £2,000.

     Likewise, employer's national insurance contributions are not paid at the time of payment of the wages; the figure is posted to an employer's NIC control account.

     The balance on PAYE and NIC control accounts are paid to the Inland Revenue usually on a quarterly basis.

(b)

A BARTON

Date 1997	Notes	Transaction detail	£	Date 1997	Notes	Transaction detail	£
1/9		Balance b/f	400	4/9	(2)	Bank a/c	380
3/9	(1)	Sales a/c	188	4/9	(2)	Cash discount allowed a/c	20
				5/9	(3)	Sales returns a/c	47
				30/9		Balance c/f	141
			588				588
1/10		Balance b/f	141				

Notes

1   Sales = £(200 × 80%) × 117.5% = £188

2   Amount received = £400 × 95% = £380
Cash discount = £(400 − 380) = £20

3   Returns = 25% × (£200 × 80%) × 117.5% = £47

C DODD

Date 1997	Notes	Transaction detail	£	Date 1997	Notes	Transaction detail	£
1/9		Balance b/f	1,200	8/9	(3)	Bank a/c	1,170
8/9	(1)	Sales	940	8/9	(3)	Cash discount allowed a/c	30
12/9	(2)	Sales	423	18/9	(4)	Sales returns a/c	141
				22/9	(5)	Bank a/c	799
				30/9		Balance c/f	423
			2,563				2,563
1/10		Balance b/f	423				

Notes

1   Sales = £800 × 117.5% = £940

2   Sales = £360 × 117.5% = £423

3   Cash received = £1,200 × 97.5% = £1,170
Discount = £(1,200 − 1,170) = £30

4   Returns = £120 × 117.5% = £141

5   Cash received = £(940 − 141) = £799

F GRAY

Date 1997	Notes	Transaction detail	£	Date 1997	Notes	Transaction detail	£
1/9		Balance b/f	340	25/9	(1)	Bank a/c	170
				25/9	(1)	Bad debts a/c	170
			340				340

Notes

1   Cash received = 50% × £340 = £170
Bad debt = £(340 − 170) = £170

(c) *Provision for doubtful debts calculation as at 30 September 1997*

Category	Value of debtors as per aged debtors' listing £	Adjust-ments £	Notes	New balance £	Rate for provision	Provision £
Current month	12,000	(60)	(1)	11,940	0%	-
30 to 60 days	7,500	(200)	(2)	7,300	5%	365
60 to 90 days	3,600	-		3,600	10%	360
Over 90 days	1,100	(240)	(3)	860	20%	172
						897

The current provision is £450. The provision required is £897. The provision must therefore be increased by (credited with) £(897 – 450) = £447.

Notes

1   We need to reduce the debtors value by £60 as this discount does not form part of the amount receivable.

2   Because GL also owes this debtor £200, the provision does not need to cover it since it does not form part of the amount receivable.

3   Debts to be written off are included in the value of debtors used to calculate the general provision.

(d)   The principal accounting concept which governs the provision for doubtful debts is prudence. The prudence concept states that where alternative procedures, or alternative valuations, are possible, the one selected should be the one which gives the most cautious presentation of the business's financial position or results. Profits should not therefore be anticipated before they have been realised. The other aspect of the prudence concept is that where a loss is foreseen, it should be anticipated and taken into account immediately. When applied to debtors, the prudence concept therefore requires the following.

(i)   Any debts which are reasonably certain to be recovered should be included in the debtors balance sheet valuation

(ii)   Any irrecoverable debt should be written off as soon as it is foreseen.

The provision for doubtful debts is therefore used to ensure that the balance sheet valuation of debtors reflects the likely level of recoverable debt.

4

> *Tutorial note.* You might have found that you could do part (b) in less than the 14 minutes you would normally allocate to it (8 marks x 1.8 = 14 mins approx), thus leaving you with more time for part (a).

(a)   Financial accounts drawn up using the principles of historical cost accounting cannot be fully relied upon if PM wishes to arrive at a valuation of the business. The valuation of the following items in the balance sheet may present particular problems.

(i)   *Fixed assets.* Generally, fixed assets will be shown in the balance sheet at their original cost, less accumulated depreciation, in other words at their net book value. The provision for depreciation will have been made in line with the accounting policies of the business. Such policies are based on assumptions about the useful lives of assets which may not be realistic. The depreciation policies of different businesses provide for depreciation over estimated asset lives in different ways, for example the straight line method and the reducing balance method.

The amount at which land and buildings is stated in the balance sheet may be based on their original cost. If the property was purchased some years ago, its value may have appreciated over that time, and so the amount shown in the accounts may be very different from the current market value of the property.

The accounts of businesses which have purchased other businesses may show an amount for goodwill. Goodwill is an intangible asset which should be written off over a period of time. The valuation of goodwill is a subjective matter. PM will want to consider the value of the goodwill of the business which she is purchasing. However, any amount shown for goodwill in the accounts may be out of date, and cannot be relied upon as a guide to the actual current value of the goodwill of the business.

(ii)   *Stocks.* Generally, stocks will be shown in the accounts at their original cost. In the case of slow-moving or obsolete items, the values should be written down to net realisable value. If the process of identifying such items has not been sufficiently thorough, stocks may have been overvalued in the accounts.

(iii)   *Debtors.* The value of debtors in the accounts will have been understated if the provision for bad and doubtful debts is too low. The identification of bad and doubtful debts involves a degree of judgement in many cases.

(iv)   *Creditors.* The amount stated for creditors in the accounts includes accruals for expenses of the business which have been incurred in the period but have not yet been invoiced. If some such expenses have been omitted, the figure for accruals may be too low.

Because of valuation problems such as those identified above, PM should not place too much reliance on the figures shown in the accounts. She should seek valuations of stocks and fixed assets, and a full aged debtors listing, as well as checking that all liabilities are included in the accounts. She will also need to consider changes which have taken place since the balance sheet date and which may affect the current value of the assets and liabilities of the business.

(b)

	Fixed assets	*Working capital*	*Profit*
(i)	No change	No change	No change
(ii)	Decrease	Increase	Increase
(iii)	No change	Decrease	No change
(iv)	No change	Decrease	Decrease

5

(a)   *Receipts and payments account*

Many charities and clubs have little accounting knowledge, and only keep records of cash paid and received. Such organisations usually record their cash transactions in an analysed cash book. A receipts and payments account is effectively a summary of an organisation's cash book. Balance sheets are not produced with receipts and payments accounts

Income and expenditure account

An income and expenditure account is essentially a record of income generated and expenditure incurred over a given period. Such accounts include prepayments and accruals and distinguish between capital and revenue items. Organisations which are not run for profit, such as charities, produce income and expenditure accounts which show the surplus of income over expenditure (or a deficit where expenditure exceeds income).

(b)   MONARCH SPORTS CLUB
INCOME AND EXPENDITURE ACCOUNT
FOR THE YEAR ENDED 30 JUNE 1997

	£	£
Income		
Subscriptions (W1)		18,400
Life membership fees (W2)		300
Surplus on competition receipts (W3)		3,200
Entrance fees		2,500
		24,400
Expenditure		
Transport to matches	3,700	
Coaching fees (W4)	2,400	
Repairs to equipment	800	
Bad debts written off (W5)	100	
Loss on disposal of equipment (W6)	200	
Depreciation of equipment (W7)	800	
		(8,000)
		16,400

Workings

1   *Subscription income*

	£
Subscriptions received in year	18,000
Less: subscriptions in advance at 30.6.97	(900)
Add: subscriptions in arrears at 30.6.97	300
Add: subscriptions in advance at 1.7.96	1,100
Less: subscriptions in arrears at 30.6.97	(100)
	18,400

2   *Life membership fees*

Fees received in year = £3,000

$1/10 \times £3,000 = £300$ (life membership fees are taken to cover 10 years)

3   *Competition receipts*

	£
Receipts in year	7,500
Competition prizes	4,300
	3,200

4   *Coaching fees*

	£
Payments in year	2,100
Less: fees outstanding at 1.7.96	(150)
Add: fees outstanding at 30.6.97	450
	2,400

5   *Bad debts*

50% of subscriptions in arrears at 1.7.96 = $50\% \times £200 = £100$.

6   *Loss on disposal of equipment*

	£
Net book value at 1.7.97	1,200
Income received on sale of equipment	(1,000)
Loss on disposal	200

7   *New equipment*

	£
Purchase cost of equipment	4,000
Annual depreciation (20% per annum straight line)	(800)
Net book value at 30.6.97	3,200

(c)   In the accounts of a not-for-profit organisation, the capital or proprietorship is referred to as the *accumulated fund*. This fund is equivalent to the capital account of a business organisation. Any surpluses from the income and expenditure account are added to the accumulated fund, whilst any deficits from this account are deducted from the fund.

(d)   With the exception of land held on freehold or very long leasehold, all fixed assets wear out over time, and should therefore be depreciated. The pavilion is no exception, since it too has a limited life and will need replacing at some stage in the future. Although depreciation is charged as expenditure in the income and expenditure account, it is unlikely that any funds will actually be set aside in order to pay for replacement assets in the future.

The accounting concepts which govern the charging of depreciation are the prudence concept and the matching concept. The purchase price of an asset should be written off over a *prudent* estimation of its useful life (this is the depreciation charge). The subsequent charging of depreciation to the income and expenditure account is in effect the *matching* of the cost of using the asset with the revenue that has been generated from it.

ORDER FORM

If you have not already used the companion BPP Study Text, you may now wish to do so. Published in June 1997, it contains full, structured coverage of the CIMA's syllabus, plus plenty of opportunity for self-testing and practice.

To order your Study Text, ring our credit card hotline on 0181-740 2211. Alternatively, send this page to our Freepost address or fax it to us on 0181-740 1184.

You may also wish to make use of our latest revision product, CIMA Passcards. Designed to act as last-minute revision notes and memory prompters, the third editions will be available at the end of February 1998. Please call for details.

To: BPP Publishing Ltd, FREEPOST, London W12 8BR   **Tel: 0181-740 2211**
                                                         Fax: 0181-740 1184

Forenames (Mr / Ms): _____

Surname: _____

Address: _____

_____

Post code: _____   Date of exam (month/year):_____

Please send me the following books:	*Quantity*	*Price*	*Total*
CIMA Stage 1 *Financial Accounting Fundamentals*			
Study Text (6/97)	....	£17.95	....
CIMA Stage 1 *Financial Accounting Fundamentals*			
Passcards (2/98)	....	£4.95	....

Postage and packaging:

UK: Texts £3.00 for first plus £2.00 for each extra	....	....
Passcards £2.00 for first plus £1.00 for each extra	....	....
Europe (inc ROI): Texts £5.00 for first plus £4.00 for each extra	....	....
Passcards £2.50 for first plus £1.00 for each extra	....	....
Rest of the World: Texts £8.00 for first plus £6.00 for each extra	....	....
Passcards £5.00 for first plus £3.00 for each extra	....	....

I enclose a cheque for £ _____ **or charge to Access/Visa/Switch**

Card number

Start date (Switch only) _____   Expiry date _____   Issue no. (Switch only)_____

Signature _____

To order any further titles in the CIMA range, please use the form overleaf.

ORDER FORM

To order your CIMA books, ring our credit card hotline on 0181-740 2211. Alternatively, send this page to our Freepost address or fax it to us on 0181-740 1184.

To: BPP Publishing Ltd, FREEPOST, London W12 8BR   **Tel: 0181-740 2211**
Fax: 0181-740 1184

Forenames (Mr / Ms): _____

Surname: _____

Address: _____

_____

Post code: _____   Date of exam (month/year):_____

Please send me the following books:

	Price			Quantity			Total
	6/97	2/98	2/98				
	Text	Kit	Passcards	Text	Kit	Passcards	£
Stage 1	£	£	£				
Financial Accounting Fundamentals	17.95	8.95	4.95	....	....	....	....
Cost Accounting and Quantitative Methods	17.95	8.95	4.95	....	....	....	....
Economic Environment	17.95	8.95	4.95	....	....	....	....
Business Environment and Information Technology	17.95	8.95	4.95	....	....	....	....
Stage 2							
Financial Accounting	17.95	8.95	4.95	....	....	....	....
Operational Cost Accounting	17.95	8.95	4.95	....	....	....	....
Management Science Applications	17.95	8.95	4.95	....	....	....	....
Business and Company Law	17.95	8.95	4.95	....	....	....	....
Stage 3							
Financial Reporting	18.95	9.95	5.95	....	....	....	....
Management Accounting Applications	18.95	9.95	5.95	....	....	....	....
Organisational Management and Development	18.95	9.95	5.95	....	....	....	....
Business Taxation (9/97 Text, 2/98 P/c, 2/98 Kit)	18.95	9.95	5.95	....	....	....	....
Stage 4							
Strategic Financial Management	18.95	9.95	5.95	....	....	....	....
Strategic Management Accountancy and Marketing	18.95	9.95	5.95	....	....	....	....
Information Management	18.95	9.95	5.95	....	....	....	....
Management Accounting Control Systems	18.95	9.95	5.95	....	....	....	....

Postage and packaging:

UK: Texts £3.00 for first plus £2.00 for each extra ....

Kits and Passcards £2.00 for first plus £1.00 for each extra ....

Europe (inc ROI): Texts £5.00 for first plus £4.00 for each extra ....

Kits and Passcards £2.50 for first plus £1.00 for each extra ....

Rest of the World: Texts £8.00 for first plus £6.00 for each extra ....

Kits and Passcards £5.00 for first plus £3.00 for each extra ....

I enclose a cheque for £ _____ **or charge to Access/Visa/Switch**

Card number ⬚⬚⬚⬚⬚⬚⬚⬚⬚⬚⬚⬚⬚⬚⬚⬚⬚⬚⬚

Start date (Switch only) _____ **Expiry date** _____ **Issue no. (Switch only)**___

Signature _____

REVIEW FORM & FREE PRIZE DRAW

All original review forms from the entire BPP range, completed with genuine comments, will be entered into one of two draws on 31 July 1998 and 31 January 1999. The names on the first four forms picked out on each occasion will be sent a cheque for £50.

Name: _____ Address: _____

_____

_____

How have you used this Kit?
(Tick one box only)

☐ Home study (book only)

☐ On a course: college _____

☐ With 'correspondence' package

☐ Other _____

Why did you decide to purchase this Kit?
(Tick one box only)

☐ Have used complementary Study Text

☐ Have used BPP Kits in the past

☐ Recommendation by friend/colleague

☐ Recommendation by a lecturer at college

☐ Saw advertising

☐ Other _____

During the past six months do you recall seeing/receiving any of the following?
(Tick as many boxes as are relevant)

☐ Our advertisement in *CIMA Student*

☐ Our advertisement in *Management Accounting*

☐ Our advertisement in *Pass*

☐ Our brochure with a letter through the post

Which (if any) aspects of our advertising do you find useful?
(Tick as many boxes as are relevant)

☐ Prices and publication dates of new editions

☐ Information on Kit content

☐ Facility to order books off-the-page

☐ None of the above

Have you used the companion Study Text for this subject?   ☐ Yes   ☐ No

Your ratings, comments and suggestions would be appreciated on the following areas

	Very useful	Useful	Not useful
Introductory section (Study advice, key questions checklist, etc)	☐	☐	☐
'Do you know' checklists	☐	☐	☐
Tutorial questions	☐	☐	☐
Examination-standard questions	☐	☐	☐
Content of suggested solutions	☐	☐	☐
Quiz	☐	☐	☐
Test paper	☐	☐	☐
Structure and presentation	☐	☐	☐

	Excellent	Good	Adequate	Poor
Overall opinion of this Kit	☐	☐	☐	☐

Do you intend to continue using BPP Study Texts/Kits?   ☐ Yes   ☐ No

Please note any further comments and suggestions/errors on the reverse of this page.

Please return to: Neil Biddlecombe, BPP Publishing Ltd, FREEPOST, London, W12 8BR

REVIEW FORM & FREE PRIZE DRAW (continued)

Please note any further comments and suggestions/errors below

FREE PRIZE DRAW RULES

1   Closing date for 31 July 1998 draw is 30 June 1998. Closing date for 31 January 1999 draw is 31 December 1998.

2   Restricted to entries with UK and Eire addresses only. BPP employees, their families and business associates are excluded.

3   No purchase necessary. Entry forms are available upon request from BPP Publishing. No more than one entry per title, per person. Draw restricted to persons aged 16 and over.

4   Winners will be notified by post and receive their cheques not later than 6 weeks after the relevant draw date. Lists of winners will be published in BPP's *focus* newsletter following the relevant draw.

5   The decision of the promoter in all matters is final and binding. No correspondence will be entered into.